ELECTRONIC SECURITY SYSTEMS

ELECTRONIC SECURITY SYSTEMS

SYSTEMS

A Manager's Guide to Evaluating and Selecting System Solutions

Robert L. Pearson, PE

AMSTERDAM • BOSTON • HEIDELBERG • LONDON
NEW YORK • OXFORD • PARIS • SAN DIEGO
SAN FRANCISCO • SINGAPORE • SYDNEY • TOKYO

Butterworth-Heinemann is an imprint of Elsevier

ELSEVIER

Acquisitions Editor: Mark Listewnik
Assistant Editor: Kelly Weaver
Marketing Manager: Christian Nolin
Project Manager: Jeff Freeland
Cover Designer: Eric DeCicco
Compositor: SPI Publisher Services
Cover Printer: Phoenix Color Corp.
Text Printer/Binder: The Maple-Vail Book Manufacturing Group

Butterworth–Heinemann is an imprint of Elsevier
30 Corporate Drive, Suite 400, Burlington, MA 01803, USA
Linacre House, Jordan Hill, Oxford OX2 8DP, UK

Recognizing the importance of preserving what has been written, Elsevier prints its
books on acid-free paper whenever possible.

Library of Congress Cataloging-in-Publication Data
Pearson, Robert L.
  Electronic security system : a manager's guide to evaluating and selecting systems
solutions / Robert L. Pearson.
    p. cm.
  Includes bibliographical references and index.
  ISBN 0-7506-7999-9 (alk. paper)
  1. Electronic securitysystems. 2. Office buildings–Security measures. 3. Business
enterprises–Security measures. I. Title.

TH9737.P43 2006
621.389'28–dc22   200649578

British Library Cataloguing-in-Publication Data
A catalogue record for this book is available from the British Library.

ISBN 13: 978-0-7506-7999-2
ISBN 10: 0-7506-7999-9

For information on all Elsevier Butterworth–Heinemann publications
visit our Web site at www.books.elsevier.com

Printed in the United States of America
06 07 08 09 10 11 10 9 8 7 6 5 4 3 2 1

Working together to grow
libraries in developing countries

www.elsevier.com | www.bookaid.org | www.sabre.org

ELSEVIER   BOOK AID International   Sabre Foundation

Table of Contents

Preface

The technology and sophistication of electronics has exploded. Digital cameras on cell phones and the Internet have affected everyone. It was not many years ago that a cell phone was a luxury; today it is becoming a necessity. The Internet has become part of the majority of households. Preschool children can operate personal computers and grandparents send messages and JPEG pictures over the Internet. Online purchasing and banking have become big-time businesses, seriously impacting brick and mortar stores' sales. These enhancements and advantages in technology have been a benefit to our society by providing more capabilities, more automation, and less physical effort to accomplish a task at a reasonable cost. A microwave oven is the appliance of choice for most families today. Technology has impacted all aspects of our work and play.

These enhancements in technology have also affected security equipment. Enhanced sophisticated electronics is part of virtually every electronic security functional system. Processing capability has been added to the alarm sensors to mitigate false alarms and intelligence has been added to access cards/badges (smart cards) which process duplex communication via a reader. The card can be updated by the reader, can internally process information, and communicate back to the reader. Entire electronic functional systems have incorporated features that allow improved operation and integration into a total electronic security system solution. Even communications between field equipment and a central station have become faster and more sophisticated. The Internet/Intranet is part of many access control, alarm, and closed circuit television, CCTV, systems available in today's market.

The sophistication and intelligence in the systems have forced the end user to become more technically oriented. Unfortunately, the typical security professional's knowledge of these various systems has not kept pace with the changes. Over the years, there have been many seminars, books, and training classes related to physical security with the primary emphasis on personnel, legal issues, facility considerations, management, and interfacing with law enforcement. In the early days, the physical security profession focused on the physical issues while the electronic systems possessed very rudimentary capabilities. Since many security professionals in the private business sector originally came from a physical security/law enforcement background, this training was appropriate. With the expanding technology, the security professional tended to consider the electronic security applications based upon functional solutions versus a holistic approach. Little consideration has been given to a key sophisticated component of the security program as to ongoing issues, maintenance, system configuration, and system philosophies.

Even today, the information that is available is primarily constrained to an electronic security functional area. For example, CCTV systems information is available that explains the different camera technologies, digital video recording, matrix systems, different communication techniques, lighting issues, and so on. There is limited information as to how all these components of any one function should operate with other functional security systems. There is a need to provide information about these different electronic security functions with a focus on integration, philosophies, tradeoffs, and ongoing issues for the end user in a corporate environment. A holistic view will incorporate these concepts as well as the perceptions of employees, visitors, contractors, management, and various business units within the company. The electronic security concerns needed to address all the different electronic security functions in a corporate central monitoring facility must be evalvated.

Electronic security is a vital aspect of any security program. It is usually a major investment and should receive a high level of scrutiny by the security professional. Often the security professional accepts a new system or has an existing system upgraded without becoming personally involved, relying on the designer, manufacturer's representative, an alarm company, or an integrator. After the installation is complete, the security professional will become the system owner from upper management's viewpoint. For a security professional to be effective, he or she needs to understand the electronics and the interactions of various electronic security functions to some level as they are integrated into a total security system solution. With this knowledge, many pitfalls can be avoided. It is a mistake to believe that a new integrated security system is top quality based solely on the fact that several electronic security components are connected together. To be successful, the security professional does not have to be the designer; however, all aspects of a holistic view must be incorporated. Since the security professional does inherit the designer's system, thus becoming the system owner, it is imperative that a holistic view is taken and the capabilities of the various electronic systems are fully understood. Further, if the security professional is fully involved in system planning, establishing data input standards, functional expectations, training of staff, and so on, a significantly better end product is assured. Short cuts, intentional or not, will undermine the foundation on which the entire system rests. If the electronic security system functions poorly, is poorly maintained, or is poorly installed, every employee, visitor, contractor and manager will become aware of the problems and be critical of the security program.

The focus of this book is to help the security professional understand the various electronic security functional components and the ways these components interconnect, as well as provide a guide to a holistic approach to solving security issues with various technologies. Issues associated with integrating electronic functions, developing a system, component philosophy, possible long-term issues, and the culture within a corporation which will impact the final system design will also be discussed. The book includes a collection of practical experiences, solutions, and an approach to solving technical problems. Electronic security solutions are as much an art form as a science; there is not just one answer to a given problem.

This book is not meant to be an engineering text, but is offered as a text for providing a solid understanding of the systems and issues that need to be addressed. Issues and information covered in this book will apply to many different environments. A corporate setting is used as its example; however, the basic issues can be applied to virtually any environment. It is my sincere hope that this book will provide you with insights into the various electronic systems and approaches to address electronic security issues by providing a lifetime of acquired experiences gained through designing, installing and maintaining electronic security systems.

Acknowledgments

It is difficult to accomplish any task totally by oneself. We are all an accumulation of experiences, information, and insights provided by other people. This book would not have been possible without the understanding, knowledge, and wisdom of the many people I have worked and collaborated with over the years. It is not possible to thank all of them by name due to the length of such a list. I do, however, want to give recognition, and my sincere appreciation, to those who helped me in reviewing the chapters in this book. Two colleagues who spent their personal time and effort to provide the needed perspective were Jim Phillips and Christine Stark. Jim provided a technical perspective and Christine provided an administrative manager's perspective, both of which were helpful in providing a balance in the material presented.

I am always thankful for the support and encouragement provided by those that are close to me. My family and my wife, particularly, encouraged the concept as well as the day-to-day work required. My final thanks go to Elsevier and Mark Listewnik for their initial interest and ongoing support in publishing this book. They have been patient and supportive and have provided the necessary assistance to bring this book to fruition. The encouraging notes from Kelly Weaver, Assistant Editor, were especially appreciated.

Electronic Access Control

You might be asking why access control is the first chapter in this book. The answer is that the access control system is the most exposed component of an electronic security program. Employees, contractors, customers and visitors are all aware of your electronic access control system. Normally the employees utilize the system via a badge every day to gain access to their work area. The employee badge is typically composed of a picture, company logo/name, employee's name and a technology to provide a unique Identification (ID). The contractor may have a badge with or without a picture, or picture and ID technology. Either way, the contractor will be impacted by the quality of the access control system. A customer or a visitor are often "badged" at a lobby and escorted through the facility. The access control system will have an impact on the customer and/or visitor as to the quality and thoroughness of the security program. Some companies are now addressing the various groups of people visiting or working at their facility as employees and nonemployees. This chapter will address the access control system and consider the groups separately. The different types of badges and technologies will be addressed in Chapter 2.

A review of the basic components that comprise an electronic access control system is important. There are readers throughout a facility which connect to an electronic panel in the field or an electronic interface. If an electronic interface is used, it connects to an electronic panel in the field. In either case, the signals are then sent from the electronic field panel to a computer, which is usually a server. Different manufacturers take different approaches. There are many options for the communication path between the field panel and the server, which will be discussed later in this chapter. Hardware and communication path redundancy between the electronic field panel and the server/computer may be added to minimize loss of communication. Badge data may be stored locally in the field panel and/or in the server/computer. Typically some level of badge data is kept in the field panel and a total badge database is kept in the server/computer. In this scenario, when a person uses a badge in a reader for the first time or a badge that has not been used for an extended period of time, the badge data is not in the electronic field panel. The field panel then communicates with the computer to verify the authorization via the badge database. If authorization is allowed, the badge data is sent to the field panel which operates in a First In First Out (FIFO) manner. The oldest badge data loaded into the field panel will be dropped when new badge data is loaded and the memory is full. By having badge data in the field panel, personnel who normally enter or leave using badge readers attached to the field panels will be allowed to enter and leave even without the server/computer being operational. In a normal operating system, a reader communicates to an electronic field panel and then to the server/computer for logging the transaction. Simply put, the reason for an electronic access control system is to provide a way for a badge to grant a person access. The badge technology provides a unique number that allows the access control system to verify authorization for a specific person via a database. If access is granted, then an electric door strike is energized, a magnetic lock or electrified crash bar is released, or a revolving door is activated. The transaction is then logged into a history file in the computer/server database.

In the past, most security professionals have selected an access control system at a trade show or from a salesman visiting the company. The manufacturer is important, but the installation company may have more to do with the success of the project than the manufacturer. The decision to purchase a system has often been made based upon a limited exposure to the product. There are many issues and decisions that should be evaluated prior to purchasing a system. These issues may not have been thoroughly considered and may not be obvious. Choosing the best system, for a given application, depends upon properly developing the requirements.

To have a quality electronic access control system, it is important to select a system that meets the requirements developed for a given facility. The requirements will vary with different industries, buildings or corporate cultures. Choosing the best electronic access control system is much more than choosing a manufacturer or brand. Areas to consider in the selection process are (1) technology, (2) culture, (3) access philosophy, (4) management commitment, (5) total cost of ownership, (6) system flexibility, (7) durability of system components, and (8) securing the database.

TECHNOLOGY

As with all these factors associated with choosing the best system, there are many possible options. There are four widely utilized technologies: (1) magnetic stripe, (2) Weigand, (3) proximity, and (4) contact-less smart card. The technology chosen will affect the way the badge interfaces with the reader. With magnetic stripe and Weigand technology the badge must be swiped. With proximity and contact-less smart card technologies the badge may be placed a short distance in front of the reader. (Smart card technology can also be purchased as a contact type, which must be slid into a reader.) The technology chosen will affect several other aspects such as cost, ease of counterfeiting, badge encoding equipment, and reader mounting locations. Specific technology details will be covered in Chapter 2.

CULTURE

You might be asking yourself, what does culture have to do with choosing the best access control system? The answer to that question is somewhat subjective, because some access control systems will be more acceptable to employees within a given company than others. For example, the prevailing view today is to use a badge technology that is presented to a reader versus being swiped through a reader. This is often referred to as "hands free" or "touch-and-go" technology. Another example is the "one-badge-does-it-all" culture. Gaining access to the workplace, parking in the garage, time keeping, logging onto one's computer and automatically charging meals in the cafeteria may all be accomplished with a single badge. This type of approach or culture could force the badge technology to be a smart card. Smart card technology has more data storage capability than the other technologies discussed and contains processing capabilities. The culture will also affect the badge's appearance, the information printed on the badge, colors used, photo, and so on. The important thing to remember is that the culture—where the badge is used—will affect its design and technology. This topic will be discussed in more detail in Chapter 2.

ACCESS PHILOSOPHY

The access control philosophy will be affected by culture, as well as which portals are controlled and in what way they are controlled. For example, most companies have a lobby in a major building with a security person/receptionist. Often these lobbies are used to access the building via a doorway or elevators. In the case of a doorway leading to the interior of the facility, the access philosophy might require a badge to be read to gain access. The receptionist might utilize a door release button or key switch to release the electric door strike for access. Or both approaches might be utilized between business and nonbusiness hours or when heightened security is required.

The philosophy should address issues such as whether badges will be used to read in as well as out of the facility. A badge read can be required to enter, and free egress be allowed via a motion detector or a pushbutton mounted on the doorframe (mullion). Is anti-pass back control necessary? If so, then every person must use his or her badge to enter and leave an area. The system will assume the last badge read indicates where the person is located physically. Should pedestrian dock doors be controlled differently? If so, how should they be controlled? How should doors for material movement be controlled, or doors for persons with disabilities? There are literally hundreds of variations of options associated with different types of access into and out of the facility. Some access points will most likely be affected by local building and/or fire codes. This will be covered in Chapter 19.

The chosen philosophy must consider human nature—people will always follow the easiest path as is true with water and electricity. For example, if emergency exit doors are closer than a designated portal, efforts must be taken to assure that the emergency exit is not used in place of the designated portal. There are several ways to accomplish this.

Place signage that indicates that the door is being monitored and is only for emergency use.

Place a breakable security seal on the crash bar indicating it is secured and not for general use.

Cover this type of information in a new hire orientation under the topic of security.

Normally several approaches are utilized to assure success. Another example of human nature is the placement of readers in reference to the door that the reader controls. The reader should normally be placed on the same side of the opening as the doorknob. Since most people are right handed, the reader should be on the right side when a double door is used. In addition, both of the double doors should allow movement when the badge allows authorized entry.

MANAGEMENT COMMITMENT

On the surface this appears to be an unnecessary concern for choosing the right system, but, in fact, there are many reasons that management commitment is critical. One of the reasons for this commitment is that following the philosophies that are developed as part of the access control, senior management ultimately must enforce the plan. These philosophies must apply to everyone equally. If a manager refuses to use a badge when everyone else must use a badge, the level of support by upper management becomes important. If some employees are allowed to bypass the "rules," then the word gets out and no one really cares about following the "rules."

There is one item that is a sure thing in any access control system—problems will develop that require management's support. For example, a hardware failure at a portal prevents employees using their badges from leaving the building, making it necessary to walk a long distance down a hallway to another portal or crash out an emergency exit that is only several feet away. If they crash out the emergency exit, then upper management is needed to support a message to the employees notifying them that the emergency exit should not be used except in an emergency. If they go to the other portal down the hall and start complaining to or about security, upper management is needed to support security. Either way, upper management support is critical.

TOTAL COST OF OWNERSHIP

Total cost of ownership is an area that is often not considered. Typically an access control system is designed, funding is approved, the system is installed, and sometimes a maintenance budget is established. With this process, many aspects of the total cost of ownership are overlooked. Some of the costs overlooked are (1) ongoing badge stock purchases, (2) database administration, (3) software modifications, (4) software upgrades and (5) system configuration management. Total cost of ownership can exceed the total cost of the original system installation. For this reason, care must be taken to select the system that provides the best total cost of ownership, not simply the cheapest solution.

Often an alarm company installs the electronic access control system. To maintain the system after installation, either the alarm company provides that service or trained company employees maintain the database and make the badges. The installing alarm company usually handles software modifications, software upgrades, and software configuration. If the access control system is large, complex and constantly changing, several full-time technicians may be required to keep the system operating properly, the software up-to-date and the database cleaned up. The level of effort required will vary based upon the activity in each of these areas.

There are costs associated with keeping the system going, whether provided in-house or by the installing alarm company or some combination of in-house and contractor. One truth to note at this point is that the selected alarm company that installs the access control system may be more important than the manufacturer of the access control system as far as the success of the system's ongoing operation. Ultimately, the technical knowledge and availability of installation and maintenance qualified technicians is the limiting factor.

CODE AND SPECIAL REQUIREMENTS

There are many special requirements that may apply to an access control system. Many of these requirements are universal, such as fire codes that are covered in more detail in Chapter 19. These code requirements will vary depending upon the municipality and area of the country. The Authority Having Jurisdiction (AHJ), or the Local Authority Having Jurisdiction (LAHJ), can force requirements that might be very different from those in another city nearby. There are other requirements that will apply to different industries, agencies, or companies. For example, hospitals, prisons, power plants, refineries, and so on have special requirements that must be considered when designing the access control system. There are issues associated with union and nonunion employees that must be considered. Also government contracting companies must comply with UL2050, which primarily applies to alarms, but can impact access control. Manufacturers, their representatives or the alarm company may not know the specific requirements that apply to a specific installation. To assure the best results, it is important for you to be part of the philosophy, functional requirements, initial design, scope of work, and implementation decisions.

AESTHETICS

Aesthetics can be a very serious issue with upper management, the architect, and/or building owner. For example, an executive area with wood paneling and glass doors can be a challenge for installing an electronic access control system. The readers must provide the desired appearance and the door-locking hardware must be hidden. This is normally a very serious challenge, because glass doors are often used and they must swing in both directions. To mount a shear lock, in the floor or a wooden header is a physical and operational challenge. First, a hole for the lock must be provided. Since the doors often rest directly upon concrete, this can be a troublesome installation. Second, the door closer must be installed to allow the door to swing both ways and the door must be set to stop or "home" directly over the shear lock. Finally, there is a critical timing issue. The lock must be energized precisely at the moment the door is directly above the sheer lock. If the door is not energized at the correct time, the door will be compromised because it will not be properly secure. To be successful in securing the door, the steel plate or armature mounted on the bottom of the door must be pulled down to the energized shear lock. Figure 1.1 shows an example of shear locks and door sensors for a double

Figure 1.1   Shear lock in wooden header.

glass door installation using a wooden header. These doors are normally a constant maintenance problem.

There are many examples of aesthetic issues that must be considered in the design of the access control system. An elegant lobby, for example, where many employees must pass every day, requires an access control approach that is unobtrusive. Optical turnstiles are often used to address this challenge. The turnstiles are aesthetically pleasing and can be modified to fit many applications. Figure 1.2 shows an optical turnstile that incorporates a glass partition. These turnstiles process a large number of people quickly, and can incorporate badge readers. When badge readers are utilized, some type of visual indication is provided for a successful authorized badge read as seen in this figure. There are also slots on the sides that incorporate motion detectors to minimize the tailgating issue. Security staff is required to view the area for the visual indication of an authorized badge read and verify the turnstiles are not compromised. (Jumping over the waist-high turnstyle can be easily accomplished.) Figure 1.3 shows a revolving door and a physical disability/material movement door adjacent to it. (Depending upon the company impairment/material movement doors can be added to allow easier access for the physically impaired via a badge reader that only allows access for these particular individuals and/or materials.) Revolving doors provide a more aesthetically pleasing appearance compared to a rotating bar-type turnstile. There is additional cost with a revolving door versus the rotating bar-type turnstile, but if aesthetics are paramount, then the decision is easier. Revolving doors also have power assist capability and aid in controlling door speed and ease of use.

SYSTEM SUPPORT

This has been addressed to some extent under the topic "Total Cost of Ownership." The challenge is to decide early on which way system support is to be provided. Not many companies have the in-house staff to provide this support, especially early on in the installation phase of the project. The types of support needed include (1) database support, (2) badge making support, (3) new installations and (4) system configuration control, on the more technical side. After the initial installation, system configuration,

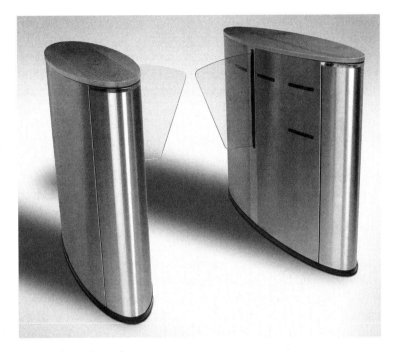

Figure 1.2   Optical turnstile. Courtesy of Smarter Security Systems.

system upgrades and troubleshooting will be important support areas. A typical problem that will arise after system installation is that an individual's badge may not be working. The answer to the problem can be in the badge or in the access control system electronics. The person with the nonworking badge will typically go to a badge room and state the problem. Often the badge room will produce another badge, assuming that the badge is the problem which sometimes fixes the problem and sometimes does not. To find the root cause of the problem, the badge room requires some training and technical support. The badge room personnel should test the badge in a local "test" reader. Then they should verify that the number read by the badge reader is what is in that database for that person. The badge room should verify that the reader the person wants to access is authorized for that person's use. After checking all of the above and if the badge appears to be operating correctly in a test reader, the field-testing effort must start. Security personnel

Figure 1.3   Revolving door.

must go to the reader in question, assuming the person's authorization has been verified, and verify proper reader operation. This tends to be more critical when a swipe-type reader is utilized. The problem should be addressed from an electronic technical view at this point and proper test equipment should be incorporated. Often, the culprit turns out to be a faulty ground. The problem could also be from an improperly grounded shield on a reader cable or a floating ground or from inadvertently grounding both ends of the shielded cable. Whatever the source of the grounding problem, electronic noise can cause misreads. Misreads often appear to be a random problem because the cause of the electronic noise is often random. It is amazing how many badges are made and remade to solve a problem, when the badge was not the problem to start with. This wastes time and money, adds to the frustration of the badge user and the badge room personnel, and degrades the perceived value of the security program.

In addition to this general approach to solving the "badge-does-not-work", the technology used within the badge must be considered. For technologies that must be swiped through a reader, the problem can be as simple as the badge's owner not swiping the badge through the reader in a smooth, level manner. Sometimes when the badge is held at an angle when run through the reader, nothing is recognized by the equipment that verifies the protocol (this will be covered in Chapter 2) or the wrong bit pattern is read. So the badge owner may gain access sometimes but not at other times, because the bit pattern read could appear to match a credential number that has approved access. Normally the number read does not match the desired protocol and is not recognized at all. In most access control systems, faulty reads are recorded into a history file in the server/computer. The badge room or technician can check the access control log for this type of information.

For badges that are simply held in front of the reader, such as proximity badges, the issues can be the same. For example, proximity readers are subject to electronic Radio Frequency (RF) noise problems. This noise can come from many electronic devices or machinery. Since the technology operates on a frequency-based RF technology, any interference from frequencies close to its radiation or receive frequencies can present problems. Sources of frequency problems can be a personal computer (PC) located too close to a reader. (PCs use a sprayed or plated proximity RF shield; however, in this case they still emit noise that can be detected at the reader itself.) The cables leaving the proximity reader can experience the same RF noise problem as swipe readers. One difference in the proximity reader electronic RF noise issue is that a proximity reader actually transmits frequencies that can interfere with other equipment in close range of the reader. This must be considered in the placement of proximity readers. Chapter 8 covers frequencies and electronic wave transmission.

SYSTEM FLEXIBILITY

This particular requirement is more subjective than the other issues covered up to this point in choosing the right system. Electronic access control systems perform more tasks or should have more capability than simply allowing access to authorized badge holders. Among these are reports that need to be generated as well as expandability and communication issues. Report generation may be very limited to certain predefined variables by a given manufacturer. For a report program to be flexible, the database should be a commercially available database management system, such as MS Structured Query Language (SQL), and not a proprietary database management system supplied by the electronic access control manufacturer. There are several proprietary protocols and software products that are part of access control systems that limit which products will operate together, thus forcing the purchaser to continue buying a given product. More will be covered on this topic later in the chapter. Using MS SQL or some other common open database management system should enable reports to be run from any of the data fields in the database and in any desired arrangement. With an open database you can use third-party reporting and designers, such as Crystal Reports or even MS Access, to create your own designs and reports, thus providing tremendous flexibility. There is always a report that would be beneficial to the end user that was not envisioned at the beginning of the installation project. To pay the installing company or the access control manufacturer to modify their software so that a report can be run is very expensive and is usually unnecessary.

Another concern is the expandability issue. Most manufacturers produce various sizes of access control systems based upon number of readers, number of workstations, number of servers and/or number of cardholders. If the smaller system is not scaleable, or upward compatible, then money is wasted. The computer software, and sometimes the interface electronics, must be replaced to expand the system. Some manufacturers use the same software package, but enable capabilities and charge the end user based upon the number of active features. Expansion is normally inevitable. Initially, when the access control system is first installed, there is reluctance to use the readers. As employees gain confidence in using the system, they see benefits in using their identification badges to gain access since they must be worn anyway. A badge is often easier to use than remembering to bring a key. Once a system is installed and provides reliable service, request for additional readers is commonplace. It is not unusual after the initial installation for a system to expand to five or ten times the original number of readers. This does not count new security requirements that may emerge, such as mergers, acquisitions, or major events such as 9/11. System growth must be contemplated from the time the first badge reader is installed.

Then there is the issue of communication. The communication from the reader to the field interface electronics uses, in most cases, a de facto standard—Weigand communication language (not to be confused with the Weigand data residing on a Weigand badge). The Weigand interface is composed of a minimum of four shielded wires. [One for power, one for ground, one for data 1 and one for data 0. To operate Light Emitting Diodes (LEDs) or audible devices, additional wires are needed.]

The communication that is used between the electronics in the field to the computer/server is usually a proprietary protocol. (Protocols and Weigand technology will also be discussed in more detail in Chapter 2.) For now, consider a protocol as a language that allows two people to communicate. For instance, the protocol used in this book is English. Manufacturers send their own unique protocol between the field electronic panels and the computer/server. That means that the only open architecture pieces of equipment used in an electronic access control system are the reader (not so for proximity and smart card readers), the computer and the printer used for report writing. The ways to send the protocol between the electronic field equipment and the server/computer include (1) RS485, (2) RS232, (3) RS422, (4) TCP/IP and (5) dialup. For a system to be flexible, it is desirable to use a manufacturer that produces equipment that is capable of multiple communication formats. Otherwise, interface equipment must be purchased from a third party that makes the conversions. The application software used in this third-party hardware is also usually proprietary. Third-party hardware/software becomes more critical if the access control system field electronic interface is part of the alarm system and must comply with a standard imposed by regulations such as UL. The total system configuration must be UL approved and each component that makes up the system must be listed in the case of UL.

DURABILITY OF SYSTEM COMPONENTS

To be durable and/or reliable, systems available today must comply with different regulations and, as such, normally contain lightning protection, fuses, and so on—so the field panels that connect the reader to the server/computer normally have the needed electronic protection. When manufacturers sell "noncompliant" equipment, damage can result when nonpower wires are crossed or mistakenly connected. Additionally, RF in the area could unnecessarily impact the equipment operation or, worse, damage the equipment. For instance, keying up a two-way radio near the electronic field panels can cause this type of interference/damage problems. Durability also applies to the longevity of a given access control product line. In the access control manufacturer's world of mergers and acquisitions, this can cause product lines to disappear because of a merger or they may not have the financial base to compete with larger companies in the market place. Even the recent acquisition of access control manufacturers by large companies does not assure continuing production or even support of a given product. For example, when a large company purchases more than one electronic access control company, the company doing the acquisition tries to determine ways to blend product lines. This saves money and produces a product that has more features and is hopefully more reliable. The problem is that different acquired electronic access control companies often take different approaches in designing and building their product. (This includes the protocol used between the electronic field panel and the server/computer.) When the new product is released, it is doubtful that multiple protocols will be incorporated, thus making one or all of the acquired access control systems obsolete. Then technical support as well as the purchase of hardware and software will have a cut-off date and your company can be left with an orphan unsupported system.

The amount of openness of the architecture will also play an important part in system durability. Most electronic access control systems today are moving toward commercially available application software packages to run on the server/computer. This is a great step in the right direction. As an example, MS SQL as a database management software package provides needed flexibility. The reality is that the commercial computer industry moves much faster than the electronic access control industry; so a software package that is a perfect application today may be totally outdated tomorrow. One example is OS2 versus Windows, where the eventual winner was Windows. Even though OS2 had many benefits it is now extinct. A less extreme example is MS Windows 98 versus MS Windows XP. Being an early adaptor or a Beta test site can be exciting, but it can also be fraught with problems, so most security professionals prefer the tried and true. The tried and true approach places you behind the commercial software development curve and future support may be a problem.

When all these issues are considered at the start of the project, it is possible to still have surprises because it is impossible to know every potential problem or every question to ask. For example, there is an electronic access control manufacturer that allows a defined pixel size for the photos in their database. (A pixel is a rectangular diminution of a CCTV screen or video picture. This will be discussed in greater detail in Chapter 7.) When a photo in the form of a JPEG file, with a larger-than-defined pixel size, is loaded into their database, the JPEG file is accepted. If the personnel record of the individual with that oversized JPEG file is retrieved from the database for any reason, the server often locks up or does not display the stored photo correctly. This can be a major problem. A second example of the same manufacturer's product is very slow loading of badges into the database, which occurs when the system is composed of many server/workstations/computers interconnected together. This particular manufacturer holds a badge database resident in each server; so all servers must reconcile their databases with a master server. This reconciliation process can take up to ninety seconds or longer in large systems—a serious delay in a badge room with employees and contractors backed up waiting to receive their badges.

These two examples show that it is impossible to know all aspects of an access control system before it is purchased. The only way for these details to surface is by using the system; however, many of these problems may never be obvious because of the way the system is used. Normally the larger the system, the more likely that problems will be encountered and require adjustments. Smaller systems are often not taxed to their limits or used by many different personnel in multiple badge rooms, so the problems do not surface. By the time these types of problems are known, it is too late to choose a different manufacturer. Once purchased, then there is a marriage of sorts. You must live with a given manufacturer, because the systems use proprietary hardware and software. Replacing a system is costly and different manufacturers will have unknown limitations in their equipment. It would be embarrassing at best for you to request funds from upper management to replace a recently purchased access control system. This is where it is important to have a top quality installation company and/or in-house staff to address problems as they arise.

SECURING THE DATABASE

The access control system by definition requires unique credentials for the badge so that the authorized person using the badge will have access to the sites, buildings, and areas interior to the buildings. On the other hand, unauthorized employees/contractors will not be allowed access to areas not approved. In the database that contains the unique badge credential numbers, the person carrying the credential is identified and linked to the credential number. Normally the database contains their name and a unique identifier; sometimes the identifier is an employee number. The number may be unique to the company or it may be a Social Security number. If Social Security numbers are used for anyone in the access control database, special precautions must be taken to assure that privacy issues have been properly addressed. Access to the database must be restricted, which is typically accomplished with passwords. The server/computer, where the database resides, must be protected from physical theft and should have all Social Security numbers encrypted "at rest." If the server is connected to the company intranet, then the database must be protected from hacking, viruses and worms.

As with any electronic security product, marketing will paint a very desirable picture of their product and assure you that their system will do whatever needs to be done. Appendix A has a list of questions that should be considered when evaluating an enterprise-wide electronic access control solution. The integrator, designer, and/or architect may have managed the installation process, but when all is said and done the entire project belongs to the security professional. The success or failure of the electronic access control system rests upon the security manager's shoulders, and senior management will look there if anything goes wrong. Since most security professionals spend a tremendous amount of effort to purchase a new access control system, it is in their best interest to be part of the project from the start and ask the right questions. It is not necessary to be an electronic security expert to ask many of the questions addressed in this chapter.

2

Badge Making

Everyone considers badges an important part of identification for employees, contractors and visitors. The badge provides identification both visually and electronically; however, the actual badge-making process is one of the most underrated tasks within security. The effort required to develop a new badge, make badges reliably, re-badge a major facility, or standardize badges across a company can be overwhelming. Selecting a new badge design and producing that badge for a given company requires many decisions to be completed satisfactorily and these decisions are affected and exacerbated by three basic areas: (1) appearance, (2) technology and (3) manufacturing process. Badge making will be addressed in this chapter based upon cost issues and the impact of company culture as well as from the more traditional approaches of appearance and technology.

Badge cost is a recurring cost that never ends and is usually underestimated. The numbers of badges that will be made in the badge room over time will far exceed any initial estimate. It is easy to assume that some number of replacement badges will be based upon employees losing and damaging badges; however, there will be other employee badge replacements based upon the company's business and culture. For instance, if the company is a government contractor, then badges will be replaced when government clearances change; or the company culture may dictate that a badge be changed every five years to coincide with service anniversaries. These topics will be covered in more detail later in this chapter. Some badges will be replaced based upon employees not liking their photo on the badge and request another badge be made. Then there are badges that must be changed due to name changes associated with marriage or divorce. Employees may have changed their appearance by growing a beard or mustache, changing hair color or losing weight. The above may also apply to contractors, a much more dynamically changing group because of the constant turnover.

The company's culture drives much of these costs. As already mentioned, if the company maintains government security clearances, these clearances are normally part of the badge. As an individual's clearance status changes, a new badge must be made and the old badge collected. Then there is the inevitable problem of needing to utilize a new employee before their clearance is through the final approval process, so there is often an additional badge that must be manufactured that shows the individual has a clearance "in process." This is usually accomplished with an interim clearance badge. The badge might have the word "interim" over the clearance designation or use a special color. As far as the cost issue is concerned, an additional badge is required that must be replaced at a later date when the clearance is final. As is true with college graduates, the clearance process proceeds in steps, which means several clearance and interim badges may be required for any given individual.

Years of service is another area that is often designated on the employee badges that will also affect cost. At first glance changing a badge every five years or so does not appear to be a significant problem. After five years of service, most badges are starting to show their age and probably should be replaced anyway. What often happens is that the employee loses a badge or misplaces a badge and a new badge must be made. If the new badge is given to the employee one month prior to an anniversary, then the new badge is only in service for one month, because another new badge is produced to indicate longevity. Now consider changing government clearances during the anniversary process and it becomes obvious that many more badges will be produced than originally planned or anticipated.

Many companies today want an enterprise-wide badge solution. The desire to have all badges the same across the enterprise will affect cost based upon exactly which equipment and badge technology is presently being used across the enterprise. Any other groups (customers, visitors and contractors) within the company that use a badge will impact cost by standardizing. This is an especially acute problem for companies that have made acquisitions and have been part of mergers where the various merger companies have different badges and different protocols. The solution that is easiest to implement is to replace all badge readers with a given manufacturer and a given technology with a defined protocol. This approach, while it is the most comprehensive, is also the most costly approach and, for a large corporation, often impractical. It is referred to as a "fork lift" replacement. Compromises must be made to reach a standard badge, technology and protocol. A transition plan might include multitechnology badges and/or dual technology readers (contact-less smart card and proximity).

Most enterprise solutions incorporate other departments in the corporation. Information Technology (IT) is normally one of the groups that want to use the badge that security has already provided to save cost. The problem is that most applications in which IT wants to use the badge require a contact type smart card badge, because the readers are more in-line with an office PC application. IT may want to use the badge to gain access to the company's computer network via an office PC. They would want a badge to insert into a reader and the badge would authenticate itself using some form of Public Key Identification (PKI). If smart cards are used by Security, they usually want to use contact-less type smart cards, because Security wants the convenience of "hands free" (also called "touch-and-go") operation. (Technically the operation of a contact-less smart card is not hands free, but swipe free.) This will be addressed more in detail later in this chapter. (This is just another variable in the total badge solution that must be considered.) To better quantify some of the issues that must be considered, when implementing a single badge solution, many questions must be answered. To properly cover the subject of badge use by various departments in a company would require a book unto itself; however, some basic assumptions must be established that will limit the length of this example. First, there is a selection of technology and a protocol. Then, there is the decision to select or not to select a single manufacturer. Finally, there is a decision as to the company-wide access control system architecture. These are covered in Appendix A.

APPEARANCE

The technology impacts the way badges are manufactured and used by employees. An issue, which is often overlooked, is the effort necessary to develop the badge's appearance. There is usually a tremendous amount of concern about the badge's appearance and about the information that is available on the badge. In fact, this aspect becomes an extremely emotional issue with various stakeholders. It can even be more difficult if an access control system is already in place and it may need to be changed. In this case, all previously agreed upon issues of appearance must be reevaluated.

This is a typical list that shows the type of questions that must be addressed:

1. Should the badge be a visual identification of the individual?
2. Should the picture of the individual be digitized or a photograph?
3. Should different colors be used to designate years of service or clearance levels?
4. Should employee numbers or Social Security numbers be used?
5. Should statistical data such as height, weight, hair color, and so on be used?
6. Should a company logo or special design or pattern be used?
7. Should tamper proof seals, holograms, micro printing, reverse image printing, or special inks be used?
8. Should data be on both sides of the badge?
9. Should the badge be laid out in a landscape or portrait format?

10. Should special badges be made for visitors, contractors, strategic alliance partners, and so on?
11. Should badges be distributed and retrieved by Security or Human Resources (HR) or the cognizant department supervisor?
12. Should retired individuals get a badge if they wish to visit the facility?
13. Should certain nonemployees be allowed to escort other nonemployees?

Depending upon the type of facility affected, the numbers, types and colors of badges can become overwhelming. This is an area that can easily get out of control because there are always special cases that someone wants to add. For example, a company may have a contract to produce a product for a large customer; the customer needs to be treated in a way that indicates support and trust. The problem is that the customer is not an employee. If they are given a standard visitor's badge, the customer may resent the feeling of being a "second hand" citizen. What usually happens is a "special" visitor badge is developed that allows the customer free access (no escort required) to minimizing the feeling the customer may have about not being trusted or always being watched.

Along with the above issues, another problem that often develops is the choice of colors, design, or logo to be used in the badge. The mere resolution of choosing colors can require months of often emotional meetings. In addition, colors can be very difficult to reliably duplicate. Problems can also occur with the different dye sublimation printers that are to be used, quality of ribbons used, and types of materials on which the badges are to be printed. Polyvinyl chloride (PVC) is easy to print on, but polyester lasts longer. Badge stock is available in many combinations of these materials. The texture, level of gloss, and surrounding materials can affect the colors. If special anticounterfeiting efforts are incorporated, such as Ultraviolet (UV) ink, holograms, and micro text (1 point font or smaller), special manufacturer printing will be required. Some level of upper management usually approves the choice of colors, patterns, logos and other images. Then, when an effort is made to duplicate the design, all sorts of problems develop: very dark colors and colors with a metallic appearance are often difficult to reliably duplicate; pastel backgrounds can appear to be washed out; a solid color background after shows surface flaws in bright primary colors (this is true for less flashy colors such as blue). It is always best if these colors can be defined by one of the standard color charts, such as Pantone, which will increase the likelihood of success.

A lack of technology standardization as well as badge design is an area often overlooked within many multinational companies. Often a given location is free to pick and choose vendors because they are an independent business unit. This philosophy is okay if there is virtually no employee movement between facilities a standardized badge is not necessary. When employees move from location to location special efforts must be made to allow their access because the badge systems may not be compatible for interconnection or manual badge data entry. Standardized badge appearance can be achieved even if different technologies exist. Developing the standard between sites can be a challenging task: meetings must be held and the issues of badge materials, colors and printed information must be resolved. Everyone has their favorite and each has a vested interest in keeping things just as they are presently. Overcoming this situation requires a team of stakeholders from the different sites to gather with a technical manager who can help to separate myth from reality.

TECHNOLOGY

The technology chosen for a company badge should be based upon cost, culture and ease of counterfeiting. The roll of technology is to provide a credential number that is unique to an individual. All technologies utilize a binary numbering system to provide a unique number. Binary numbers are composed of combinations of 1s or 0s. There are rules for coding the numbers and different manufacturers may use different systems. As a point of explanation let's assume there are four binary digits in our unique credential number. The numbering scheme is shown in Table 2.1. From the table, it is obvious that with four binary digits there are sixteen possible decimal numbers and thus sixteen possible unique credential numbers. (Zero is a zero in binary and decimal.) When four binary digits are grouped together, the number is a hexadecimal number. In Table 2.1, after the hexadecimal number 10 is reached, then hexadecimal

Table 2.1 Binary, decimal and hexadecimal numbering schemes.

Decimal	Binary	Hexadecimal
0	0000	0
1	0001	1
2	0010	2
3	0011	3
4	0100	4
5	0101	5
6	0110	6
7	0111	7
8	1000	8
9	1001	9
10	1010	a
11	1011	b
12	1100	c
13	1101	d
14	1110	e
15	1111	f

uses an alphanumeric numbering scheme. For example, the decimal number 1101 is a "d" in hexadecimal. An electronic access control system would need more than four binary bits to allow a company to issue badges to employees and contractors. Credential numbers vary in length, although standard lengths are available. A badge that is thirty-one bits long will have a credential number of around one million, depending on the protocol. Twenty bits of a 31-bit number will provide slightly over one million unique credential numbers.

The grouping of bits used for the credential number, company/site code and parity bits combine to provide the total data stream making up the badge protocol. To better illustrate the protocol of badges refer to Figure 2.1. In this figure, the parity bit is the first bit; the company code is bits 28 through 38. The credential number is bits 10 through 27. Protocol definitions add protection and security. When a badge number is read, the company/site codes are checked first. If they do not match with the correct company/site bit pattern, then the badge is denied access. When a badge is denied because of incorrect company/site bit patterns, the credential number is not even necessary. For this reason, many access control systems strip off the company/site code first for a match. If there is a match, the credential number is then verified. The credential number will normally reside in the electronic panel in the field. If the company/site code matches, but the credential number is not in the electronic field panel, then the access control server is checked for a match. If a match is made, the server sends a door release command to the electronic field panel and downloads the credential number to the electronic field panel. This is referred to as dynamic loading, and it usually only happens the first time a badge is used at a given portal. The initial download may take tens of seconds. After the credential number has been downloaded from the access control server to the field panel, the next time the badge is used the processing time should be three-quarters of a second or less.

In the 31-bit example, some of the other bits are used to provide additional information and assure proper transmission of the data from the badge to the electronic panel in the field. Then the data is verified from the electronic panel in the field to the access control server/computer. These additional bits fall into two categories. The first bit type is a grouping of bits that defines a company, site or both. They are referred to as company code and/or site code. The manufacturer will establish this when the company

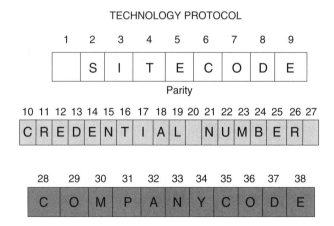

Figure 2.1 Binary breakdown of protocol.

places the initial badge order. If a company is small and its badge orders will be small, the badges may be ordered from an alarm company or badge manufacturing service generally with a common protocol that will be sold to many companies. If this is the case, the actual company/site code numbers may be the coding of the alarm company that supplies the badge. The company/site code will not be unique for the purchasing company. The alarm company or badge manufacturing service does its best not to duplicate numbers, providing unique numbers in the credential field. If for some reason a badge number is duplicated, then it would be possible for someone to gain unauthorized access to a different company via the duplicated number that is in the other database.

The second bit type denotes the parity (the quality or state of being equal). It is used in an access control system to assure that the data sent from the badge reader to the field panel is correct. There are several variations as to how this is done. For simplicity, one way to accomplish the task is by counting the number of 1's in the entire data stream. If the number of 1's is an odd number, a parity bit can be defined as an odd parity bit. When the badge is encoded, the parity bit is programmed into the badge data. Then when the reader sends the data to the field panel it is again counted and the parity bit checked. If the odd parity bit is set and the number of 1s is odd, then the field panel assumes that the data received is correct. To better explain parity refer to Figure 2.2.

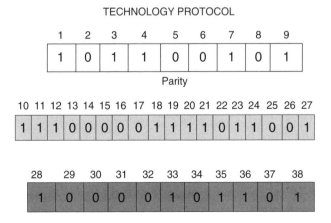

Figure 2.2 Binary breakdown of protocol.

In this example, the parity bit is the first bit in the data steam. In Figure 2.2, bit #1 covers bits 2 through 38. The parity bit is set to 1 because there are nineteen 1 bits in the data stream or data word. Many times more than 1 parity bit is used. In this case, the parity bits cover half the data word to improve the odds that the data being sent is correct. There are now two samples being checked in the same data stream or word to verify parity.

There are several badge technologies available and each has advantages and disadvantages. The majority of the access control market has been magnetic stripe, because of cost. Weigand has been used for high security applications. Now there is a strong move toward proximity and contact-less smart cards. To better understand each of the four primary badge technologies, they will be discussed one at a time.

Magnetic stripe is basically the same material as a Video Home System (VHS) cassette tape used in a home video recorder and the material used on a standard credit card. When initially encoding a badge, a write head magnetizes the information on the magnetic stripe. A read head in the badge reader is used to read the written information much like the read head in a tape player reads the audiotape. The maximum number of bits in any protocol utilizing magnetic stripe technology is 75. There are three standard tracks on each tape for recording the data. The first track is for the Air International Transport Association; the second is for the American Bankers Association; and the third track is for the Savings and Loan Association. Security does not follow a standard, so the information could be on any of the three tracks. Magnetic stripe badges are often recorded on all three tracks to minimize reader track issues. The data loaded or written onto the magnetic stripe is resistant to electromagnetic fields. This capability to resist being erased is referred to as coercivity, and the magnetic stripe material used on badges has a high coercivity. It is possible to erase the information, as some have found, on their credit cards when they are placed on the counter of a department store that uses EAS (Electronic Article Security) tags to protect their products. The store has a large degaussing (demagnetizing) device often mounted under the checkout counter that destroys the EAS tags so that you can leave the store without an alarm going off. Your credit card might also get erased by this same device, if set on the checkout counter. *Pro:* This technology is inexpensive, fairly reliable, and easily programmed. Although this technology provides limited security, it is easy to reprogram badges. *Con:* This technology can suffer from environmental problems and abrasion due to swiping. Badge life is reduced because of reader abrasion to the technology itself as well as the employee/contractor picture on the badge. Exterior reader heads especially tend to get dirty and require frequent cleaning. The magnetic data on the badge can be inadvertently erased. A credential number and protocol can be easily counterfeited when this technology is used.

Weigand is a technology that uses a wire made of a special twisted alloy that retains magnetism for a very short period of time. The wires are placed in two rows with one above the other. The presence of a wire represents a "one" on the lower row and a wire on the upper row represents a "zero." The wires are installed at the manufacturer's facility so they cannot be changed. The wires are not permanently magnetized on the badge but are temporarily magnetized by a head in the reader (for a short period of time) and then immediately read by the reader. The readers contain two heads: one head is used to magnetize and one head is used to read the wires. *Pro:* This technology is moderately priced, reliable, and factory preprogrammed. The manufacturer strictly controls distribution, coding and badge production for any given customer. Some proprietary standards were available to large users with a numbering scheme large enough for the entire company for 10 years, without repeating numbers. (Ten years is somewhat arbitrary, but badges are distributed faster than anyone plans for and repeat numbers cause problems in the database.) This technology provides a high level of security and is very difficult to duplicate. The manufacturer physically sets Weigand wires in a pattern before the badge is shipped to the customer. Weigand readers are hermetically sealed and are not subject to most environmental issues (rain, frost, magnetic fields caused by plant electrical systems, lighting, etc.). *Con:* The numbering scheme is set at the manufacturer and cannot be altered by the end user. The technology requires swiping the badge through a reader. There is some abrasion to the badge if protective film is not employed, which may affect the employee/contractor picture depending upon picture placement.

A *proximity badge* utilizes an RF technology, 125kHz (125,000 hertz) that receives the RF energy from the reader. The energy charges a capacitor within the proximity badge and "wakes up" the electronic chip embedded in the badge. The chip then sends the data stored inside the badge to the reader at one-half the frequency generated by the reader. Most badges are passive; that is, they do not have a battery that supplies the energy for the chip to transmit. The capacitor that is on the badge acts like a short-term battery providing power to the chip so that it will "talk" to the reader. There are active proximity badges that contain a long-life battery, but most proximity cards in the security market are passive. The advantage of active cards is that they transmit further, so the distance the card can be held from the reader is greater. Passive badge read distances are normally in inches and active badge read distances are in feet. The data stored in a proximity badge is about 96 bits of information. *Pro:* This technology is moderately priced, reliable, and partially preprogrammed by the manufacturer. This price is dropping and will continue to drop as more applications for proximity applications expand. There are several notable areas for proximity in addition to the typical door control access: the transportation industry and the government logistics area, specifically. This technology provides medium security and is fairly difficult to duplicate. The technology allows "hands free" or, more accurately, "swipe free" badge reads at short distances. Readers are not subject to most environmental issues (rain, frost, abrasion). Some proprietary standards were available to large users with a numbering schemes large enough for the entire company for 10 years, without repeating numbers. (Ten years is somewhat arbitrary, but badges are distributed faster than anyone plans for and repeat numbers cause problems in the database.) *Con:* The distance between badge and reader for reliable badge reads is normally 3 inches or less. This technology is susceptible to high levels of electromagnetic fields that can destroy the badges. Reader placement (on metal vs. wood) can adversely affect the "read" distance between the badge and the reader.

   Contact-less smart cards are similar to proximity badges in that they utilize RF energy, the price is going down and both technologies are often referred to as Radio Frequency Identification (RFID). RFID is available in several different frequencies and has been used primarily in applications where a long read distance is needed (except for tagging animals). RFID has been used in the toll tag and the material inventory/movement markets. The frequency used by contact-less smart cards is also different from proximity badges: smart cards utilize 13.56 mHz (13,560,000 hertz). They also differ from proximity badges in that they have much more data storage, can be segmented for different tasks, can process and modify information stored in the card, contain cryptographic functions performed when the card and reader communicate and transmits at a different frequency. One note is that each manufacturer of contact-less smart cards has a proprietary protocol. When a manufacturer says that they can read other manufacture's smart cards, what they really mean is that they can read the serial number of the card, not what is stored in the card. (The best way to visualize the serial number limitation is to consider a house address. Anyone can read the address, but only the home owner can see what is inside the house.) There are standards such as the European standard (MIFARE), but for security access control applications the protocols are proprietary. *Pro:* Smart cards could be partitioned to provide a one-card solution across the company. For example, security as well as the IT department could use the same card. 128 Kbits+ cards/badges are available with many partitions possible. Going to one new standard for both IT and Security could save money. *Con:* Security could lose control of the data being entered on the smart card. If Security was the only data entry point controlling the card, personnel would need to be added to make the constant changes necessary from an IT standpoint. IT could control their own data entry, on their partitions, by downloading that data each time the badge was used to activate a computer.

MANUFACTURING PROCESS

Even after the badge design is agreed upon, there is the issue of production and distribution. These can both be formidable tasks. To produce the badge, equipment must be selected and purchased that will make the badge production process reliable. There is always a desire to use a "one step" badge making process which usually involves a PVC badge stock that will be printed with all employee information including a photo in a single process. The photo is digitized and printed on the badge when the company logo, and so on is being printed. Note that not all printers are created equal.

They can be purchased to encode the technology used in the badge, provide card-cleaning mechanisms, provide operator display, print both sides of a badge, and process high volumes of badges. But these "one step" high volume double badge stock side printers with encoders are expensive and do require maintenance. The printer will be one of the major expenditures of the badge-making system. The heads in the printer will be the primary failure point. The cost of the heads, the critical way they are installed, and the complexity of pinpointing failures within the printer should be compared among manufacturers. Even the quality of the card stock can impact printer head failure.

The second issue with printers is the adjustments required to process badges. The printer must be adjusted for the thickness of the badge stock to assure proper flow through the printer. The type and thickness of the clear laminate that is to be used must be adjusted so that the laminate attaches properly to the badge stock. This adjustment refers to the heat used to make the badge. Then there are issues of properly reproducing colors, patterns and logos. The color will vary based upon the number of badges run through the printer at a given time and the temperature of the print heads. The large areas of solid color on the badge are also difficult to duplicate accurately. The settings on the computer program must be correct and quality ribbons must be installed in the printer. The number of badges the manufacturer states can be made in a given time period with a certain printer may not be valid when large quantities of badges are processed at one time.

One way to minimize these problems is to select the proper printer, design the badge without major areas of color, or preprint portions of the badge stock. Any of these approaches will work and the badge can be individualized (with name and photograph) during the final step using the "access badge" printer. There are many ways to resolve these potential problems as long as they are considered early in the process.

Another potential problem for "one-step" badge making is that badges made by this process do not normally work well in readers that tend to cause abrasion such as a swipe reader unless a clear overlay laminate is utilized. Some manufacturers provide a clear laminate from .1 to 1 mil. (A mil is a thousandth of an inch or .001 inch.) This provides some level of protection, normally the thicker the better for swipe readers. Some printers work better with one thickness over another, so the printer can be a limiting factor as to which clear laminate thickness is used. The cost of making the badges, the level of effort to distribute the badges and the desired usable life of the badges must be weighed against each other. Some applications may well warrant an inexpensive badge because there is not a concern with badge life expectancy or effort needed to distribute the badges. (A badge can be designed to last from a few days up to 10 years.) The environment in which the badges will be used, as well as the person using the badges, will affect the life expectancy. For example, a manufacturing company's blue collar employees will have badges that do not typically last as long as a company that is made up mostly of office workers, because of the work environment and employee handling of the badge.

Another option is to print onto a 14-mil adhesive-backed "stick-on." The stick-on is printed and then attached to the PVC badge stock that contains the technology. This approach allows for a more reliable printing process because the probability of flaws increases when printing on top of a technology that is embedded inside the badge. For example, badges typically have minor flaws when printed on top of Weigand, proximity or smart cards. With the adhesive-backed stick-on the thickness is exact, the surface is perfectly smooth, and a clear laminate can be attached during the printing process just as it can be attached to a PVC badge. This approach also allows for a badge to be reused. The old stick-on can be removed and a new stick-on attached to the badge. This removal process often includes removing the old adhesive which adds labor time. This is the argument manufacturers use in their advertisements; however, it is my opinion that the benefit is in the printing process not the reusing of badges. (The potential security issues with reusing a badge are strongly debated.)

We have addressed components and issues associated with manufacturing a reliably producible badge. What has not been addressed is the badge room itself, which is a critical component in reliably producing and distributing badges. Figure 2.3 shows a badge room with all the usual equipment. There is a standardized colored background mounted on the wall that provides the picture background of the badge; a camera to take pictures of employees and contractors; a mirror on the side door for people to check their

Figure 2.3 Typical badge room.

appearance prior to having their badge photo taken; a flat screen monitor that allows the person receiving the badge to view his or her picture prior to printing the badge. This way, if there is a problem the picture can be retaken and avoids wasting badge stock and printer ribbon. There is a printer and an enrollment system in the badge room. On the left hand side, just out of view, there is an enrollment reader. These are used so that the personnel in the badge room are not entering the credential numbers on the badge. Manual data entry is a source of errors, which needs to be avoided. There is also a proximity encoder that can encode the badge and automatically load the database. Lastly there is a reader on the wall by the picture background material that allows the user to test the new badge in the access control system to make sure the badge works and the data in the database is correct.

Distribution has been mentioned earlier; however, in a large company implementing and distributing a "new badge" can be a challenge. The replacement or issuance of a large number of badges in a relatively short period of time requires careful planning.

A digitized badge station can use multiple printers to increase throughput for the manufacturing of badges. This requires the badge station to be able to handle multiple printer ports. There is, of course, a limit imposed by the speed of the PC and by the number of printers that can be run in an optimal situation. When there is an existing badge system in use and the new badge technology is not compatible, distribution issues multiply. This is normally addressed with a multitechnology badge that will provide a bridge that spans the reader technology conversion. Some of the questions that arise when an existing system is to be replaced are:

1. When does the switchover to the new badge start?
2. Is the switchover accomplished at the site, building, or department level?
3. How are employees who are visiting from other sites allowed access?
4. What is the time frame to cut over all company facilities?
5. What happens to the old badges?
6. Could someone gain access through a lobby with an old badge?
7. What changes must be made in the access control hardware and software?
8. How will the access control database be cleaned up?
9. Can multiple records be created for each user in the database so that new badges can be distributed prior to cutover?
10. Should the employees and contractors be required to have new photos taken?

The challenges of installing a new access control system that will be readily accepted by the employees are extremely difficult. The results of system design and implementation can be compromised or even destroyed if the less technical side of the access control system is not carefully considered. The way the badge will look and be reproduced must be part of the initial plan. Time to incorporate the badge design must be allowed for, as well as making and distributing the badges. These pieces of a successful access control project must mesh with the project installation schedule and budget. It is important to develop a team of stakeholders that represent all aspects of Security as well as HR, Facilities, Management, and Legal to assure success. Appendix A lists questions to address when planning an enterprise-wide badge.

To sum up, the badge decisions associated with technology, design and reliable/dependable manufacturing processes are very complex. The solution as to the perfect badge is a compromise of many options and impacts a wide range of topics. The badge appearance, technology and uses will depend upon company culture and philosophy. (A great deal of detail was provided about binary numbering schemes and protocols. This information applies to all binary signals and will be referred to in other chapters.) The choice of badges and applications will impact a company's capital expenditure. For an item that symbolizes security to everyone that interfaces with a company, the choice of that symbol is not a simple process. Even with a thorough program that evaluated all the topics addressed above and included all the right stakeholders, sometimes a simple error or omission can cause havoc with the enterprise-wide badge program. For example, the discussion has not addressed one simple issue that may arise: should the badge be punched for a clip to allow the employee/contractor to wear it? If proximity badges are utilized, it is possible to punch the hole in a location that cuts through the antenna, which makes the badge unusable.

Biometrics

3

Biometric sensors for security applications has been a hot topics for years. They have a mystique and aura of high tech devices that would be utilized in super secret government applications. They conger up in one's mind the technologically advanced devices used by spies like James Bond. The truth is that many movies do depict high tech biometric devices similar to those available today used to gain access to sensitive areas. Biometric devices used to identify an individual use various identifiers of the individual, such as fingerprints, hand geometry, retinal or iris scan, voice, dynamic signature, and facial features to name a few. Biometrics has been around and evolving for a long period of time. Its acceptance into the security market has been slow primarily due to cost. The biometric devices available today have a great deal to offer and can provide very solid security in many company applications. To understand and evaluate each of the biometric products in a given security environment requires a look at each device's background, strengths, and weaknesses. In this chapter, we will review many of the biometric devices on the market and their potential issues.

One of the selling points of biometrics is that it eliminates the need for items that must be carried around with you, such as identification badges and keys. For example, if a fingerprint biometric reader were used, then you would only need to have your finger, which should always be available. A finger, unlike a key, could not be mistakenly left on the kitchen table. In the security market, the heart of the biometrics concept is access control through individual biometric measurements and individual distinguishing identifiers. This might be one's finger, hand, signature, face, weight or eyes. (It can also be a combination of more than one identifier.) As mentioned above, these are all items that do not have to be remembered and can't be left at home. The use of a biometrics identifier to allow access to a given area has a persuasive sales pitch and has indeed been a large part of the reason that biometric devices have been used in high security applications for years. As cost for these devices decreases, they will be used in more and more applications. The goal for expanding the use of biometric devices is ease of use and accuracy.

Their primary use in the past has typically been in high security, low volume applications. The use of biometric devices was driven by the value of equipment or sensitivity of information contained in a controlled area. The number of users that would access the area via the biometric device was normally a small group, because the biometric systems tend to be a slower means of access. This is changing as biometric devices are being added to check people entering the United States. The border patrol applications of one or more biometric devices are expanding due to the phony documents and heightened security developed because of 9/11.

A badge reader can process the information contained in a badge in less than three-quarters of a second. If the time is longer than one second, people will complain about the access control system being too slow. Biometric devices can process much faster than they used to; however, they still take a few seconds. They also require the presentation of the biometric item to be presented—a finger, a hand, an eye, and so on. The total process of presenting the biometric item and processing time to verify access will normally be longer than reading a badge; however, the positive verification of an individual is substantially more likely with biometric applications than with a badge read only. In the case of border checks, where multiple biometric technologies are used to verify individuals, the results approach total verification.

There are of course other advantages of biometric devices that make them desirable.

1. The systems are smart and can update the database with each "read." For example, a weight sensor system modifies the database with each access request. In this way, the database is adjusted as an individual adds or loses weight. (This of course works best when the system is used on a daily basis.)

2. The system will minimize the possibility that any unauthorized person will gain entry. In a conventional access card system, an unauthorized person can gain access by using a lost badge that has not been removed from the database. Biometrics, on the other hand, requires the measurable item of an authorized person to be present. For example, if a fingerprint system is used, the finger must be present. In fact, some fingerprint systems measure temperature to assure that the finger indeed belongs to the living authorized individual.

3. The database can be contained within the reader electronics. The digitized information that reflects the biometric item is stored in the equipment's database. Normally a personal identification number (PIN) and/or badge are used as a second source of identification and that information also is stored in the database. This allows the biometric system to stand alone or to be integrated into a larger access control system. Biometrics can be used in place of any other access control product from a badge reader to a door key. These products are not limited to a specific architecture like badge readers that require a field panel to control doors. The database and decision-making process can be contained within the biometric device itself. When the biometric item of an authorized user and the biometric information stored in the electronics are a match, the device provides a switch closure similar to an electronic field panel that is part of a badge reader system. When a match of the biometric item and a PIN occurs, a relay is activated that can send power to an

electronic door lock or remove power to a magnetic lock directly. The data is normally resident in the biometric device. When data is remotely stored and a central server is not required to house the data, the system is referred to as a distributed processing system. Distributed processing simply means that all the information needed to grant or deny access is in the field (at the door) and no information must be sent and received from a remote server/computer. Smart cards are sometimes used to store the biometric information and PINs. If this approach is used, the card owner in essence carries the database with him or her. This database can be modified and reloaded into the card to address weight change that was discussed earlier. If smart cards are utilized, the data is normally encrypted. With this technology, the applications are only limited by one's imagination.

Even with these advantages, biometric applications have been slow to expand in the security market. There have been predictions for years that these technologies would take over the security access control market. There are limitations that have impacted biometrics that will be explored in more detail. Some of the limitations have been mentioned already in this chapter. As the limitations are discussed, you will see how different technologies are trying to overcome their particular limitations. There will always be improvements, so it is important to study these limitations to better understand the past performance of the different biometric technologies. There have been five major limitations of biometrics in access control.

1. Price
2. Usability/intrusiveness
3. Enrollment
4. Biometric variations
5. Processing speed

PRICE

Biometric devices are more intricate in hardware and software than the typical access control device, which makes them more expensive. Over time the price of biometric devices has gone down due to increased sales, reduction in production cost, utilization of better designs and changes in technology. Prices will continue to drop as these factors are optimized and the biometric applications expand. The use of biometric devices and biometric systems is growing within commercial applications also. These include scanning an iris for access to an Automated Teller Machine (ATM). There is no doubt that many other large applications will soon be coming. This applies to government security applications and the simple drivers license. A Global Positioning System (GPS) was fairly unknown and expensive until it was used on cell phones and by OnStar in vehicles.

USABILITY/INTRUSIVENESS

Because biometric devices measure one's distinguishing identifiers, there are issues of usability. For example, voiceprint has in the past used a telephone handset to talk into for enrollment and authorization. A handset was used to eliminate ambient noise levels, which could cause errors in allowing access for an unapproved person or denying access for an authorized person. (These errors for biometric devices are referred to as Type/Class I, an authorized user is rejected, and Type/Class II, an unauthorized user is accepted.) Some employees/users do not want to use a handset that someone else has used. The handset could spread colds or flu. This type of user reluctance can apply to other biometrics technologies as well.

The other major issue was the ease of using the device itself. In the example of voiceprint, when an employee tries to gain access, the process is fairly cumbersome. The employee is required to pick up a handset, talk into it, usually put in a PIN and then hang it up to gain access. The PIN is used to index the memory of the biometric device that allows faster processing associated with the biometric data. This is referred to as a one-to-one match (versus a one-to-many match caused by comparing the biometric data from and individual against the entire database of individuals). With this level of effort, you could argue against ease of use. This difficulty was typical for many of the biometric devices, not only voiceprint.

When a smart card containing the biometric data is used, there is some concern for protecting the data. By carrying the biometric matching information around within a smart card there is some level of exposure to the data being extracted or modified. The extraction could be an unauthorized removal or modification performed on a lost or stolen card. The extraction could also be electronically activated covertly while being in the possession of an authorized party. (It takes a sophisticated effort to compromise a smart card.) Most smart card manufacturers minimize this by encryption techniques within the card. Passwords are often required during the interrogation of the software loaded in the smart card. The concern is having the data reside in the card instead of it being safely stored in a biometric device or server's database within a protected facility.

ENROLLMENT

The enrollment in most biometric devices requires several attempts to assure that good data is obtained. The level of data required depends upon the percent limits desired for Type/Class I and Type/Class II errors. For example, retina scan employs a spinning disk that the enrollee has to focus on to assure the retinal pattern is processed by the biometric electronics using the same view in the same way each time. Typically, the enrollment requires three attempts. After completing enrollment, the user is then asked to process an access control request using the retinal scan. If there are problems gaining entry, the enrollment process has to be restarted. Although time consuming, this enrollment process is similar for most biometric devices.

BIOMETRIC VARIATIONS

The challenge for biometric devices is to allow access for authorized individuals every time they request entry. The goal is *not* to reject authorized individuals, Type/Class I error. The biometric device should always deny access to unauthorized individuals. Said another way, there should be no false accepting or false authorization of unauthorized individuals, Type/Class II errors. The goal is to adjust the parameters of the various biometric devices so that there is a total elimination of both types of errors. This is normally not accomplished if the database is very large. A typical access control system will have a high 90+ percent elimination of both types of errors. To reach this goal, of eliminating Type I and Type II errors, the electronics and software must be sophisticated enough to handle the problems that the "real world applications" provide. For example, fingerprint biometric devices require a reliable fingerprint to compare to the database. There can be issues with the finger being too dry, too wet, too greasy or too smooth. These limitations can be employed in a covert effort to avoid detection or just a simple real-life everyday problem that prevents access. For example, an employee has been working all weekend on painting his or her home and has been sanding the wood on the soffitt to get ready to paint. The fingerprint may have been abraded to the point that it will not reliably compare with the sample in the biometric devices database. Other biometric devices can each have similar issues that make totally eliminating Type I and Type II errors impractical. One solution is to utilize more than one biometric device or include PINs, badges or passwords.

PROCESSING SPEED

Biometric devices require several seconds on average to verify authorization. The smaller the database when performing a one-to-many match the faster the processing speed. The sophistication of the technology will also affect processing speed. Different technologies and different manufacturers will claim different processing speeds. For example, a fingerprint biometric device will vary from one-half a second up to less than 3 seconds. This reflects the speed of the actual device after being presented with the biometric identifier. Time associated with entering PINs or placing a finger on the device is normally not included. In Chapter 2, when we discussed badge reading speed, the goal was to process the badge read in less than three-quarters of a second. This does not include the time required for an employee to find the badge and present it to the reader. When considering personnel flow through a portal, the total effort time must be considered. In the case of a badge reader and a revolving door, a five-second-per-person time frame is assumed when deciding the number of revolving doors needed for a given portal. This 5 seconds allows enough time to open the coat (in the winter), find the badge and present the badge; then system verification of the badge and energizing a light and/or a buzzer that acknowledges verification; and finally the person stepping into the revolving door and processing through to the other side. If the revolving door allows movement in both directions (entering and leaving), then the largest number of personnel in any one direction is all that must be counted to determine the number of revolving doors needed at a given portal. This approach is used to assure reasonable flow without queuing. Properly allowing for the total processing time for personnel applies to biometric control portals also, although the number of users in a biometric portal is normally less in a company-type environment.

The limited applications for biometrics systems in security are changing and have been discussed to some level already in the chapter. The causes for this change come from a wider acceptance/applications and need for a higher reliability of verification, such as border control, which has already been mentioned. There are other causes for the renewed interest in biometric applications:

1. Many new biometric technologies have appeared in recent years that are less obtrusive. An example is facial recognition and finger blood vessel imaging. Facial recognition technology can be a camera and associated software at a portal that allows entry to an area. It can also be sophisticated software that processes video information from one or many cameras that view an area. This type of application can be used in public areas such as airports or casinos. Fingerprint technology is available that plugs directly into a Universal Serial Bus (USB) port on a PC that can be used instead of passwords to obtain access to a company's application software and network.

2. The various technologies have found new ways to measure biometric identifiers in less obtrusive ways, thus enhancing usability. They have also found ways to overcome the detrimental modifications that have had a negative impact on the access control systems. For example, in the past, retinal scan required a user to place an eye on a rubber cup that was part of the biometric device. Now the eye can be processed without touching the device. Changes in the types of technologies used, such as iris scans and facial

recognition systems, have also appeared in the market. Even with facial recognition there is a major difference in the technology used to develop the image that is digitized. One technology utilizes a standard Closed Circuit Television (CCTV) camera and the other is infrared. These are diverse approaches to process the same distinguishing identifier. Other identifiers will be found that will be cost effective and less obtrusive.

3. Speed of processing has been enhanced; in fact, some biometrics systems are extremely fast compared to where they were several years ago. This trend will continue as hardware speeds increase and software becomes more efficient while minimizing Type I and II errors.

4. Teaming partners are being used more now than in the past, such as system integrators that incorporate biometrics into a larger access control system and companies that incorporate privately labeled products as though they were part of their own product line. The newer approach is to have a teaming partner that actually works directly with the manufacturer and end user to develop software and hardware that meets a specific market need. Another teaming approach is a joining of several companies where each has the expertise needed to develop a product for a specific market. This concept has been used for years in the defense and computer industries.

5. Biometric systems are being used to replace other technologies. For example, biometric fingerprint technology is attempting to match the quality of hard copy ink images. The new twist is in using the biometric fingerprint to obtain such a high quality image that it can replace ink fingerprinting and link many different law enforcement databases together. One aspect of the biometric market has become high quality fingerprint images versus simply allowing access as part of an access control system. The changes in the biometric systems as well as their applications have reached an all-time high. Iris scan, for example, is a technology that measures differences in the iris pattern of the eye. A bank chain has chosen this technology for use in its ATM machines and this concept is now being tested.

In the bank ATM system, user inconvenience is minimized and processing speeds are very fast. This biometrics concept of controlling ATM transactions is also being accomplished using fingerprint technology. Biometrics has been primarily used for access control, but today new products are being developed for applications where a card technology may have been used before, for example, time and attendance access to computer networks, activation of encryption software, and so on. These applications can be part of a larger computer network or stand-alone. Even the arming and disarming of home security systems is available with biometrics. Fingerprint technology can help prevent car theft by storing the owner's fingerprint data in the automobile computer. When the door is opened, the biometric sensor on the inside of the door handle will verify the fingerprint profile against the profile stored in the automobile database.

For high security applications, the thought process has been to provide "something you have" plus "something you know" plus "something that is you" to confirm identification. The something you have has been a badge; the something you know has been a PIN; the something you are has been a biometric identifier. The system was a way of assuring that several components were compared before verification could be accomplished. If any one of the components was compromised, the user would be denied access. This approach has worked very well. In less demanding applications, a single or even dual method of authentication might be used. To better understand which application in a given technology should be utilized requires an understanding of each technology and the knowledge that each biometric identifier used is a unique identifier to each individual. There can be subtle differences in different manufacturers' claims. Some consider one-to-one comparisons as an "authentication" and a one-to-many as "identification." Some of the more common biometric technologies are addressed below.

IRIS SCAN

The iris is the colored part of the eye surrounding the pupil and is just as unique for every individual as a fingerprint. The areas that can be measured are pits, furrows and striations of the iris. A black and white video camera is used to obtain the iris image. This normally requires a distance between the individual and the camera of a few inches to a couple of feet. There is a low power near-infrared illumination that enhances the video. (Infrared and cameras are covered in Chapter 7.) The software must define the iris area and remove information that obscures/modifies the image, such as eyelashes, glasses, reflections and so on. The software then develops a pattern of data that is compressed and usually encrypted to protect the data. The storage needed for each individual will be in the range of 512 bits.

RETINAL SCAN

The retina is the surface on the back inner wall of the eye where the images we see are focused and in turn processed by our brain via the nervous system. The blood vessels attach to the eye in the retinal area. This vascular pattern is what is used to develop a template. To properly see the vascular pattern, the eye must be properly focused. This is accomplished with a spinning wheel that is viewed in the biometric device. Since the human eye cannot "see" in the infrared frequency range and protect itself from exposure, there has been some concern that the infrared scanning device used to obtain the vascular pattern would damage the eye. This has not been an issue because of the extremely low power used. This technique has been used for years with newer systems allowing the vascular pattern to be scanned without having to place one's eye directly on the biometric device. There are over 300 distinct points used to develop the template that is digitized and stored for comparison.

FINGERPRINT

Fingerprinting requires either an actual image of a fingerprint or a capture of minute ridge endings to develop a template. Some manufacturers use as many as 500 points per inch to develop a template. The devices are very reasonably priced and are also available in many configurations that add to their flexibility. For example, a fingerprint device can be purchased to allow access to a PC via a USB port. There is some concern about the device storing a fingerprint as far as privacy issues are concerned but the device actually

Figure 3.1 Fingerprint. Courtesy of Ingersoll Rand Recognition Systems.

stores points in the fingerprint and not the actual fingerprint itself. The obvious potential limitation of the device is poor print quality. About 5 percent of the population has fingerprints that are not of the quality needed for the device to provide a reliable match. There are an additional number of people who damage their fingerprints for a short period of time unintentionally (by sanding wood to get it ready to paint). Then there are those who intentionally damage their prints. To overcome defective prints, multiple fingers must be scanned. It takes eight to ten fingers to get a 95 percent Type/Class I and Type/Class II rate. Dry, greasy or dirty fingers can also be a problem to properly read. See Figure 3.1.

HAND GEOMETRY

This technology utilizes a plate with guide pegs that properly position the proper hand for scanning. There are left- and right-handed models. The device measures the fingers' widths and lengths, proportions of the hand, curvature, and webbing between the fingers. A camera is used to obtain the three-dimensional image (this is usually accomplished with one camera and a mirror to obtain a second view), which is made into a template and digitized. Various points

Figure 3.2   Hand geometry. Courtesy of Ingersoll Rand Recognition Systems.

become the data that must be matched to obtain access. The number of digital points is in excess of thirty thousand. This data is compressed and loaded into memory. The data utilizes a vector algorithm to regenerate the uncompressed data. Since hand geometry units take a side view of the hand, a person wearing a large number of rings can present a problem with false rejects. See Figure 3.2.

FACIAL RECOGNITION

This biometric approach is used every day to identify people. The difference between a biometric device and the way a human recognizes a face is that a camera and software are used in place of our eyes and our brain. The camera requires good lighting, but no special lighting requirements. The software is designed to address issues such as a photo being used, glasses being on or off, and changes in facial hair. (There is a limit to the amount of hair covering the face, particularly around the center of the face.) The facial evaluation can vary in complexity and data storage requirements. The most basic two-dimensional system evaluates the geometry of the face including the relative distances between predefined features such as the nose, mouth and eyes. The most complex two-dimensional system evaluates skin texture, and randomly defined features. The frontal angle for proper identification can vary as long as both eyes are clearly visible. There are also three-dimensional systems that develop an image based upon multiple two-dimensional images. The final variation is a newer, more sophisticated type of facial recognition system that scans lobbies, casinos or airports, identifying people that are in a controlled database.

DYNAMIC SIGNATURE

This technology utilizes a process that is common to everyone who signs his or her name. People's signatures have been studied for years to evaluate personality. Three different aspects and capabilities that can be utilized with signature dynamics are (1) capturing signatures, (2) authenticating signatures and (3) binding signatures. Capturing signatures is used by many different industries already, including the checkout line at Wal-Mart. Authenticating signatures is often used in the security environment. Binding signatures is the capability of locking the signature with other biometric data as part of a document. It cannot be removed without making the document invalid and is used in the financial industry for documents such as applications, mortgage closing documents, and so on. See Figure 3.3. A biometric dynamic signature device measures the pressure, speed/timing, shape, stroke order and motion of a signature and can be accomplished with a sensitive platform or a sensitive pen. The sensing component develops a template based on pressure, speed and motion. This template is compared to the one stored in memory. If they match, the device activates a relay to open a door and/or the signature can be verified and loaded into a computer as documentation. Some manufacturers have difficulty matching left-handed people's signatures.

With biometric devices there is always the concept of spoofing the devices in the back of people's mind. There are articles that are published from time to time expressing concern about potential

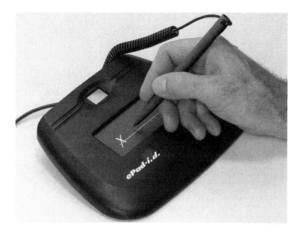

Figure 3.3   Signature dynamics. Courtesy of Interlink.

vulnerabilities of a given biometric technology. There are Web sites dedicated to spoofing and counterfeiting other types of identification. A biometric technology that almost always receives some spoofing exposure is fingerprint technology. There are potential counterfeit fingerprint materials that are reported to be successful in allowing access. Biometric fingerprint manufacturers have developed ways to overcome the actual counterfeit finger. They include a temperature sensor to verify that at least the "finger" is close to 90°F, and a time limit on verification to make using a counterfeit finger difficult to maneuver. They are even testing an electronic "nose" to sense silicon, gelatin, latex and Play-Doh. The level of effort required and the likelihood of spoofing a biometric sensor should be part of the risk assessment for the area being protected. The sophistication of the biometric sensor will be associated with the price of the device. The less expensive, the more likely it is that the device can be easily compromised. For example, some fingerprint readers on the computer mouse can be compromised by providing moisture from your breath to enhance the latent fingerprint that is already there. These potential problems appear to be more sinister, probably because of the mystique of the biometric field. In reality, all devices and technologies have strengths and weaknesses. Any installation should consider the technology and the application with an eye on possible compromise and the needed level of security required. There is no perfect solution or product, so do not depend on any one approach to gain 100 percent success. Biometric devices will continue to become more sophisticated and the government will help fund applications and development. If we think about the way the human brain recognizes someone, we can better understand the direction of biometric applications and solutions. The brain looks for patterns that match the way a person walks, holds him- or herself, and general appearance. When the person comes closer, the brain uses facial recognition and/or other biometric features. The brain also recognizes people by the environment they are in. Have you ever failed to recognize someone or were not sure if they were the person you thought they were because of where you saw them?

4

Electronic Alarm Systems

Most security professionals think of alarm systems first when securing a facility. Alarms are an important aspect of any security program. The goal of a security program is to provide cost effective detection, assessment, delay, and response. A properly designed alarm system will provide the first component goal, which is detection. Assessment is accomplished with closed circuit television (covered in Chapter 7). To delay a potential intruder, the physical side of security [such as fencing, barriers, open expanse and techniques such as those used in Crime Prevention Through Environmental Design (CPTED)] typically accomplishes this goal. The response goal is not discussed as such in this book because it is primarily a security officer issue. However, by properly incorporating all the topics in this book, the security officer is much more likely to provide a timely response. The correct designs, maintenance, systems selection, philosophy, integration and automation provide systems that allow the operator in the Security Control Center (SCC) to effectively handle all situations efficiently. The first major goal of detection is accomplished with the electronic alarm system. This chapter will cover the alarm system with a focus on design concerns and selection issues. The alarm system with its associated sensors should detect an intruder as early as possible. This requires both exterior and interior sensors (discussed in Chapter 6). The electronic alarm system collects the sensor inputs and provides the alarm and location information to the operator in the SCC. The reason for separating the alarm system from the sensors in different chapters is to provide enough detail for both components of the detection system to be properly understood. The approach is similar to the first two chapters, where one chapter covered the access control system and the other covered badge manufacturing.

A review of the basic components that comprise an electronic alarm system is the first place to start the discussion. There are sensors throughout and around a facility which connect to an electronic panel in the field. (The field panel is typically connected to other field panels.) The sensors' alarm information is then sent from the electronic field panel to a server/computer. Figure 4.1 represents the typical alarm system architecture. The sensors in the field, no matter how sophisticated, provide a simple switch closure when

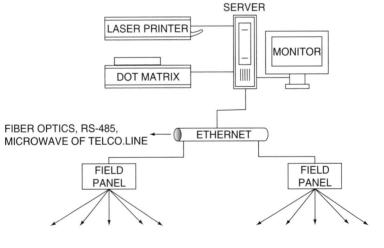

Figure 4.1 System architecture.

they alarm. The wiring from the sensor terminates in the electronic field panel. To keep all installation wiring in the field panels can be difficult, so punch blocks are often installed adjacent to the field panel to help control the wiring (Figure 4.2). The field panels are typically designed to incorporate a normally closed loop from the alarm sensor in the field as the input to the electronic field panel. The alarm sensors/devices are arranged in zones/loops that cover a certain geographical area. For example, all emergency exit door switches on the northwest side of the building might be zoned/looped together. In this way, the security officer would know where to respond in the building. The wiring of the door switches can be reduced by being interconnected in one loop versus requiring each door switch to be wired back to the field panel and requiring an input on the panel for each switch. The limiting factor of a zone/loop is that any one of the door switches might have been activated, requiring each door to be checked. For example, if someone exited through an emergency exit door and there are several doors on the zone/loop, then each door must be checked. Often, by the time the security officer responds, the doors are all closed and

Figure 4.2   Punch blocks.

no one is in sight and no one knows exactly which door was used or who used it. So zones/loops should be limited to a reasonably sized grouping. (In this book, the term loop and zone will be used interchangeably. In the strictest sense, a zone is a location on the field panel. The field panel is designed for a given number of zones—they are often multiples of eight—and the zone may have one or more sensors/devices. A loop is normally more than one sensor/device that makes up the zone.) When the sensor is activated, the field panel senses the activation and reports the alarm condition to the alarm system server/computer in the SCC.

To understand the way a sensor notifies the field panel that an alarm has occurred, we must look at the electronics. Figure 4.3 shows a typical sensor with an end-of-line resistor, R_1. These resistors should be placed on the last device/sensor in a given loop so that the panel will sense all devices/sensors that comprise the loop. The purpose of the resistor is to supervise the loop. When current, C_1 flows from the field panel to the sensor it travels through the resistor when the sensor is in its "normal" state (door closed). The field panel monitors this current flow to indicate that the sensor is in a normal state and that the wiring of the loop is intact. The sensor

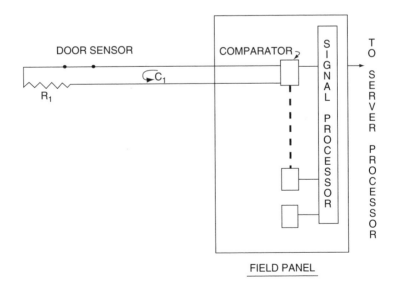

Figure 4.3   One end-of-line resistor.

should be normally closed when the door being sensed is closed. When the door opens, so does the sensor, which causes the current to stop flowing. When the sensor opens, the current flow stops indicating an alarm to the field panel. If the loop wiring to and from the sensor becomes shorted together then the current flowing in the loop will increase (no resistor when door is shut), because the sensor is bypassed by the wiring short. This situation causes the field panel to send a trouble signal to the server. This supervision approach notifies the operator of a normal state (door closed), an alarm state (door open) and a trouble state (wires shorted). A single end-of-line resistor loop does have one problem: there is no way to distinguish between the sensor opening and a break in the loop wire going to the sensor from the field panel.

To solve this problem, another resistor, R_2, is added. Figure 4.4 shows the double end-of-line resistor design. (The original resistor, R_1, functions as discussed earlier.) When the door opens there is still a current flow, C_2, through the second resistor. If the wire is cut between the field panel and the sensor, there is no current flow. This situation causes a trouble signal to be sent to the SCC indicating that something has happened to the wiring in this zone (either cut or shorted). For this dual resistor plan to work, end-of-line resistor

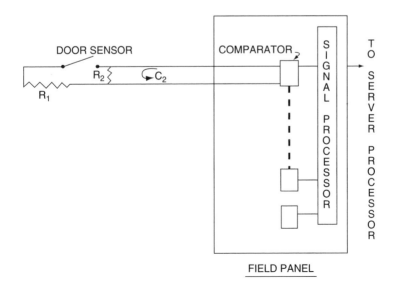

Figure 4.4 Two end-of-line resistors.

R_1 must be a different value from end-of-line resistor R_2. With the voltage to the sensor being a constant value and the resistors being different values, the currents will be different through each resistor. Current C_1 is the desired steady state value (door is closed) for the alarm system to know that everything is working properly, thus the door is secure and the wiring is intact. Current C_2 lets the panel know that there is an alarm and the wiring is intact (door is open). The field panel is constantly monitoring the current to notify the SCC of the sensor's status.

The actual alarm number sent to the SCC is defined by the wiring in the field panel. The field panels are assigned an address that simply provides an electronic naming scheme for each field panel. Inside the field panel is a circuit board (sometimes more than one) with connections for each zone/loop. Figure 4.4 is a loop. The loop leaves the field panel, goes to an end-of-line resistor through the sensor and returns to the field panel (two wires). Each loop is connected to a given physical location on the circuit board. These physical locations are defined by the circuit board and given an address. The first loop might be designated on the circuit board as zone #1. Electronically the loop has an address, which is added behind the field panel address to provide a total sensor address. The security server/computer receives this address as a series of numbers that are defined in a database in the server. The field panel/loop address in the database provides a description as to the type and physical location of the sensor. For example, the address that defines loop #1 might be programmed to display "main lobby motion." When the address is sent to the server as a series of numbers, the computer program translates the address to "main lobby motion" for the operator in the SCC. The SCC operator can then send a security officer to investigate the alarm at the main lobby.

Now that the basic architecture and operation have been discussed, let's address the selection of an alarm system. Alarm systems, as with access control systems, are often selected at a trade show or from a salesman visiting the company. The decision is often based upon a limited exposure to the product. Every alarm system will meet your requirements according to the salesperson. There are many pitfalls that we will be discussing in this chapter. The alarm system manufacturer is important, but so is the installing company. In fact, the installing company may have more to do with the success of the project than the manufacturer. There are many issues and decisions that should be evaluated prior to purchasing a system. Choosing the best system, for a given application, depends upon properly developing the requirements, understanding what is available in the marketplace, provide solid bid documents, pre-qualifying bidders and managing the installation project.

Alarm systems have a similar architecture to access control systems; thus, it is reasonable to evaluate alarm systems using a similar approach as that used in Chapter 1. We will evaluate the same characteristics as discussed in Chapter 1. In this chapter, they will apply to the electronic alarm system. The examples may be different than those used in Chapter 1 but they can apply to both systems. To have a quality electronic alarm system, it is important to select a system that meets the requirements developed for a given facility. The requirements will vary with different industries, buildings or corporate cultures. Choosing the best electronic alarm system is much more than choosing a manufacturer or brand. Areas to consider in the selection process are (1) technology, (2) culture, (3) alarm philosophy, (4) management commitment, (5) total cost of ownership, (6) system flexibility, (7) durability of system components, (8) component replacement cost and availability and (9) maintenance cost including maintenance callouts.

TECHNOLOGY

For the corporate security professional there is a strong interest in utilizing systems that communicate on an Internet Protocol (IP) based architecture. The push has been to minimize cost by using existing IT infrastructure in the company. Since IT normally has a wiring infrastructure already in place through the enterprise, it makes sense to capitalize on it. In addition to having infrastructure in place, IT often has unused communication system bandwidth. The combination of infrastructure and bandwidth that is in place and paid for could easily be used by Security. The idea of combining Security and IT to use common cabling networks and work together is often refered to as convergence. Convergence can go much further depending upon the company culture. IT has experience in PC products, network solutions, securing networks, software problems, and so on. Security typically does not possess such expertise. There are benefits and potential issues with convergence, some of which were addressed in Chapter 1.

Another aspect of technology is that used in the SCC server/computer. The PC market drives what will be commercially available for the Security market. The problem for most security alarm system manufacturers is keeping the application software that they sell with their system up-to-date with what is happening in the PC market. Even casual observers know that the PC market has been operating at a frantic pace. What was considered super fast three years ago is now considered obsolete and is being thrown away or being given to young children to help them become computer literate. New operating systems require substantially more memory than the previous software releases. There are two main points that need to be made. First, in the security world, "tried and true" is normally better than "cutting edge." To be cutting edge requires you to be a beta test site which can be rewarding, but also very painful. The difference between tried and true and cutting edge is also a major philosophy difference between IT and Security. IT must purchase the latest and greatest if they expect any sort of life cycle to their hardware, software and networks (Return On Investment or ROI). The demand from the employees and business pressures force early adoption of faster and faster PCs, networks and feature-rich software. Every year or so there is a major change in PC operating systems, PC speed and PC memory requirements. This has recently slowed to some extent, but will always be an issue. Second, there is no way to know which operating system, database management system, or PC will provide the best results for your security alarm server. The PC marketplace will decide most of the parameters for these three areas. It is not necessarily which product is the best, but which one becomes accepted. Examples of this phenomenon are VHS versus Sony's Beta, IBM versus Microsoft, and Macintosh versus open architecture. A security alarm system can easily be in place for eight to ten years. In order to continue to receive support from the alarm system manufacturer, care must be taken in choosing the technology, because of a possible long-term manufacturer support issue. If the alarm system and access control system are integrated, which is usually the case, the processing speed of the server becomes more important. If the server cannot properly handle the needs of a large access control system and still process alarms quickly, the system will be a failure. This is discussed in more detail in Chapter 1.

CULTURE

You might be asking yourself, what does culture have to do with choosing the best security alarm system? The answer to that question is somewhat subjective and applies primarily to the implementation of the alarm system. Some alarm systems' philosophies will be more acceptable to the employees than others. Employees' movement through and around a facility is like water; it will always take the most direct route. If that means crashing out an emergency exit to get to a smoke break area, then they will, unless there is management support that prevents or discourages that type of activity. The alarm system should be designed in such a way as to incorporate this human tendency. This specific example can be solved in several ways, one of which is to provide an area outside the building adjacent to a location in the building that would be conducive to a smoker, such as outdoors by the cafeteria. The adjacent area should provide some protection from the weather and utilize a door between the cafeteria and the smoking area for easy access. The door should have a badge reader on the inside and outside as well as a door alarm. During breaks and at lunch, the badge readers could be bypassed, thus allowing free entry and exit. At all other times, the badge readers would be active. If the door is forced open, there will be an electronic security alarm sent to the SCC. The cultural aspect of an alarm system affects the decision of where the alarms are placed and when they are activated. This design will be tempered with the needs of the corporation to protect its personnel and assets while meeting code and company/customer requirements. The design will be significantly different for a government contractor versus a corporation that is in the nongovernment supplier business. The type of business will affect the design of the alarm system, but an effective design that incorporates human behavior and protects the company is very important to the integrity of the security program as a whole. Designing a security alarm system is much more involved than simply installing a few door switches and motion detectors.

ALARM PHILOSOPHY

Alarm philosophy will be affected by culture, as well as the requirements that are developed to address the security needs.

(Alarm philosophy has been addressed to some extent in the culture section above.) Developing a solid alarm philosophy requires an understanding of the functional requirements. These requirements are developed by understanding the security vulnerabilities, business risks and appropriate levels of protection, and knowing the key assets and threats. Functional requirements apply to security and fire alarm, access control, CCTV, intercoms, and so on. Functional requirements provide the basis for a holistic security solution. They are addressed here because of their impact on alarm philosophy.

Functional requirements are developed into statements that define the desired goal. They are not a statement of what devices will be installed where. For example, a functional requirement might be: provide restricted access to the executive floor. There are many approaches to solving this functional requirement. They may include badge readers on the elevator to gain access to that floor or panic buttons on the executive secretary's desk or alarms on doors leading into or out of the area. Closed Circuit Television might be utilized to comply with the functional requirements. The goal is to record the required security needs in a statement that can then be combined with the other needs into a list. The list is then prioritized and solutions are developed based upon the critical functional requirements.

MANAGEMENT COMMITMENT

This appears on the surface to be an unnecessary concern for choosing the right system, but, in fact, there are many reasons that management commitment is critical. One of the reasons for this commitment is that following the philosophies that are developed as part of the alarm system, senior management ultimately must enforce the plan. These philosophies must apply to everyone equally. If a manager refuses to use an approved exit to take a smoke break when everyone else must use the designated door, then by upper management becomes important. If some employees are allowed to bypass the "rules," the word gets out and no one really cares about following the rules. Management commitment also applies to the funding needed to meet the functional requirements.

TOTAL COST OF OWNERSHIP

Total cost of ownership is an area that is often not considered. Typically an alarm system is designed, funding is approved, the system is installed, and sometimes a maintenance budget is established. With this process, many aspects of the total cost of ownership are overlooked: (1) database administration and backup, (2) software modifications, (3) software upgrades, (4) system configuration management, (5) system expansion costs and (6) data entry. For these reasons, care must be taken to select the system that provides the best total cost of ownership. Depending upon the manufacturer, ongoing support and cost for adding and replacing components of the system can become a problem.

Often an alarm company installs the security alarm system. To maintain the system after installation, either the alarm company provides that service or trained company employees maintain the database, repair the system and add new sensors as needed. The installing alarm company usually handles software modifications, software upgrades and software configuration. If the alarm system is large, complex and constantly changing, several full-time technicians may be required to keep the system operating properly, software up-to-date and the database cleaned up. The level of effort required will vary based upon the activity in these areas. There are costs associated with keeping the system going, whether provided in-house by the company itself or by the installing alarm company or some combination of in-house and contractor. One truth to note at this point is that the selected alarm company that installs the alarm system is more important than the manufacturer of the alarm system as far as the success of the system's on-going operation. Ultimately, the technical knowledge and availability of installing and maintenance qualified technicians is the limiting factor.

CODE AND SPECIAL REQUIREMENTS

There are many special requirements that may apply to an alarm system. Many of these requirements are universal, such as UL compliance for various industries. For example, government contractors must comply with UL 2050 (covered in more detail in Chapter 19). There are requirements that vary depending upon the site location. There are other functional requirements that will apply to different industries, agencies, or companies, for example, hospitals, prisons, power plants, refineries, and so on have special requirements that must be considered when designing the alarm system. To assure the best results, it is important for you to be part of the philosophy, initial design, scope of work, installation contractor selection, implementation decisions and system installation and commissioning.

AESTHETICS

Aesthetics can be a very serious issue with upper management, the architect, and/or the building owner. For example, an executive area with wood paneling and special interlocking ceiling tiles can be a challenge for installing an electronic alarm system. The door sensor must be hidden and wiring for alarm sensors must be planned and incorporated early in the project to assure proper aesthetics. Another example is a lobby receptionist desk with a panic alarm. Often, the lobby receptionist desk is in the center of the lobby area and the desk resides on a marble floor. To provide wiring to the panic switch, conduit should be installed before the concrete is poured for the lobby; otherwise there is no way to conceal the wires (unless the marble is cut and relayed) leaving a wireless transmitter as the only option. Another example is a door switch on a concrete wall or a steel doorjamb that is concreted in place. If a polystyrene block is placed in the top of the jamb or conduit prior to the concrete pour, then the door sensor can be recessed in the doorjamb. If these steps are not taken, the door sensor must be surface mounted, which does not provide an aesthetic installation.

SYSTEM SUPPORT

This has been addressed to some extent under the topic "Total Cost of Ownership." The challenge is to decide early on which way system support is to be provided. Not many companies have the in-house staff to provide this support, especially early on in the installation phase of the project. The types of support needed include (1) database support, (2) new additional installations and (3) system configuration control. After initial system installation, system configuration, system upgrades and troubleshooting will be important support areas. A typical problem that will arise after the system is installed is that additional new sensors must be added, removed or relocated. In any of the three scenarios, the database must be modified to reflect the changes. Sensors that are removed should be taken out of the database, the wiring removed, and a resistor added across the terminals on the field panel to replace the end-of-line resistor. The resistor assures that the unused zone will not be in trouble and provides a visual indication that the zone is available for future use. If new sensors are added, they must be connected to a field panel and properly defined in the database to assure that the SCC operator will know where the sensor is located. Relocating a sensor is a combination of additions and deletions even though the actual sensor and its assigned zone may be reused.

An administrative procedure should be developed for processing these types of changes to assure that the database is accurate and up-to-date. The procedure needs to define additions, deletions and relocations of sensors. It is best to utilize a data sheet for these changes. The actual location listed on the datasheet is defined by the installing technician; however, the location should be verified and modified by a security officer (the responder) to be certain that the sensor can be easily located during an actual alarm. This can be a challenge in large buildings which many times use a grid system. The exact grid location is often not obvious because a technician usually defines the sensor location initially, based upon the installation paperwork, and often the security officer will call the area by a different name or will come from a certain direction, which may change the perception of the sensor's location. By allowing the security officer to review all locations, the best description can be generated.

SYSTEM FLEXIBILITY

This particular requirement is more subjective than the other issues covered up to this point in choosing the right system. Electronic alarm systems perform more tasks or should have more capability than simply monitoring a given facility. There are also expandability issues and communication issues as well as reports that need to be generated. Report generation may be very limited to certain predefined variables by a given manufacturer. For a report program to be flexible, the database should be a commercially available database management system such as Microsoft Sequel, MS SQL, and not a proprietary database management system supplied by the alarm system manufacturer. Several proprietary protocols and software products are available that are part of the alarm systems that limit which products will operate together, thus forcing the purchaser to continue buying a given product. More will be covered on this topic later in the chapter. Utilizing MS SQL or some other common open database management system reports should be capable of being run from any of the data fields in the database and in any desired arrangement. This provides tremendous flexibility as there are always reports that would be beneficial to you that was not envisioned at the beginning of the installation project. To pay the installing company or the alarm system manufacturer to modify their software so that a report can be run is very expensive and should be unnecessary.

Another issue is expandability. Most manufacturers produce various sizes of alarm systems based upon number of alarm points or zones. When purchasing a system, it is important to consider future needs and plan for the fact that the present system will need to be upgraded to the next larger model in the future. Initially when the alarm system is first installed, it is based on existing functional requirements that will over time change and grow. If a smaller system is not scaleable, upward compatible, then money spent on the system is probably wasted. In many cases the computer software and sometimes the interface electronics must be replaced to expand a system.

Then there is the issue of communication. This applies to the communication from the electronic field panels to the server/computer which is usually a proprietary protocol. (Protocols are also discussed in Chapter 2.) For now, consider a protocol as a language that allows two people to communicate. For instance, the protocol used in this book is English. All manufacturers send their own unique protocol between the field panels and the server/computer. That means that the only open architecture pieces of equipment used in many electronic alarm system are the sensor, the server/computer and the printer used for report writing. The ways to send the protocol between the electronic field panels and the server/computer include: (1) RS485, (2) RS232, (3) RS422, (4) TCPIP and (5) dialup. For a system to be flexible, it is desirable to use a manufacturer that produces equipment that is capable of multiple communication formats. Otherwise, interface equipment must be purchased from a third party that makes the appropriate conversions. The application software used in this third-party hardware is also usually proprietary. Third-party hardware/software becomes more critical if the alarm electronic field panel is part of the alarm system and must comply with a standard imposed by regulations such as UL. The total system configuration must be UL approved or approvable and each component that makes up the system should be UL listed.

DURABILITY OF SYSTEM COMPONENTS

To be durable and/or reliable, systems available today must comply with different regulations and, as such, normally contain lightning protection, fuses, and so on. So the field panels that connect the sensors to the server/computer normally have the needed electronic protection. The lightning protection on many panels is required by UL and is accomplished with Metal Oxide Varistors (MOVs). These devices clamp the lightning spike to a predetermined level but they do not assure that the microprocessor is totally protected. When manufacturers sell "noncompliant" equipment, damage can result when nonpower wires are crossed or mistakenly connected. Additionally, RF in the area could unnecessarily impact the equipment operation or, worse, damage the equipment. For instance, keying up a two-way radio near the electronics panel in the field can cause this type of interference/damage problems.

The amount of openness of the architecture will also play an important part in system durability. Most electronic alarm systems today are moving toward commercially available application software packages to run on the server/computer. This is a great step in the right direction. As an example, MS SQL as a database management software package provides needed flexibility. The reality is that the computer industry moves much faster than the electronic alarm system industry; so a software package that is a perfect application today may be totally outdated tomorrow. One example is Windows versus OS2. In this software battle, the eventual winner was Windows. Even though OS2 had many benefits it is now extinct. A less extreme example is MS Windows 98 versus MS Windows XP. In this conversion, within the same manufacturer there will typically be some level of upward compatibility. Being an early adaptor or a Beta test site can be exciting, but it can also be fraught with problems, so most security professionals prefer the tried and true. The tried and true approach places you behind the commercial software development curve and future support may be a problem.

COMPONENT REPLACEMENT COST AND AVAILABILITY

Replacing system components applies to the availability and longevity of a given alarm system product line. In the world of mergers and acquisitions, this can cause product lines to disappear or they may not have the financial base to last in the marketplace. Even the recent acquisition of alarm system manufacturers by large companies does not assure continuing production or even support of a given product. For example, when a large company purchases more than one electronic alarm system company, the company doing the acquisition must then determine ways to blend the various product lines individually purchased. This saves money and produces a product that has more features and is hopefully more reliable. The problem is that different acquired electronic alarm system companies take different approaches in designing and building their product. This includes the protocol used between the electronic panel in the field and the computer. When the new product is released, it is doubtful that multiple protocols will be incorporated, thus making one or all of the acquired alarm systems obsolete. Then technical support as well as the purchase of hardware and software will have a cut-off date. In this case, the security professional will be left with an unsupported orphan system.

MAINTENANCE COST INCLUDING MAINTENANCE CALLOUTS

Several of the topics already discussed will affect the maintenance and the cost of that maintenance for a given alarm system. The difference in cost from one alarm system manufacturer to the next will depend primarily on two areas. First, some alarm system manufacturers make their profit margin on software so their component parts are less expensive. Some of these manufacturers sell their software based on a system size and configuration. When the system is expanded there is additional cost for software keys that allow the needed expansion. Second, some alarm system manufacturers' costs are higher on their system components. This might be because of the way their system is marketed. All manufacturers want authorized/trained installers to support their products to you. Some are sold through their dealership network, some force exclusive area protection for their installers and some allow a more competitive environment. The degree that your company can take advantage of more competition depends on the area of the country, the dollar size of the contract, whether the contract is a nationwide contract, whether a preferred supplier arrangement can be established or the alarm system can be purchased and sold by "any" company. Components such as sensors will be consistent across the security industry.

Keeping the cost of maintenance "callouts" down requires that the SCC operators be trained and understand the impact of a failure so that callouts and associated fast response requirements are minimized. Often on new installations a maintenance contract is added as part of the initial bid. It is usually a percentage of the total project cost and may include parts, software upgrades and labor. The problem is that these maintenance agreements are often expensive and do not cover the cost of after hour/weekend or holiday callouts. On new or existing alarm systems an outside alarm company often supplies the actual responding technician. This requires agreements and contracts that specify such items as (1) hourly rates for business hours, after hours/weekends and holidays and (2) hourly rate start time—when they get in a vehicle to drive to the location and return to their original location, when they arrive and leave the company's site, or a minimum number of hours that they charge for each callout.

When all these issues are considered at the beginning of the project, it is possible to still have surprises because it is easy to overlook possible potential problems. For example, when there is a security alarm system retrofit project, a plan must be developed to keep the old system operating until the new system is ready to cut over. There is a tremendous amount of planning to assure a smooth transition to the new system. With the correct planning, development of solid functional requirements and proper execution, one item often overlooked is the end-of-line resistor. This was discussed earlier in the chapter. Different electronic alarm system manufacturers utilize different end-of-line resistor values. (In Figure 4.3, the value of resistor R_1 changes between different manufacturers.) A system that requires a 1,000 ohm end-of-line resistor does not work properly with a 2,000 ohm end-of-line resistor or vice versa. The only solution is to replace all end-of-line resistors when installing a new alarm system, which is an expensive process. Adding to the expense is the fact that larger alarm systems have two extra problems: the location of the end-of-line resistor is not obvious and these systems are often not documented as to the end-of-line resistors' locations.

An example of a new or retrofit installation problem that can add major costs to a project deals with the system architecture. Most of the time the alarm system is integrated with the access control system. In this case, a system is sized and electronic field panels ordered based upon the number of alarms, badge readers and badge holders (employees and contractors). For an example, we will assume the system being purchased will allow 128 alarm points or 16 readers per field panel. Assuming that the number of alarm and badge readers will be handled by a given number of panels, the number of panels has allowed for expansion and that the panels are properly distributed within the building and are accessible. There are still two possible oversights that can cause major cost overruns. First, it is assumed that each field panel will handle the proper number of alarms and badge readers as advertised; however, when badge readers and alarms are located in the same field panel, the number of one or both will often be reduced. The number of readers might remain at 16 for a given field panel, but the number of alarms might drop to 32. Second, the memory allocated to an electronic field panel that incorporated badge readers may not be large enough to store the number of badges. The manufacturer's advertisement will state that each field panel will handle 12,000 badge credentials. This assumes that PINs are not used. If PINs are used, half of the 12,000 badge credential numbers will be reduced because of the need to store a PIN with each badge credential. Sometimes memory can be added to the field panels to resolve this problem; however, there is a limit to the addressable memory locations. If the panel is at a maximum memory size when this problem is discovered, the only way to solve the problem is to add another field panel.

5

Fire Systems

Fire and emergency response is important to every security professional. Monitoring these systems may or may not be part of the Security Control Center (SCC) function; however, the response and evacuation systems are part of the security tasks. Therefore, it is important for you to understand the inner workings of a fire alarm system. By understanding the physical piping, sensors and electronic panels, the mystery as to why these systems sometimes cause false evacuations in the buildings that you are responsible for will be addressed. They are not overly complex, but they do operate differently than the typical security alarm system. Fire systems do have sensors in the field that connect to a central panel. The panel might be in the SCC or in an area within the building. On larger systems, where multiple panels would be required to properly cover the building, the central panel is actually a sophisticated computer with many field nodes that connect to it. The additional nodes in the field can be thought of as a security or access control electronic field panel. The nodes are used to expand the number of devices in a given loop. Fire systems are composed of two basic but distinct functional areas. One is the plumbing/mechanical side and the other is the electronic side. The sprinkler system delivers the water to the fire and the electronic system senses, monitors and warns of a fire. We will discuss both aspects of a typical fire system, but our primary focus is with the electronic side.

THE SPRINKLER SYSTEM

The sprinkler system is what actually extinguishes the fire. Most of the readers of this book will have sprinkler systems in the various buildings within their company. The concept of a sprinkler system is simple: fires develop heat that rises; when that heat reaches the same temperature as the sprinkler head rating, the fusible link in the sprinkler head melts and the water is released. This, of course, is oversimplified. There are many different types of sprinkler heads and code issues about their spacing, size of piping used to distribute the water, and so on. The layout of a sprinkler system, fire ratings of doors and walls, controlling airflow, combustibles under raised floors, the type of construction, piping penetrating fire walls, and so on, will not be discussed in this chapter. To cover these topics would probably require an entire book. For this chapter, we will assume that all these items are in place and correctly addressed. I will occasionally refer to some of these types of issues, but our focus will be primarily on the electronic side. We cannot totally segregate ourselves from the mechanical piping side of fire systems because we will be monitoring some of the mechanical piping systems (such as water flow alarms). The construction of an area will affect the electronic systems, and the lack of a sprinkler system in a given building will cause you to add more electronics as well as change the way some of the sensors impact evacuation of a building. Again, we will assume that the sprinkler system is in place.

Before we "dive" into the electronics side of fire protection, another part of the mechanical piping system that you need to be aware of is the way that the sprinkler system assures that there is enough water pressure to put out a fire. The water for most facilities is supplied from some municipality or water district. That water will arrive at your site or building in a large pipe or main line. The pipe will normally have a shutoff either outside the building or where it enters the building; these shutoffs are called Post Indicating Valves (PIVs) or Wall Indicating Valves (WIVs). Their purpose is to cut off water to the sprinkler system while it is being installed or when there are major repairs being performed on the system. The older codes allowed you to wrap a chain through the valve and padlock the chain. This kept the valves in the "open" position to be sure that if a fire occurred, there would be water available. The more recent codes require a sensor (tamper switch) on these valves to provide a supervisory alarm when the valve is closed there by shutting off the water. Many municipalities require these valves be both alarmed and chained. Buildings will normally have multiple main pipes that come off the main city water supply in the building and rise vertically into the building space to supply the various sprinkler loops. These vertical supply pipes are called "risers." They will be plumbed with a control check valve (clapper valve) that keeps the water from draining down from the sprinkler heads, a cutoff valve called (PIV or WIV), pressure gauges and piping to test the sprinkler system. See Figure 5.1. In addition to the various plumbing components at the riser, there will be a flow switch which will indicate when water is flowing in the sprinkler system, and, in theory, will indicate that there is a fire (or possibly a leak in the system). There are several ways to electronically monitor water flow. One way is with a vane switch (see Figure 5.2). When water flows the vane moves with the water flow and activates a switch closure. There are also pressure switches that provide a switch closure to indicate water flow, but we will not go into this type in this chapter. Additional valves in the building that control branches of the sprinkler system are called control valves. They can be of several types: Stem and Yoke (OS&Y), butterfly, ball and so on.

The water supplied to the building from the city will normally be rated at a pressure of about 60 pounds per square inch (60 psi). Before we go any further, we need to make a simple analogy. When a garden hose is connected to a hose bib (water faucet) at your house, the pressure at that connection will also be at about 60 psi. If everyone is watering lawns in the summertime, the pressure will drop to about 30 psi and you will get less water over a given period of time through the same hose because there is less pressure. If the pressure is really low, it is visually obvious to you because the water seems to be coming out slowly compared to the usual forceful stream of water. When several lawn sprinklers are connected to a

Figure 5.1   Fire riser.

long length of hose, the sprinkler farthest from the house hose bib will have very little water squirting on the lawn because the pressure drops with each sprinkler. Now transferring these thoughts to your company's building: if the pressure is low, the sprinkler system will not deliver enough water to put out the fire. Pipe size and sprinkler installation should be designed assuming that there would also be a certain water pressure and volume capability at the sprinkler head no matter the length of the loop. There are two potential fire-extinguishing problems with low pressure. One problem has to do with the pressure above and below the clapper valve in the riser or standpipe. For example, if the pressure was 60 psi when the sprinkler system was initially filled, and the pressure is now 30 psi water will not flow past the clapper valve to the sprinkler if there is a fire. When a sprinkler head is activated, no additional

Figure 5.2 Vane switch.

water will flow through the riser until the water above the clapper valve has gone below 30 psi. The other problem is a water volume issue based upon the reduced pressure. The only code requirement is that there must be a certain minimum pressure at the last sprinkler head in any one branch of the sprinkler piping.

Sprinkler systems in many buildings actually operate at a much higher pressures than 60 psi. Normally the pressure is in the 140 psi range. Since water supplied by the city system will not go to that pressure, a pump or multiple pumps are used. Most buildings have an internal pump called a jockey pump that provides the needed pressure for the building's sprinkler systems. Sometimes multiple jockey pumps are utilized based upon the size of the building. For a large campus facility, there will also normally be diesel pumps that supply a fairly high pressure to the risers and then the jockey pumps keep individual building sprinkler systems pressurized. Another reason for pumps is the need to push water up the standpipe in high-rise buildings. Since city pressure will not typically supply a building greater than three stories, pumps are needed to get the water to the sprinklers on upper floors. Sometimes there are large reservoirs on the top of the building to hold water that adds capacity to the fire system. Jockey pumps, diesel pumps and water storage tanks usually have electronic sensors that are monitored in the Security Control Center (SCC), even though they may not connect directly to the building fire panel.

Most of you are familiar with these types of wet sprinkler systems. There are also dry systems which have pressurized air in the pipe between the clapper valve and the sprinkler heads. The air pressure is high enough to keep the clapper valve closed and water out of the sprinkler heads. When a fire causes the fusible links in the sprinkler head to melt, air starts to flow out of the sprinkler head. When the air pressure is reduced to the point it will not hold back the water, water flows in the pipe and out the activated sprinkler head/heads. Otherwise the system works the same way as a wet system. The primary reason for using a dry system is for applications when the water sitting in the sprinkler head's piping might freeze—for example, the system protecting an unheated warehouse or protecting gas storage that is outside the building. One more slight variation to the dry system is one that uses an antifreeze solution in the sprinkler piping. The clapper valve has water on one side and antifreeze on the other.

Most mechanical sprinkler piping systems include a water gong that will sound when water flows through the sprinkler system. The sound is developed by a paddle wheel in the pipe that rotates and clangs the bell by pushing water into the system. See Figure 5.3. In most large building environments, these gongs are not loud enough to initiate an evacuation because they are normally on an outside wall of the building. The important thing to remember for the electronic side of a fire system is that the water gong and the flow switch will activate based upon the water volume flow through one sprinkler head. Flowing only one sprinkler head of water should be enough to active the water gong. When the Fire Marshall tests the systems, the inspector test valve and the associated water pipe incorporates a restriction that allows the equivalent of one sprinkler head of water to flow above the clapper valve. See Figure 5.4.

THE ELECTRONIC SYSTEM

Now we need to discuss the electronic side of fire systems in more detail. We will start with a basic system and move on to a larger

Figure 5.3 Water gong.

complex system that connects to the mechanical sprinkler system (both types of systems are used in the corporate environment). The basic system that might be used on a stand-alone area such as a computer room is composed of smoke detectors, heat detectors, speaker/strobes or horn/strobes and fire pulls that connect to a fire alarm panel and can be arranged into loops or zones. In this basic configuration, the loops can be a single detector, or multiple detectors can be in a loop. The number of loops is based upon the fire panel that is selected and the desired grouping of devices. A common small panel would accommodate four loops. Figure 5.5 shows a typical smoke detector loop. As you can see there are two wires for powering the loop. Each detector is wired so that removal of the detector causes the power to disappear from any detectors that are farther down the loop. Power is looped through the detectors in such a way that any one detector provides the power connection for the next detector. There are two wires that connect to the alarm side of each detector. The detectors are wired on the normally "open" side of the detector output relay. Fire detection devices should provide a normally open signal when they are powered and not in

Figure 5.4 Inspector test.

alarm. This type of smoke detector connection is refered to as a four-wire circuit and is composed of two power wires and two alarm wires. There is an end-of-line resistor that is across the normally open alarm circuit to provide supervision similar to that used in a security alarm system (discussed in Chapter 4). The only difference is that the resistor's presence in the circuit is controlled by a relay. When power is removed, the relay holding the end-of-line resistor in the circuit drops out and the panel will receive a trouble alarm because there is no longer an end-of-line resistor in the circuit.

Since most of you will be somewhat familiar with a basic four wire fire system, this is a good starting point. To completely understand this configuration, let's take a closer look into each component in the system. The initiating devices for this type of stand-alone system are smoke detectors, heat detectors, manual pull stations, duct smoke detectors, beam smoke detectors and various other specialty devices. Let's start with smoke detectors. There are two types of smoke detectors. The photoelectric smoke detector is the most

4 Wire Detectors
4-wire Smoke Detectors wired Style B

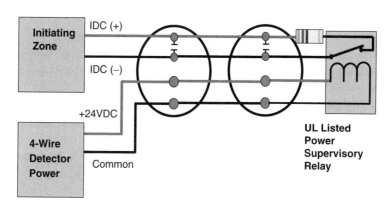

Figure 5.5   Smoke detector loop. Courtesy of Fire.Lite.

widely used type of smoke detector. See Figure 5.6 for the inner workings of a photoelectric smoke detector. The Light-Emitting Diode (LED) or emitter radiates into a dark chamber that is divided between the LED and a photosensitive diode or detector. When particles of combustion enter the chamber, the particles reflect the light and the detector starts to receive the light from the emitter. As the reflection increases, more current will flow in the detector and cause an alarm. This type of photoelectric detector utilizes a light scattering approach. The amount of current that the manufacturer has set in the smoke detector to assure that the smoke detector will cause an alarm is designed to meet UL standards. The color of the smoke, humidity greater than 93 percent, temperatures less than 32°F and greater than 100°F will make a difference as to sensitivity of photoelectric-type smoke detectors. It may be noted that particles other than smoke particles can and do cause these types of smoke detectors to go into alarm. For this reason, these smoke detectors come from the factory with a plastic head cover to keep the detector head clean, but keep dust and other debris out of the detector head during construction, as this will cause false alarms. There is also a

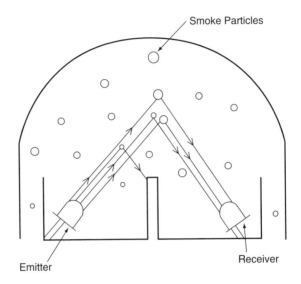

Figure 5.6 Photoelectric smoke detector.

light obscuration type of photoelectric detector where the transmitter and receiver face each other and smoke causes the current to decrease for an alarm condition.

The ionization smoke detector is less expensive than a photoelectric style and can be susceptible to some environmental false alarms such as dust. This detector is shown in Figure 5.7. The ionization detector has a very small radioactive element inside that generates ions into the air. There are two charged plates in the sampling chamber that attract the ions generated by the radioactive element. The ions that are attracted to the plates cause current to flow. When particles enter the chamber they attach themselves to the ions which slows the movement of ions in the chamber, thus reducing current flow. When the current flow is reduced to a predetermined level, the detector goes into alarm per the manufacturer's design. These detectors work best with small particles of combustion, and they are effective when used in areas where there are not large amounts of fabric, carpeting, upholstery and so on. The detector sensitivity can be affected by air velocity greater than 300 feet per second, humidity greater than 93 percent, altitude above 3,000 feet, and temperatures less than 32°F and greater than 100°F.

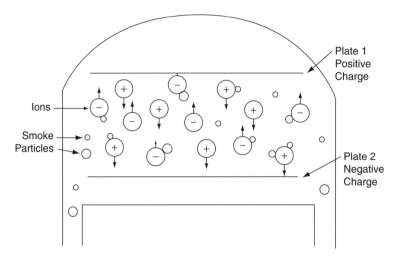

Figure 5.7 Ionization smoke detector.

Heat detectors are another initiating-type detector used on many fire systems. They tend to be used in areas that might contain smoke as an acceptable part of the daily operation and/or areas where the air quality cannot be controlled. For example, heat detectors are recommended in mechanical rooms where generators, boilers and pumps can cause some level of smoke that is not fire related. An example, closer to home, would be a residential kitchen. There are two types of heat detectors: fixed temperature and rate-of-rise. Fixed temperature heat detectors will only detect a fire one time and must be replaced. Rate-of-rise heat detectors can be used continuously like smoke detectors and can be reused. In many cases, the rate-of-rise detector will detect a fire condition faster than a fixed temperature detector. The reason for one-time use in the fixed temperature type is that there is a fusible link, similar to those used in sprinkler heads. An example of this device is shown in Figure 5.8. A spring places tension on a plunger which is held in place with solder that melts at a given temperature. When the solder melts, the plunger is forced upward into the alarm contacts. This type of heat detector is selected based upon the melting point of the solder and is available in a wide range of temperatures. A typical heat detector that might be used inside conditioned space would be a 135-degree detector. There are times when it is desirable

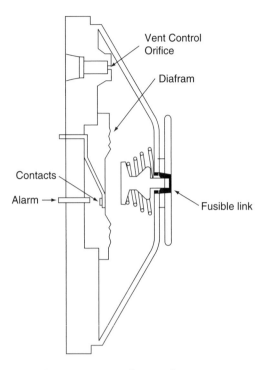

Figure 5.8 Fixed temperature/rate-of-rise.

to know when a fire is rapidly expanding before the 135-degree temperature is reached. This is addressed with a rate-of-rise heat detector. This can be a separate device or combined with a set temperature heat detector. You should also notice in Figure 5.8 a small hole at the upper end of the detector. This is a vent hole to allow the heated air inside the detector to escape. If the temperature is rising faster than the vent will allow the air to escape, the membrane holding the spring and plunger in place swells and the alarm contacts touch causing a fire alarm.

The next device is a manual pull station. This device is activated by physically pulling the handle on the pull station and is designed for an easy one-motion activation. The benefit of these devices is that they can allow anyone in the area to activate an alarm immediately. They are placed throughout an area and must comply with code. They will be located within five feet of an exit in a protected area and every 200 feet in an unobstructed emergency exit hallway, for example. Theses devices are manufactured to require a manual reset. The reset is typically a special key operation. Figure 5.9 shows a typical manual fire pull. There are covers available to minimize false activations caused by inadvertently bumping into the fire pull. This may sound unnecessary; however, it is surprising what excuses you will get as to why someone pulled the fire pull. I have seen these devices activated during construction of a large building, and no one admits to activating them. In one case, the building under construction was dumped several times, and it was blamed on the fire system malfunctioning. Invisible ultraviolet dust was placed on all fire pulls in the building. When there was another evacuation, everyone in the building, including all contractors, had to place their hands under an ultraviolet light. When the person causing the alarm was identified, the excuse was that they wanted a "smoke" break. There are accidental activations that can also occur accidentally; however, if no one admits causing the alarm, then a physical guard cover of some type can be a cost effective alternative.

The next device is a duct smoke detector which is basically a smoke detector that is packaged to mount on HVAC ductwork and utilizes sampling tubes that extend into the duct. One tube (inlet) contains holes that allow the air in the duct to flow through the tube via the venturi effect. A second tube (return) extends into the duct-work to provide a suction that causes the air in the first tube with

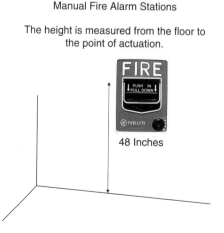

Manual Fire Alarm Stations

The height is measured from the floor to the point of actuation.

48 Inches

Figure 5.9   Fire pull. Courtesy of Fire.Light.

the holes to draw air into the sampling chamber. The smoke detector portion of the duct detector allows the detector to work just as any other smoke detector. The correct placement information for these detectors is available from the manufacturer. The goal is to place them in the ductwork where the airflow is moving with very little turbulence. This is referred to as laminar airflow and is typically six duct diameters from a bend, damper or any other discontinuity that causes turbulence. This requirement is expected to be removed in newer code releases because testing has shown turbulence to have less impact than originally thought. The size of the air handler will affect the number of the detectors needed. If air flow is greater than 2,000 Cubic Feet per Minute (2000 CFM), a detector is placed on the supply side of the unit. If air flow is greater than 15,000 CFM, a detector is installed on the supply and return side. (Some municipalities require both supply and return duct detectors above 2,000 CFM.) The goal of a duct detector is to detect smoke in an air handler and then to turn the air handler off. The air handlers can be purchased from the manufacturer with the duct detectors already mounted on them. In this case, only the duct auxiliary alarm points are needed to connect to a fire alarm system and notify someone that an air handler has been shut off versus a "fire alarm" causing an evacuation of the area. The actual Air Handler Unit (AHU) shut down has been pre-wired and taken care of by the AHU manufacturer. This type of alarm is called supervisory and it will be discussed in more detail later in the chapter.

The beam smoke detector utilizes a transmitter and a receiver. A light beam is generated in the transmitter and detected by the receiver. When the beam is partially obscured by smoke, the received signal is reduced and the receiver generates an alarm. These devices are used in applications where large areas must be covered, such as in a warehouse or where unusual ceiling designs are incorporated, such as atriums. The beam detector, which is actually a transmitter and a receiver, can cover distances hundreds of feet between the transmitter and receiver. The beam detectors are mounted just below the ceiling trusses and cover an entire warehouse with one beam detector. The detector relies on a partially blocked signal to detect smoke. If the signal is totally blocked or stopped, a trouble alarm is generated. In this way, if the transmitter fails or a box is placed in front of the transmitter or receiver, a trouble signal is sent instead of a fire alarm. There are variations of the beam detector. In a typical arrangement, the transmitter and receiver must be wired separately. Both the transmitter and the receiver require power and the receiver also requires alarm lines. The typical variation uses a reflector at the end where a receiver would be and the transmitter also includes a receiver. In this case, the beam travels from the transmitter to the reflector and back to the receiver that is built into the transmitter. Again, if the beam detector were totally blocked, the detector would cause a warning alarm or a trouble alarm.

The next group of detectors is referred to as specialty detectors. This is a very lengthy list, so only a sampling of types and their operation will be discussed. The first in the group are flame detectors which are used to detect very early stages of a fire. They are very effective and used where flammable liquids are stored, such as in an airplane hangar. They are also expensive and their applications are somewhat narrow. Two sampling technologies are available: one is ultraviolet and the other is infrared. (The sampling capability of flame detectors utilize both ends of the light spectrum.) The device watches for either ultraviolet or infrared frequencies and when the frequencies are present and they match a signature of a fire, then there is an alarm. There are possible nuisance alarms that can develop with these detectors. For example, lightning produces ultraviolet frequencies. This would appear to the detector to be a fire condition. One precaution that the manufacturers have made with ultraviolet detectors is a three-second delay. The device waits three seconds to verify that the ultraviolet signature is still present before sending an alarm. If there are multiple lightning strikes, then the detector may still false alarm. It is best to place this type of detector where it cannot view the outside of the building.

Another specialty detector is the heat sensitive cable. This device uses a specially manufactured cable that contains two conductors. A voltage is applied to one conductor and a ground is applied to the other. When the heat from a fire reaches a specified level, the insulation on the cable fails allowing the two wires to touch each other. The short that results causes a current flow and the detector causes an alarm. Sensitive cable is used in applications that require a large coverage area and there is a requirement for an extremely stable device. An application might be along a wall or ceiling of an aircraft hangar. When the device goes into alarm, the only way to reuse the device is by replacing the section of cable that was damaged with another piece of the special cable. The strength of this device is its stability. Nuisance alarms are basically nonexistent. The only nuisance alarms would typically be due to physical damage to the cable where the two inner conductors became shorted together. This device is also fairly expensive, so its applications are limited.

There are other specialty detectors such as spark and ember detectors which monitor exactly what their names imply. Their operation is very similar to the flame detectors that we have already discussed as they also monitor for infrared or ultraviolet emitting sources. These detectors require a dark environment and natural or artificial light sources will cause nuisance alarms. An application would include a conveyor system that transports combustible materials. These detectors are also very expensive and have a very limited application. The uniqueness of these devices is not that they are monitoring infrared or ultraviolet, but that they will only operate in a dark environment.

All the devices to this point have been initiating devices, or devices that initiate an alarm. The next group is annunciating devices or, as they are called in the code, notification appliances. These are the devices that notify area occupants that there is an alarm. They are available in several forms. They might be bells, horns, sounders, chimes, sirens, speakers and/or strobe lights. Audible devices must be code compliant. Code requires that three separate distinct audible signals or tones must exist for the different types of alarms: one for trouble, one for supervisory, and one for fire. We have already discussed fire alarms and trouble signals. Supervisory alarms were mentioned in the discussion of monitoring PIVs or Sectional Control Valves (SCVs). If a PIV or SCV is closed, not allowing water to get to the sprinkler heads, then someone should know that the valve is in a closed position even if the sprinkler system is being serviced. These valve alarms are supervisory alarms. Fire codes and the Authority Having Jurisdiction (AHJ) define the way that initialing devices are connected to the alarm panel and if they are defined as trouble, supervisory or fire. Fire system design is heavily fire code and AHJ driven, as these systems are considered to be life safety systems.

The notification appliances discussed above can use coded outputs for different areas in the building or a general alarm code. There are several types including Temporal code, which is the American National Standards Institute (ANSI) evacuation code number 3. The notification appliances discussed so far have all been audible types. This brings us to the Americans with Disabilities Act (ADA), which requires that wherever there is audible notification there must be visual notification. The actual evacuation alarm for a fire must provide audible and visual notification so that hearing and visually impaired occupants will both be notified. Many of the devices mentioned earlier are available with both audible and visual capability in a single device or the devices can be purchased separately. The audible devices are measured in decibels (db), which indicates their sound-producing level. This topic is discussed in Chapter 11. As a short refresher, it is important to remember that the sound level doubles for every 3 db increase. For every ten feet away from the speaker or horn there is a 6 db loss. The audible fire device should be 15 db louder than the ambient noise level. That is true up to an ambient background level of 105 db. The visual devices are measured in candle power (cd) or candela output. There are also requirements on the pulse rate, duration of the pulse, area coverage and synchronization of the strobes to comply with ADA visual notification requirements.

It is important to note that there are some differences in the NFPA 72 requirements and the ADA requirements. These differences apply to placement of devices. NFPA 72 covers placement of all initiating and notification appliances. These requirements are to assure proper detection of a fire, proper notification of area occupants of a fire and other requirements such as fire extinguishers, fire hose placement, and so on. When these diverging requirements conflict, it is important to make the best attempt to comply with both and document the issues. To better explain the possible conflicts, we will look at a real life example. NFPA requires manual pull stations to be mounted so that the part of the pull which is operated by an area occupant is 42 inches (42″) to 54″ above the finished floor. ADA requires the pull to be mounted 15″ to 48″, if the access is only from a forward wheelchair approach. If the approach is from the side or parallel, then the pull should be mounted at 9″ to 54″. If the side approach is over an obstruction, then the height should be the same as a front approach. This example should provide some insight as to the conflicting issues, although placing devices 42" to 48" above finished floor can solve this problem. This topic is extensive and there is not enough space in this chapter to address all the various environments and code requirements. It is also complicated by the AHJ because any fire system must be submitted to the AHJ for approval. The same system in the same environment in different parts of the country will vary because of the different AHJ opinions and code interpretations. It will also vary because there are two major fire codes that can be followed: one is Uniform Fire Code (UFC) the other is the International Fire Code (IFC). Finally, one more fine point about variations: codes are updated every couple of years and the different AHJs adopt a specific code and a specific year the code was written, even though a newer code might be published by the same governing body. For example, at the time of this writing, the city of Dallas, Texas adopted the IFC of a certain year and the city of McKinney, Texas, just outside Dallas, adopted the IFC from a different year. Fire codes are generally very complex and there is some level of subjectivity that must be taken into account. These issues usually arise when there are special circumstances or after a major fire disaster occurs causing a sensitivity of the AHJ to a specific application. These problems do not affect the monitoring side, but are critical to the installation side and must be properly addressed. A qualified designer that fully understands all aspects of the fire codes as they pertain to your fire alarm system is a must.

We have discussed initiating and annunciating devices (notification appliances). Now we need to discuss addressable device schemes. Devices in older systems were connected in loops and when alarms were activated and there was no fire or smoke found, it was necessary to look at each smoke detector or initiating device in the loop to find the device that was activated. When the smoke detector activated, the light on the detector was continually red. To solve this problem and provide an enhanced maintenance effort, smoke detectors and other initiating devices were given an electronic address and were connected on a communication loop back to the fire panel. The address is usually set via two wheels or dip-switches that can be physically set to an address that defines the individual device. When an alarm is received, it will be from a specific address that indicates a specific location. This allows the responder to go directly to the area where the alarm was activated, rather than trace out the entire loop of sensors. The other benefit of addressable systems is that they check each initiating and notification appliance device to make sure that they are connected to the system. This is done every few seconds by "polling" the devices on the loop. They also check each initiating smoke detector for sensitivity and when the smoke detector is dirty (that is it is close to the alarm threshold), the system notifies the operator via a remote display and/or panel that the smoke detector needs to be cleaned and or replaced. This notification prevents unnecessary alarms and evacuations in the facility. The panel employs electronic drift compensation for the detectors. If their sensitivity is changing because of the detector drifting, the panel will electronically compensate for a certain amount of drift to help keep the detectors as accurate as possible.

The new addressable systems use two wire loops. The power and communications to each device are sent on the same two wires. The panel polls each device on the two-wire loop in a similar way that the server/computer in a security alarm system polls the various field panels. The software programming that is available in even a rudimentary two-wire panel is fairly sophisticated. These programs are capable of software zoning, which is the ability to link different initiating devices with various notification appliances. Since all devices are addressable, including notification appliances, any combination of inputs or outputs can be linked together. This adds a tremendous amount of flexibility to the fire alarm system. The initiating devices and notification appliances can be on their respective loops and act electronically as if they were hardwired in several different configurations.

The last topic on fire alarm systems is the type of loops. The older standards referred to Class A and Class B circuits. Class A circuits, Figure 5.10, run the loop from the panel to each device and back to the panel. Class B circuits, Figure 5.11, run the loop from the panel to each device ending with the end-of-line resistor on the last device. The advantage to a Class A circuit is that even if there is a break in the loop, the system will continue to operate. Class A circuits are bi-directional, which means that the panel can communicate in either direction up to the loop break. The disadvantage is that there is more wiring and therefore more cost with a Class A

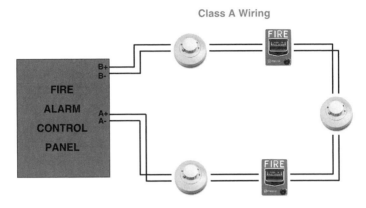

Class A Wiring

Class A wiring starts on "B" terminals and returns on the "A" terminals.

Figure 5.10 Class A circuit. Courtesy of Fire.Light.

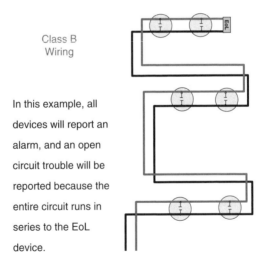

Class B
Wiring

In this example, all devices will report an alarm, and an open circuit trouble will be reported because the entire circuit runs in series to the EoL device.

Figure 5.11 Class B circuit. Courtesy of Fire.Light.

circuit. Today, the standards refer to styles instead of classes of circuits. For the most part, the new style designations are the same as the class designation except that there is a style for each type of loop (initiating and notification). For example, there are two styles for initiating circuits and two styles for notification appliance loops.

There is also a Signal Line Circuit (SLC) loop. A four wire Class A circuit is a Style D for initiating devices, a Style Z for Notification Appliance Circuit (NAC) and a Style 6 or 7 for an SLC. Class B is a Style B for an initiating device, a Style Y for an NAC and a Style 4 for an SLC.

For large, intelligent two-wire fire systems that are used to protect many company buildings across the country, it is desirable for the fire alarm system to notify Security and any repair personnel of an alarm as soon as the panel receives it. A remote display panel is often installed in the SCC for the operators to be notified as soon as possible. This remote display panel is normally capable of controlling and/or interrogating the central fire alarm panel, just as if the operator were at the central panel. The advantage of incorporating this capability into the SCC is that the operator knows exactly which alarm was received and if the panel needs to be interrogated, reset, and so on, the process can easily be handled within the SCC. This saves valuable time when alarms can affect a building evacuation. Building evacuations cost companies large sums of money in lost personnel time, not to mention any production losses. Some industries will be more sensitive to this issue than others. A building that manufactures semiconductors (a semiconductor FAB) can lose hundreds of thousands of dollars in a single evacuation. Many times these critical environment, large-scale systems use a paging system that sends pages to predetermined personnel (normally the Security, Facilities, and Safety departments) when the fire panel receives a fire alarm. If such a system is used, only fire evacuation alarms and fire nonevacuation alarms should be sent through the pager. An example of a fire nonevacuation alarm could be an under-floor smoke detector which is usually classified as a supervisory alarm. This definition will depend upon the code that the system was designed to meet. Otherwise the recipients would constantly receive alarms due to trouble, ground faults, and so on.

6

Exterior and Interior Security Sensors

The quality of any security alarm system starts with the correct selection of sensors. The sensors should be selected based upon their strengths and the application. Often sensors are installed with little regard for the environment in which they must operate. The result is a system that constantly suffers from nuisance alarms, or, worse, does not provide the detection needed. The desired goals for any security sensor are reasonable cost, high reliability, high detect ability, low nuisance alarms and no false alarms. It is obvious that not all sensors can meet this entire goal, but by properly understanding their strengths, incorporating them in the correct environment, and with reasonable expectations, the desired results will be obtained. In this chapter, we will look at exterior and interior security sensors. We will address strengths and weaknesses, environmental issues and real life problems.

You might be asked to design a security system that provides 100 percent detection in a given area of the building. The problem with this design requirement is that it is virtually impossible to design a system that will provide 100 percent detection of an intruder. An installation with an average cost might address a typical threat that detects intrusions more than 90 percent of the time. The closer to 100 percent detection you want to get, the higher the cost of the installation. This is a choice you must make given a certain set of circumstances. To develop a realistic Probability of Detection (PD) requires some testing and subjectivity. The testing is not a pure science, there is some subjectivity and quantifying required in establishing the type of test needed. Let's assume that the goal is to achieve the probability that an intruder would be detected in a computer room on the second floor of a two-story building. The detection is to be accomplished with an infrared motion detector on the ceiling. The first step is to define the number of ways that the intruders might enter the area. For example, we can assume that they could walk or run within the protected area. There are, of course, other ways that they might enter, such as crawling, rolling or even coming down through a skylight. Then each activity should be weighted, as to the likelihood that an intruder would actually use the activity to gain physical access to your computers. In our example, walking or running would be the most likely so those might each be given a 45 percent chance of being the approach used by an intruder. That is you are assuming that 90 percent of the time an intruder entering the computer room would do so either walking or running to gain access to the computers. Summarily the other activities must also be weighted. See Table 6.1. Then each activity must be tested a given number of times and the results added to the chart as a percent. Let's say we assume each activity is tested ten times. If the walk test results in the intruder being detected 95 percent of the time, it is added to the chart under the topic "tests." Each activity must be tested and the

Table 6.1 PD Chart

Activity	Probability	Test	PD
Walk	0.45	0.95	0.43
Run	0.45	0.95	0.43
Crawl	0.05	0.05	0.03
Enter roof	0.05	0.04	0.02
			0.91

results documented under the test column. To find the actual PD, each activity must be multiplied horizontally, listed under the topic PD on the chart and the PD column must be added vertically. Back to our walking example, 45 percent of the time we expect the intruder to walk through the area. The test resulted in a 95 percent detection, so 95 percent is multiplied by 45 percent resulting in a number of .43. Each activity must be multiplied in this way. Then the vertical column under the topic PD must be added. The result is a 91 percent PD that under our assumptions an intruder would be detected trying to gain access to the computers, the motion detector chosen, and its location.

Since the results did not yield a 100 percent PD of detection, the question becomes "How can the PD be improved?" There are several ways to improve the PD. They include adding more of the same type of sensors, adding a mixture of sensor technology types and limiting some of the means of entry (activities). A door switch could be added to the entrance of the computer room. The ability to enter through the skylight (or roof) might be eliminated by making access to the roof virtually impossible. The goal is to make the PD as close to 100 percent as is economically feasible. After a while, it becomes obvious that the PD of 100 percent may not make economic sense. It also becomes obvious that reaching 100 percent is unlikely. That means that there should be a reasonable expectation that the PD for any given area may not be 100 percent. It is possible to approach total detection, but the expense is seldom worth 100 percent detection.

To start our discussion on alarm sensors, we will start outside of the box. In our case, this is outside, or the exterior of the building. One of the common exterior sensor technologies is a microwave. Microwave sensors come in two configurations and are active devices. The first type is a monostatic microwave which has a transmitter and receiver in the same housing. The microwave produces a field that extends from the device. When the field is disturbed, an alarm output relay is activated. The second type is a bistatic device which has a separate transmitter and receiver. The receiver monitors the field produced by the transmitter. When the field is disturbed, an alarm relay is activated. Figure 6.1 is a bistatic microwave transmitter. The pattern or field developed by these microwaves is similar to the shape of a football. It extends out horizontally and vertically becoming

Figure 6.1   Microwave sensor. Courtesy of Southwest Microwave.

maximum size in the middle of the electronic field. One advantage of these devices is that they are difficult to go over or through without being detected. They can be defeated if the terrain is not properly graded, an intruder may crawl through a low spot and successfully tunnel under the electronic field without being detected. It is also possible to tunnel under deep snow and not be detected.

Infrared beams are another exterior active sensor type. These devices have a transmitter and a separate receiver. The transmitter sends an infrared beam to the receiver. If the beam is blocked or not received by the receiver, an alarm output relay is activated. These devices are normally stacked so that several transmitters and receivers are used. You might think of this approach as an infrared fence or wall. Infrared detectors have been included in many spy or action motion pictures, but are typically shown in interior building applications. The infrared beams would be like invisible wires connecting the two posts (transmitter and receiver) together. These stacked devices are very effective, but also require proper grading for the same reasons as the microwave sensor. Rain and fog can affect this type of sensor. Condensation inside the infrared lens also causes nuisance alarms.

Another group of open area sensors are the buried type. There are several variations of this type of sensor: seismic, seismic/magnetic, ported coax and fiber optic. Each type uses the technology associated with its name; for example, fiber optic utilizes a buried fiber optic cable with a signal being transmitted down the cable constantly. When an intruder steps on the buried cable, the cable bends slightly causing an electrical discontinuity in the fiber. The signal being sent down the fiber will be affected by this discontinuity, indicating an intruder. The transmitting equipment that sends the signal is basically an Optical Time Domain Reflectometer (OTDR). This piece of equipment is covered in Chapter 7. To provide a short description, the OTDR sends a signal down a fiber optic cable. The OTDR then compares the signal it sent with the signal that is reflected back through the fiber optic cable and also detects any discontinuities and the distance down the fiber where the discontinuity occurred. This allows the Security Control Center (SCC) operator to not only know that there is an intrusion, but where in the zone the intrusion occurred. A typical zone size for these devices is about 100 meters based upon other sensor types and Closed Circuit Television (CCTV) coverage; but they can be longer or shorter.

Other types of buried sensors measure seismic impact as an intruder walks or runs over the buried sensor. This can be accomplished by incorporating piezo sensors which produce an electrical current when they are mechanically stressed. The stress is developed when an intruder walks over or close to the buried sensors. Other buried devices produce a field that the intruder interferes with when they cross the zone. There are several versions of what is called leaky coax: cables made with a standard coax configuration of a center conductor surrounded by a dielectric, a shield and a protective jacket. The difference between this type of cable and other cables with a similar configuration is that the shield has been designed with gaps to allow the electric field caused by current flowing through the center conductor to "leak" or radiate out. The resulting electronic field is disturbed when an intruder walks next to or over the buried cable. There are buried balanced pressure sensors that incorporate a sensing device in the middle of two zones. The pressure in each zone is the same until an intruder steps close to the buried loops. Then the pressure in one of the loops will rise, indicating an intruder. There is also buried cable that utilizes two cables and a field between the cables. See Figure 6.2. This is not a total list, but includes some of the basic technologies.

The advantage of buried sensors is that they are not visible and they follow the terrain very well, which makes them difficult to see and allows for a very natural appearing zone of protection. These devices are often used in high security applications or applications where appearance is critical. For example, a typical application would be a company's corporate campus environment where the goal is to have security without the appearance of security. These devices will respond differently in different soil environments; therefore, testing is critical. There will be requirements as to the construction of the trenches addressing the base, backfill and the depth of the trench. The devices must be tested for proper operation for any given area. The manufacturer or its representative should be involved in any new installation. Many times, the depth of burial will change based upon soil conditions, as well as assuring the trench is free of any rocks or other debris. These sensors are not plug and play devices. They require care in preparing the area, care in installation and eliminating potential nuisance-causing situations, which will be discussed later in the chapter.

Microwave, infrared and buried sensors are normally used in an open area that is void of or has properly controlled vegetation.

Figure 6.2 Buried cable. Courtesy of Southwest Microwave.

In high security applications, where a double fencing is used, additional sensor technologies are used to increase the PD. The inner fence has several possible sensor types that can be mounted on it, including taut-wire, electric field, capacitance, piezo, and geophone sensors. Fence sensors require a stable fence. This means that the fabric on the fence must be taut and the post must be stable. (There will be requirements by the fence sensor manufacturer that the post and fabric must meet. These specifications must be met to minimize nuisance alarms.) The fence fabric must be tested and re-stretched every so often to mitigate nuisance alarm problems. These exterior sensors are not installed once and forgotten; they require ongoing maintenance. The fence post must be mounted in concrete for stability. If the fence is allowed to move or the fabric is allowed to flex excessively, the rate of nuisance alarms will be so high that the system will be unusable. The environment in which exterior sensors must operate is not very forgiving. There is nothing worse than having constant alarms to the point that the SCC operators ignore them. You can only cry wolf so many times before no one pays attention.

For some examples of fence sensor technology and the way they operate; let's start with the electric field, or E-field, sensor type. Three or more separate wires are used and run parallel to the fence on an insolated standoff or outrigger. On a three-wire system, one wire is at the top of the fence, one in the middle and one close to the bottom. The center wire has a signal applied that develops an electric field between it and the top wire as well as the bottom wire. As an intruder approaches the wires, the electric field is disrupted and this disturbance causes an alarm to be generated. See Figure 6.3. Capacitance fence sensor systems operate in a similar fashion to the electronic field system, except they use the capacitance between the wires as the sensing technology. The capacitance changes when an intruder approaches the fence, causing an alarm. Taut-wire uses a series of switches with a taut wire running through the top of each switch. When an intruder cuts the fence or climbs the fence, the taut wire will deflect and cause the switch/switches to activate. Piezo systems operate the same as they do in the buried environment. The mechanical stress is sensed on the fence fabric. Another variation in technology is available in a buried sensor and it is composed of an electrical coil with a magnet inside the coil. When the magnet moves, an electrical current is produced which in turn causes an alarm.

Figure 6.3 X-Field sensor. Courtesy of Magal-Senstar, Inc.

The exterior sensors mentioned usually have fairly compli-cated electronic controls that develop signals or "listen" for intrud-ers. The final result of an intruder activating the sensor is a switch closure. The actual alarm is a simple relay that activates when the electronics determines that there is an intruder. This is not 100 per-cent true, but is basically how exterior sensors operate. Some of the buried sensors will indicate the location in the zone an intruder appears, but most are just a switch closure that indicates that a zone has been activated. Fence sensors are similar and often use the same technology modified for mounting on a fence. The fence systems are also typically assigned 100-meter zones for the same reason that was discussed for buried sensors. The open area sensors are often used in combination with fence sensors for high security applica-tions. This approach allows a more positive detection because com-binations of technologies in a given zone will indicate an intruder, adding validity to any single technology alarm.

There are some basic precautions (some have already been mentioned) that must be considered with exterior alarm systems. When exterior sensors are used, it is important to incorporate Closed Circiut Television (CCTV) to view the alarmed zone. There are many potential nuisance alarms in an exterior environment. By being able to view the zone, it is possible to make an assessment as to the likelihood that an intruder caused the alarm. Without the CCTV capability, every alarm would require a response, which could become a full-time task. In fact, an exterior alarm system without CCTV coverage is impractical. Another precaution is lightning protection. Even with wires buried in the ground, they will still have lightning induced Electromagnetic Interference (EMI) which can be hundreds or even thousands of volts induced into the wires, which will cause damage to various electronic components: the electronics that allow the sensors to operate or the electronic field panel or power supplies. As a general rule, it is advisable to place lightning protection on any wire entering the building from outside; this is a National Electric Code (NEC) requirement. Remember, it is up to the end user to protect his/her equipment. This is why lightning and various Alternating Current (AC) surge protection equipment and components are sold. UL requires minimal surge protection to be installed in the field panels—primarily metal oxide varistor (MOV). These devices limit the voltage, but do not necessarily protect the electronics from failing. This is discussed in Chapter 4.

Another precaution is to control the environment so that nuisance alarms are minimized. This would include keeping fence fabric tight, to prevent animals from gaining access to the sensors, and avoiding overhead and buried power lines. Prepare areas for proper drainage so that water does not accumulate or pond. Water ponding by a microwave will cause the signal pattern to change by reflecting energy in different directions. Large trees close to buried sensors will cause nuisance alarms when the trees sway because of high winds. The swaying action stresses the tree roots, which in turn appear as an intruder to many of the buried sensor technologies. Each sensor type will have strengths and weaknesses that must be considered for its possible use to minimize nuisance alarms and assure the highest PD. Whatever the technology is, that same technology that detects intruders will also detect situations that are not intruders, but appear to be. Careful planning is very important for exterior sensor applications along with CCTV.

Now let's move on to interior sensors. They are in an environment that is much easier to control, but the correct selection of technology is still very important. The basic groupings of interior sensors are (1) door sensors, (2) motion sensors and (3) glass break sensors. We will look at each type of sensor and understand the benefits and limitations of each as well as how they operate. We will start our study with door sensors. In its simplest form, the door switch is composed of two components: a reed relay and a magnet. The magnet is installed on the movable door and the reed relay is installed in the stationary doorjamb. When the magnet gets close to the reed relay it causes the reed relay to close and the electrical contact allows current to flow. This is discussed in detail in Chapter 4. The magnet should be aligned with the reed relay vertically and horizontally. The distance between where the magnet first causes the reed relay to "make contact" and the physical distance between them is referred to as the door switch gap. Door sensors can be purchased with various gaps. The reason for using a wider gap is to allow for swelling and contraction of the door itself, as well as natural movement of the door within the doorjamb. While the door is closed the door switch must be shorted during any of this type of movement. Garage or rollup doors are notorious for needing large gap door sensors. Garage or overhead door reed relays are normally available in a heavy aluminum case mounted to the floor of the garage or warehouse to prevent them from being damaged if driven over.

A more complex and secure door switch is referred to as a Balanced Magnetic Switch (BMS). The BMS is composed of several reed relays and several magnets. The magnets are placed in such a way that the reed relays will all be shorted when properly aligned with the matching magnet pack. The polarities of the magnets are considered when the magnet pack is built for a BMS. In fact, the magnet pack and the reed relay pack components are sold as a matched pair. If several BMS magnets are mixed up, the BMS reed relays must be tested and re-matched to the magnet pack, otherwise a new pair must be purchased. It is not likely that one magnet can be exchanged for a different magnet and work reliably. These devices are typically used on doors associated with high security requirements. Often, they are used on data centers, critical or high dollar storage areas or government "closed" areas. They are required to be utilized on government DoD, Special Access Required (SAR) and Special Access Program (SAP). There are four mounting holes and screws to mount each of the two components.

In high secure areas, the screws used to mount the BMS are special and require a special tool to install them. The special securing screw cannot be removed without a special security screwdriver, which adds to the overall security of the installation.

The next type of interior sensor is the motion detector group. The best-known detector in this group is the infrared motion detector. Interior infrared motion detectors are passive devices, that is, they do not generate infrared energy; they detect the infrared energy that may be present within their viewing area. Infrared energy is heat, and humans produce heat; in fact the external skin temperate is approximately 90°F. In a room that is at 72°F, a person would stand out as a hotspot. Likewise, in a room that is 90°F a human may not be detected, so another type of motion detector might be used. Warehouses or areas without temperature control will typically need this solution. This detector is looking for both heat and motion. Infrared detectors utilize a Freznel lens that focuses the infrared energy onto a detector that is sensitive to the frequencies of heat. The lens divides the protected area into several zones which are similar to your fingers extending out from your hand. Each zone can be divided into quadrants to provide a more sensitive detector. The intruder must pass through a zone and a certain number of quadrants in the zone to assure detection. This approach helps eliminate nuisance alarms such as those caused by animals. Infrared detectors can also provide a vertical narrow wall of detection. This coverage is often referred to as a curtain. Many manufacturers allow their detectors to be changed from a finger pattern to a curtain pattern or vice versa, by simply changing the Freznel lens.

The size of the zone is based upon detecting a 6-foot-tall person at the far limit of the area. For example, if the detection pattern is for a 30-foot-by-30-foot area, a 6-foot-tall person would be detected at a distance of 30 feet from the detector. The detector will still detect an intruder that is farther away than 30 feet, but the intruder must be larger than the 6-foot person. This is the mouse and the elephant story. An elephant will be detected much farther away than 30 feet and a mouse might be detected a foot away from the detector. This target information must be taken into account when using an infrared motion detector. Another consideration is the fact that infrared energy will not penetrate materials. For example, an infrared detector will not detect an intruder on the other side of a glass window. For that matter a piece of paper can be placed in front of the detector and an intruder can go anywhere undetected. Many manufacturers have added electronic capability to their detectors to notify the SCC operator via a trouble signal if the detector is being compromised in this way. This is often accomplished with a small infrared pattern close to the detector. There are other additions to make these devices more reliable, such as bright lights and animal immunity.

Microwave is another type of interior motion detector and it works the same way as a monostatic exterior microwave. These devices are active because they produce microwave energy but at a very low level. One of the major differences between a microwave and an infrared detector is that the microwave detector will penetrate objects. For example, if an interior office belonging to a company executive was to be protected and a microwave motion detector was used, someone walking down the hallway adjacent to the protected office could cause an alarm; therefore, placement is important with this device. Even water flowing through a PVC drainpipe in the wall can cause an alarm. Microwave detectors are excellent volumetric devices, but like any other technology there are unique limitations.

Ultrasonic motion detectors are active devices that are "looking" for a Doppler shift. (Doppler shift is the change in frequency of a wave reaching an observer or a system.) A common example is the audible frequency change of a train whistle: as the train gets closer to you the frequency gets lower. The ultrasonic motion detector is a monostatic unit sending out a frequency and checking for a shift in that frequency, which ideally indicates an intruder. The frequency is above the human ear's ability to hear, but much lower than the frequency used in the microwave sensor. There are frequency-producing items within a facility that can cause nuisance alarms. One example would be a squeaky belt on an air-handling unit. A human can hear some of the frequencies produced from the squeaky belt on an air-handling unit but not all. Frequencies generated in this example are not just the ones that we can hear, but there are also harmonic and subharmonic frequencies, which we cannot hear, that will affect the ultrasonic motion detector. (Harmonic and subharmonic frequencies are multiples of the fundamental frequency. There is a decrease in signal amplitude of half for each harmonic as it is generated.) Photoelectric detectors are similar to the exterior infrared beam detectors discussed earlier. They are usually composed of only one transmitter and one receiver which are active bistatic devices. The transmitter produces an infrared beam that is detected by the receiver. When an intruder enters the protected area, the transmitter's beam is broken, producing an alarm. The beam is fairly narrow, so it is possible to jump over the beam or crawl under the beam. Most of the time beam detectors are mounted about knee height, which is usually effective, because the intruder does not realize that the detector is present. The beam of a typical photoelectric detector is invisible and the detectors are mounted fairly low; however, it is possible to purchase units with multiple transmitters and receivers stacked on top of each other similar to the exterior versions. Multiple separate units can also be used in a similar fashion to produce the same results.

Laser field sensors are active devices that produce a very thin invisible laser wall or curtain to cover the protected area. These devices are used in many different applications, but a common application would be in a museum. Let's assume that there is an expensive painting on the wall and it needs to be protected. A laser field detector could provide a detection wall in front of the painting that is inches away from the expensive work of art, but provides total coverage of the painting. For someone to take the painting, to touch the painting, or try to vandalize the painting the laser wall must the interrupted, thus sending an alarm to the electronic field panel to the server/computer in the SCC.

The next variation of motion detector types is a dual technology detector. The idea is to utilize two different technologies that will complement each other with both technologies activating before the device goes into an alarm condition. The advantage to this approach is that nuisance alarms are reduced significantly, because both technologies must detect the intruder. A common dual technology motion detector will use infrared and microwave. To reflect back to an earlier example, if water is flowing down a drainpipe in the wall, the microwave detector might detect the motion and think it is an intruder, but the infrared sees nothing. The reason being that the infrared energy is blocked by the Sheetrock on the wall. Since both technologies did not detect an intruder, there is no alarm.

Glass break is a different detection approach because it detects the frequency of breaking glass, usually between 4 and 6 kilohertz (kHz). It detects the suddenness, the frequency and the duration of the frequency of breaking glass that is produced when the glass is struck. When glass breaks, it produces distinctive sounds or frequencies that can be verified with a detector that incorporates a frequency filter tuned to the frequency range of breaking glass. Glass break sensors measure amplitude, duration and suddenness of the 4 to 6 kHz frequencies and activate an alarm when all components are present. These detectors are typically mounted on the ceiling facing the windows that are to be protected. The distance from the window will vary, but a sensor will often detect breakage at 35 feet. The reliability will vary when the detector is at right angles to the glass. A common source of nuisance alarms with these detectors is lightning or, more accurately, the thunder associated with lightning. The percussion of thunder will rattle the glass and cause both acoustic waves and frequencies that can trigger these sensors.

Glass break sensors should be tested either by actually breaking a sample of the type of glass that they will be sensing or by testing with an electronic glass break simulator (commercially available units). The frequencies produced by different types of glass will vary. There are three basic categories of glass. One type is plate glass which is typically used in homes and older buildings. The thickness will vary based upon the surface area size of the glass (plate glass is typically ¼ inch thick). When untempered glass breaks, it will shatter into large pieces. The second type is tempered or hardened glass which is glass that has been heat-treated (usually around 1,400°F). Tempered glass cannot be cut or drilled without shattering into thousands of pieces. Any work that must be done to the glass must happen before it is tempered. As stated above, when the glass breaks it shatters into thousands of small pieces, which produces a different frequency response from that of plate glass. Tempered glass is one of the two types of safety glass and is required for newer construction or remodels. Most of the glass in modern cars is tempered glass. The glass is very impact resistant and if it shatters, pieces are so small that they are less dangerous to people inside the vehicle. When someone breaks into a car, they usually use a center punch on a side window because the center punch produces a substantial force on an extremely small point which is the weak point for this type of glass. The third type of glass, which is also a safety glass, is laminated. Laminated glass uses two or more layers of ordinary glass separated by a plastic-like polymer in between. The glass will break, but the shattered pieces normally stay attached to the polymer. Car windshields are made out of this type of glass. Older cars also used this type of glass for windows as well as windshields. You may have noticed small bubbles in the edges of these old windows on antique cars. This is the laminate between the two pieces of glass breaking down with age, allowing air bubbles to form. Based upon the different techniques and characteristics of these three types of glass, it is obvious that the frequencies would be different when the glass shatters. This is the reason that the glass sensor needs to be tested and adjusted if necessary.

Another type of glass break sensor is the type that physically mounts on the glass. These detectors are impact type sensors. There are different techniques used (piezo is the most common), but they all rely on the glass shaking when it is broken. These devices should also be tested based upon the type of glass used. The number of nuisance alarms will depend upon where the device is mounted on the glass (the corners of the glass are the best), and the type of frame that supports the glass. These devices normally have sensitivity adjustments just like the other types of glass break sensors. The difference is that these devices must be mounted on the glass itself. When they are hard wired to a zone in the electronic field panel, access to the window must be available, which means that they are normally used on new construction. The devices can be wireless, but most of the time if a glass break sensor is used on existing construction it will be the ceiling mounted, acoustic type discussed earlier.

The goal of all sensors, whether exterior or interior, is to detect an intruder and have no nuisance or false alarms. This ideal state cannot be reached; however, it is possible to greatly reduce the nuisance alarms by installing the sensor technology that is best for the environment in which it will be placed. This is extremely critical for exterior sensors due to the fact that their environment is already much harsher than that of an interior detector. As mentioned previously, exterior sensors should have CCTV coverage to minimize the number of response requests sent to the responding officer. If the responses are not limited, the response will become lax or nonexistent with constant nuisance alarms. (The old cry wolf issue.) It is important to remember that the terms "nuisance" and "false alarms" are often used interchangeably. A nuisance alarm is an alarm that occurs because the sensor "sees" an event that appears to be an intruder. It is detecting what it should detect. The problem is that it is not an intruder. The solution is to utilize a reasonable quality detector for the desired application and place the detector in the environment in such a way as to minimize nuisance alarms. A false alarm might be an electronic failure inside the device that caused it to go into alarm. When a lightning storm rolls through and there are high winds, the automatic assumption will be that the alarms are weather related. That means the best time to have an attack or break-in is during times when the weather is bad. Lightning and its associated thunder produce shock waves and ions in the air that can impact various sensor technologies. There are also often high winds associated with these storms that can cause nuisance alarms. On high security environments the concern is that there will be a diversion generated with nuisance alarms to sidetrack the SCC operators and responding officers allowing intruders to gain access.

7

Closed Circuit Television

The incorporation of Closed Circuit Television (CCTV) within a company is a critical function for any security department. There have been many improvements in CCTV equipment over the years. Cameras have become capable of much wider extremes in background lighting, making fairly inexpensive cameras capable of reliable pictures even in low light conditions. Cameras have become less expensive by replacing tubes (Vidicon, Nuvicons, etc.) with semiconductor imaging chips (CCD or Charged Couple Device). The imaging devices have shrunk in size from ½″ to ⅓″ to ¼″. Today's color cameras are relatively inexpensive, will operate at night and are available at a small premium over black-and-white cameras. Cameras are available with Information Protocol (IP) technology built into the camera; so all that needs to be added to allow the camera to work on the Internet is an IP address. Cameras have become much more robust and not as sensitive to high intensity lighting suddenly entering the field of view and causing the camera to bloom ("wash out" as it tries to compromise to the high intensity light). This sensitivity can be mitigated by replacing older motorized lenses with an electronic iris. Specialty cameras are available to address several issues. For example, they allow adjustments to be made on a pixel basis (a pixel is a rectangular segment of the video display, based upon the resolution of the camera) to correct lighting problems. In early morning, light coming through a window might reflect off the floor and a camera viewing the area will have a very bright spot in part of the monitor's display while losing detail in the rest of the picture. By being able to modify the pixels in the bright area, the remainder of the viewing area will provide a reliable picture on the monitor. There are other types of specialty cameras. Another example is a camera that has been factory designed to provide a quality image of vehicle license plates. This particular camera is sensitive to the light waves reflected off the surface of a vehicle license plate and provides the needed resolution to read the license plate. In this chapter, we will consider the products that comprise a video system and understand the best ways to install these products to obtain the desired results.

There have been many advances in other pieces of equipment that comprise a CCTV system. Monitors available today are flat screen which consume less space and provide higher quality video. Digital Video Recorders (DVR) have replaced Video Cassette Recorders (VCR). The DVR can store a tremendous amount of video and includes video motion detection as well as other options not available in the standard VCR. There are no more tapes to keep up with and no more heads to clean. The DVR is being impacted by the latest technology, the Network Video Recorder (NVR). The NVR is attached to the IP network and records various IP cameras that are also on the network. Another advance is intelligent video, which provides the capability for automatic software evaluation of video from a camera to decide if there is a threat. Specialty software operating on a computer is looking for suspicious activities (the activities have been predefined in the software). If a potential problem exists, the Security Control Center (SCC) operator is automatically notified. All aspects of the video systems are becoming more digital and more sophisticated, but the basics are still the same. A solid understanding of video concepts will allow you to make any transition necessary, as the enhancements in this area continue. To understand the concepts, we must start in the field and work our way back to the SCC.

Everyone understands that video is provided by a camera and sent to a monitor to be displayed. So we will start with the camera.

A video camera can be thought of as a snapshot camera that takes thirty pictures each second. The fact is, that is exactly what is happening. This is the same process utilized by commercial television. The reason that you do not see jerkiness in the screen is because your eye cannot detect the difference between thirty pictures per second and real life motion, thus the screen appears to be real time motion. If you think back to when you were a child, you probably drew stick figures on a pad of paper. If you drew a slightly different pose on each successive page and flipped the pages of the pad quickly in such a way as to show each page in a rapid sequence, the stick figures appeared to be moving. This is very similar to what is happening in a video system. The snapshot pictures are being shown one after another in extremely rapid fashion (30 pictures each second). The speed is so fast that your eye does not detect the fact that you are really seeing a series of still pictures.

The video monitor produces these pictures by scanning the information on the monitor in horizontal lines. There are 525 horizontal lines that make up one picture. That means that 525 lines are scanned 30 times per second for a total of 15,750 lines per second. The lines scan from left to right and then retrace back to the left side of the screen ready to scan the next line. The retrace lines are not perfectly horizontal, they are at a slight angle and each time the scan sequence is run it alternates between odd and even scan lines. For example, the first scan might be the odd lines which means that lines 1, 3, 5, 9, 11, 13, etc. are scanned. The next scan is lines 2, 4, 6, 8, 10, 12, etc. The total combination of odd and even scan lines produces one of the 30 images or snapshots each second. The grouping of one odd and one even scan is referred to as a frame. Each odd or even scan is referred to as a field; therefore two fields make one frame. There are 30 frames and 60 fields. This is considered "real time" video. The reason 60 was chosen for the field was based upon the electrical power in the United States. The electrical power is Alternating Current (AC). The power cycles 60 times each second in AC. The power company carefully regulates the power to keep it extremely close to 60 cycles per second (60 hz). Each cycle change allows a scan to start. The early Cathode Ray Tube (CRT) had a phosphorescence (the ability to emit light after excitation has been removed) to hold the field snapshot long enough for the next field which kept the picture from "turning on and off." The importance of this detail will be more obvious later in the chapter.

Now that the basic concept of video scanning has been covered, let's see what affects the quality of the picture from the camera. The camera contains an imaging device. The scene viewed by a camera is actually a reflection of the actual scene. Light strikes the scene and reflects back through the lens and onto the camera-imaging device. The old analog cameras used a tube as the imaging device and digital cameras use a semiconductor chip as the imaging device. As you think about light reflecting off the scene and traveling to the imaging device, it becomes obvious that the picture quality depends upon the resolution of the imaging device, the lens quality and the amount of reflected light. We will start our discussion with the reflected light and work toward the imaging device.

If you have ever read camera specifications, one of those specifications is minimum light level. The light level in the specifications is provided in foot-candles (fc) or lumens. A foot-candle is an old measurement based upon the amount of light one foot away from a candle. When reading the specifications, you might assume that the camera will provide a quality picture when the outside lighting is equal to the fc minimum rating of the camera's specifications, but, in fact, this is the minimum requirement for the light striking the imaging device. The metric unit of light measurement is also used on some camera specifications and it is called a lux. A lux is the amount of light from a candle measured one meter away (1 lux = .1 fc). Full direct sunlight is about 10,000 fc while an overcast day is about 100 fc and twilight is about 1 fc. To help put this into perspective, let's assume that the camera is viewing a green grassy area in full daylight (10,000 fc). The light reflected off the green grass is approximately 40 percent or 50 percent of the light that is striking the green grass. In this case, we have lost more than half the light we need on the imaging device and there is additional loss through the lens, which has not been addressed. This points out the fact that an environment that will be viewed at night must include all losses associated with the camera system before the light gets to the imaging device. If the camera is mounted in a housing, there can be additional loss through the housing's glass window material directly in front of the camera. Table 7.1 is a chart that shows various backgrounds and the amount of light that is reflected.

Table 7.1 Reflection Chart

Scene	Reflectance
Asphalt (new)	5 percent
Concrete (new)	40 percent
Concrete (old)	25 percent
Red Brick (new)	25 percent
Green Grass	40 percent
Snow	95 percent

The spectrum of light is discussed in Chapter 8. As a brief overview, light is composed of various colors that together make up what we see as white light. One end of the visible light spectrum is blue and the other is red. The frequency of light is measured in nanometers (nm), which is one billionth of a meter. Our eyes can see from roughly 400 nm violet to 700 nm red. At 1,200 nm, the red spectrum disappears as far as our eyes are concerned and is what we feel as heat. Infrared (IR) cameras, which will be discussed later in the chapter, detect electromagnetic energy in this range. Black-and-white video cameras, normally used in security, detect energy in the red end of the spectrum much better than our eyes. For the most part, cameras will respond in a similar fashion to a human eye as far as what will be displayed on a monitor with the exception of energy in the red part of the spectrum. This is what allows an infrared illuminator to work so well with black-and-white cameras. IR illuminators can be used in areas where there is either low light, where the level of lighting needs to be enhanced without being obvious, or areas where an investigation is taking place. The IR illuminator will light up the area and the black-and-white camera will produce an excellent picture that the human eye cannot see. Color cameras do not have the same bandwidth and are limited to about 800 nm; therefore, the illuminator will not be as effective with a color camera.

The last topic on light we will discuss in this chapter deals with artificial light. The typical CCTV applications for artificial light are at night to allow cameras to provide reasonable quality video. Artificial light varies in color and intensity. (See Table 7.2.) Color and black-and-white cameras are affected by the amount of light

Table 7.2   Lighting Fixtures

Lighting Fixture	Efficiency Lumens/ Watt	Strike/ Restrike Minutes	Color Discrimi- nation	Lamp Life Hours
Incandescent	12 to 20	Immediate	Excellent	750–10,000
Mercury Vapor	40 to 65	3 to 7	Good	16,000–24,000
Metal Halide	80 to 100	3 to 5	Excellent	10,000–15,000
High Pressure Sodium	95 to 130	3 to 4	Fair	20,000–40,000
Low Pressure Sodium	131 to 183	8 to 15	Poor	16,000–24,000
Fluorescent	36 to 100	Immediate	Excellent	7,500–10,000

and the color of the light. As mentioned earlier, color cameras do not extend into the infrared range like black-and-white cameras do. Color cameras are, however, affected by the color of the light source. The term Color Rendering Index (CRI) addresses the ability of a color camera to properly render the colors in the scene. Sunlight has a CRI of 100 and reproduces colors accurately. Incandescent light and halogen light also have a CRI of 100, but fluorescence has a CRI of 80 and mercury vapor has a CRI of 20. When choosing outdoor lighting there are several concerns when using color cameras: the correct color rendering, the energy cost, the lighting fixture cost and lighting fixture maintenance cost. Considering CRI and total lighting costs, metal halide is a reasonable compromise for color cameras. Black-and-white cameras can use almost any light source. Lighting fixtures with the light produced in the red end of the spectrum can be an advantage.

It is important to define what the objective of the CCTV system is in the first place. This may sound ridiculous at first, but there is a good reason for this to be addressed at this point in the chapter. If the objective of the CCTV system is to see movement and be able to detect an intruder, then the lighting, camera, lens, field of view and resolution will be affected. These parameters will be affected in a different way if the goal is to recognize an individual and not merely that an individual is present. In other words, is the CCTV camera used to detect or to recognize? (Designing a system to provide recognition level video is an approach that may be used when the video might be presented in a court of law.) These distinctions will affect every part of the design. For example, the lighting will need to be substantially better for recognition versus detection. Even the background that the intruder must pass when being viewed by the camera is important from a reflectivity standpoint. Black-and-white cameras also tend to have better resolution than color cameras, which makes them desirable from a recognition standpoint. Color cameras will be beneficial in describing what an intruder is wearing. One more note on color cameras is that the less expensive color camera specification sheets may show a very low light level of operation, but they normally switch to black-and-white mode of operation at the low light end of their operation. These cameras are referred to as day/night cameras.

Another issue with outdoor lighting is the issue of spotty light. If you have ever looked down from a multistory building at a parking lot, you may have seen round dots of light across the parking area. The architect that designed the lighting might have designed the lot for a minimum light level of 1 fc to accommodate a camera system. The problem here is that a camera compensates for the brightest light in its field of view. The result on the monitor would be a series of bright spots where movement could be seen surrounded by black. It is better to have light as uniformly distributed as possible, even if that means a lower light level in the brightest areas. As much as is possible, outdoor lighting in the camera's field of view should be uniform, not pointed into the camera. The camera should be mounted below the lighting fixture and the type of lighting should match the camera's needs (black-and-white or color).

The lens is the next component that affects the loss in the light reaching the imaging device. The lenses utilized in CCTV systems are the same technology used on the old 35-millimeter cameras. There are two aspects to consider when selecting lens, one is the field of view and the other is the F-stop. The Field Of View (FOV) is the height and width that the camera views at the point where lens is in focus. There are charts for various lens sizes that can be used to pick the correct lens for a given application. The process is to define the height and width of the scene that is to be viewed and the distance that the viewing area will be from the camera. When a motion picture director holds his hands up with his forefingers and thumbs touching, looking through the box formed by his thumbs and fingers, he or she is looking at the FOV the motion picture camera "sees" in the particular scene they are trying to evaluate. There are rotating cardboard calculators that are available from lens manufacturers and even an adjustable viewing lens device that allows you to look through while standing where the camera will be mounted and focus on the desired FOV. The device is adjusted until the desired view is in focus, then the lens size can be simply read off the chart that is scribed into the body of the device. There are also formulas that can be used, but we do not have room in this chapter to address that level of detail. The other issue is F-stop. An F-stop addresses the quality of the lens. It indicates the amount of light that will pass through the lens itself. Typical F-stops for quality lenses are 1.2 or 1.4 in most CCTV applications and run up to about 4. The important thing to remember is that for each full F-stop the change in light passing through the lens is reduced by 50 percent. The lower the F-stop the more expensive the lens and the more light it will allow to pass through.

The next consideration for possible loss of reflected light is the imaging device. As technology has improved, so has the quality of smaller imaging devices. A quality low light tube type camera needed a 1" lens many years ago, today ⅓" and even ¼" solid-state CCD type imagers provide quality pictures. Obviously the cost is less with a smaller imaging device. So cameras are actually cheaper today than they were in the old 1" Vidicon tube days. Cameras with small digital imagers have become the standard. The imaging devices are simply light sensitive diodes that are arranged in a matrix. The size of the matrix affects the resolution of the camera. The imaging device is scanned by row and combined into an analog signal that is sent through the coax or other medium to a monitor. Digital cameras are digital at the imaging device only. The digital data is converted to analog before the signal leaves the camera. The only exception at this time is the IP camera that connects directly to a network. The IP camera is basically a totally digital camera. (You can think of it as a computer with a lens.) It provides a digital signal directly to the network. A "digital" camera can connect to the network although an interface box that reconverts the analog signal leaving the camera back to digital is required.

Another type of camera available today is the IR camera. As the name implies, the camera is sensitive to the IR end of the spectrum, which is heat. The monitor will display the image as white as hot or black as hot. This makes the image on the monitor considerably different from what an SCC operator would normally see as video. The image is more like a black-and-white film negative. This requires the operators to view the monitor more toward shapes and detection versus recognition. A person, for example, will have a white face (if white = hot), the exposed skin will be white and places such as around the waist will be a shade of white while the rest of the body might be a shade of black or gray (cooler). There are advantages to IR cameras, one of which is that the camera will detect people from surroundings in the total darkness. A regular CCTV camera might see only black while an IR camera could find someone hiding in a field. Police cars are starting to be outfitted with these cameras for that very reason. Another advantage is that the cameras can provide an image of where someone has gone. For example, the camera can detect the footprints of a person walking across a carpet after the person has already left the area. One more advantage is that no lighting is required for the cameras to provide a quality image. That makes these cameras ideal for emergency situations, such as power loss, or for areas where no lighting is available.

There are some negatives with IR cameras. One is that they should be tested before purchasing to assure that you receive the results that you desire or need. There are two basic areas to verify. The first is that IR cameras have a lens or a couple of lenses that can be interchanged with a given camera. The less expensive IR cameras have only one lens. That means the FOV is defined for that particular camera. The expensive IR cameras allow you to switch predefined lenses. (A CCTV camera can accept any focal length lens.) The second area to consider is the background temperature. A human's exterior skin temperature is about 90°F. If the scene background is about 90°F, a person in the scene will disappear into the background. For example, in the desert during certain parts of the year, the sand, cactus and other plants can be about 90°F. In this situation a person cannot be easily seen. On the other hand, the greater the temperature difference the better the contrast will be.

The transmission of video from the camera to the monitor can take several different approaches. The transmission can be accomplished with copper wire. For long distances, a large diameter coax might be used. The part number of the coax can indicate its diameter.

For example, a 500 coax is ½″ in diameter. Large coax is used to minimize signal loss. There are some issues with large coax such as the special connectors that must be used. The wire is stiff and difficult to work with. When there are short coax runs, the coax is usually a smaller diameter coax such as RG59. This coax is very flexible and about ¼″ in diameter. Typically, the smaller the coax, the more capacitance per foot it has and the more capacitance per foot it has the less distance it will allow a video signal to travel. For that reason, longer coax runs will incorporate 500 coax versus several hundred feet of RG59. The connectors normally used are F or BNC connectors. (BNC connectors provide a better signal quality and F-type connectors are used in commercial television work.) The other type of copper wire to send the video signal back to a monitor is twisted pair. There is a module than can be purchased commercially that allows the video to travel over twisted pair cable such as used on older telephone systems. This approach was developed in an attempt to utilize existing wire in a building and eliminate the need to run new cabling or fiber. The module converts the twisted pair impedance (analog resistance) to 75 ohms. That is the impedance of CCTV coax and the expected impedance of the line by both the camera and the monitor to assure quality signal transmission. The sales pitch used for the device is that it utilizes wiring that is often part of the existing phone system that is distributed throughout a facility with data gathering areas in the Intermediate Distribution Frame (IDF) rooms. This allows a convenient network of cabling to use with collection points in rooms where equipment can be added to the video system.

Although sometimes expensive, fiber optics is also a favored transmission medium because it has less loss than coax and is more immune to electromagnetic interference than copper cable. Fiber optics cable is available in two types of configurations. The first is single mode, which is a small diameter cable with light being transmitted straight through the cable. Thus the bandwidth is very high, in the neighborhood of 2000 mega hertz (2000 mHz). The second is multimode, which is a larger diameter cable and the light reflects off the inner edges of the cable thus reducing the bandwidth. This cable has a bandwidth of between 50 and 500 mHz. The multimode fiber optic cable is typically larger in diameter, which makes it less expensive to manufacture. The most widespread use of fiber cabling in the security industry is multimode 62.5 microns in diameter. A micron is an antiquated (yet widely used) form of a micrometer, which is one millionth of a meter. (A human hair is about 80 microns.) The core with a protective jacket would be 125 microns in diameter. The manufacturer will specify a number in relation to the core or glass diameter and the protective jacket, or cladding, around the core.

There are several benefits of fiber optic cables:

1. Low loss
2. Immunity to EMI/RFI
3. Secure communications
4. Lightweight
5. High data rate capability
6. No ground faults

LOW LOSS

When information must be transmitted long distances, then fiber is the primary choice. As the distance between the camera and monitor increases, the signal loss in the cable increases. To overcome the signal loss in coaxial cable as mentioned earlier, a larger size cable is used. For example, when transmitting video over a standard distance, say, 1,000 feet, the losses can be measured and different types of cabling can be compared and presented in chart form. Most charts are set for transmission of video at a given frequency. For a relative comparison, let's assume the video is transmitted as commercial television channel 6. The loss is measured in decibels, db. A three-db loss in signal power means the power is half of what it was at the start. RG59 is a standard, small diameter flexible coax, and the loss in 1,000 feet for this type of cable depending upon construction of the cable is 24 to 31 db. Low loss coaxial cable referred to as 500, as mentioned previously, has a db loss per 1,000 feet of cable of 6 to 7 db. Fiber, on the other hand, has a loss of about 1 db per 1,000 feet and is much more flexible than 500 coaxial cable. When transmitting video over fiber there must be a transmitter at the camera end and a receiver at the monitor end. The fiber transmitter and receiver pair will affect the overall signal quality. (A higher quality pair will exhibit a high signal to noise ratio.)

IMMUNITY TO EMI/RFI

Interference voltages can be induced in the coax or copper twisted pair cable via external sources. The induced interference utilizes the same process as an antenna operates. Induced signals are discussed in Chapter 8. The problem with these induced voltages is that the signal is not desired and it degrades the video signal. Electromagnetic and radio frequency interference, EMI/RFI, can induce voltages in copper wire. These voltages totally distort or destroy the information being sent down the coaxial cable. This is an inherent problem with copper cables even when shielded. This means that in areas such as mechanical rooms, where high voltage switchgear and motors are located, it can be extremely difficult to process reliable information over coax. To address this problem, some type of additional shielding must be used. The coax or twisted pair cable can be run through conduit or in a shielded cable tray for additional protection from EMI/RFI. There should be physical separation between the communication copper cable and any power lines that might be in the same tray. When crossing a power line with copper cable, it should be crossed at a 90° angle and if possible, separated vertically as far as possible. The higher the level of twist (more twist per inch in copper cable), the higher the capacitance between the two wires being twisted. The longer the run of the twisted pair wire, the higher the inductance. Higher level of twists, in say CAT 5 cable versus CAT 3 for instance, produces cables that can be run much farther distances because the capacitive reactance in the cable tends to cancel out the inductive reactance in the cable at a given frequency range. Reactance is a dynamic resistance measured in ohms and is associated with frequency. Higher resistance in cable tends to attenuate cable electrical signals, thus lower cable resistance is the desirable mode when transmitting long distances. This is the primary reason CAT 5 and 6 cables were developed. Fiber optic cable is immune to EMI/RFI.

SECURE COMMUNICATIONS

When information is moving on coax cable, the current flow through the cable causes a magnetic field to develop around the center conductor. The magnetic field will have the same signal relationship as the occurring current flowing through the cable.

This means it is possible to monitor what is going over the cable by what is radiating out of the cable. With sophisticated equipment this information can be obtained without physically "tapping" into the cable. The shielding in the cable improves the security of coax cable, if it is properly grounded. Fiber, however, does not radiate because it uses light or photons instead of electrical current or electrons to send information. To "tap" a fiber cable and not drastically affect light loss in the cable would be very difficult, but it can be done. Since fiber does not use electrical current, it is not possible to radiate causing the information to be accessible by others without approval. Fiber will not allow EMI/RFI interference due to induction. Fiber eliminates these issues by being made of glass and utilizing light as the transmission medium. The lack of electrical current flow has another advantage in certain applications, such as hazardous environments where a spark could be a serious problem.

LIGHTWEIGHT AND HIGH DATA RATE CAPABILITY

To provide a comparison of the weight of copper and fiber we will look at the typical twisted cable used by the telephone company to run major lines. The cable is about 1.5" in diameter and carries 5,000 two-way communications. This cable weighs about 5.5 pounds per foot. A fiber cable that is capable of the same number of communications is about ½" in diameter and weighs about 3 ounces per foot. The fiber cable is composed of 6 fibers. The large number of communication paths on each fiber is possible, because of the bandwidth characteristics of fiber and the electronics that connects to each end of the fiber. Most security applications do not have the same density of signal transmissions as the telephone company cable, but there are multiplexers readily available that control multiple video cameras over a single fiber. These properties of fiber optic cable explain why it has been used in many applications including security video.

NO GROUND FAULTS

Ground faults are common in coaxial video cabled systems. The cameras and monitors are connected together via the coax cable. Cameras and monitors also require a connection to electrical power. The electrical receptacle or transformer that supplies the cameras and the monitors with power are usually separated by a long distance, which allows the electrical grounding at one location to be slightly different from the grounding at a different location. For example, the electrical ground potential at one end of a building is often different from the ground potential at the other end of the building. The slight differences in ground potential cause a current to flow from one ground at one end to the other through the coax shield that connects the camera to the monitor. This is referred to as a "charged shield." The current that develops in the charged shield distorts the video image. To overcome the problem, isolation transformers, that isolate the power from ground, are often used at one end of the line (usually at the monitor side). With fiber optic cable, the grounds are isolated because there is no electrical conductor running between the camera and the monitor that would allow a difference in ground potential.

The desire to use fiber optic cable in various applications is driven by equipment being separated by long distances, adverse environments, and readily available components to connect existing equipment. This hardware can be purchased fairly reasonably and allows data as well as video to be transmitted. Even small multiplexers are fairly inexpensive allowing the fiber cable to carry data or video from several sources. Based on the information to this point it would appear that fiber optic cable use should be the only choice. The above properties make fiber appear to be the perfect solution for all applications. You would think that copper cable should be a thing of the past with no future in the electronic security market. The very positive properties discussed make fiber appear to be the perfect solution for all applications; however, fiber optic cable does have its dark side just as any other technology. Fiber optic cable has the following potential negative properties:

1. Splices are critical and can be difficult to make properly.
2. It requires proper handling and skill.
3. It requires long term protection.

SPLICES ARE CRITICAL

The low loss of fiber optic cable is what makes its use so popular. The truth is the splices in the cable can easily add more db loss than the cable itself if not installed properly. Fiber optic cable uses a glass conduit for the light to travel down. When two pieces of glass are spliced, they must first be cut or cleaved and then highly polished before the actual splice takes place. The two pieces of glass should be perfectly mated with an exact match of the total surface area of both pieces of glass. This is accomplished via fiber splice kits/connectors and has been a process that required a great deal of skill and practice to be effective. (There are machines available that fuse the two fiber optic cables together; however, they are expensive.) The newer connectors are more forgiving than earlier units, which speed up the process and provide a faster connection; however, it is still important to do a quality job in cleaving and polishing the glass. Some of the newer mechanical splices cleave the cable and utilize an optically conductive gel to assist in minimizing transmission losses. A quality connection can be .5 db or less and a poor connection can be 3 db or more.

IT REQUIRES PROPER HANDLING

Installing fiber optic cable requires care in two areas. One is stretching the cable and the other is bending the cable. The cable is fairly strong, but no motorized pullers should be used. When making turns in conduit or the cable tray, care must be taken to prevent bending the cable because sharp bends develop small fracture lines. These lines will distort the signal, which adds to the db loss. When purchasing the cable the manufacturer will supply bend radius information for that particular cable which will define the sharpest turn that can be made before damage occurs. This is typically 25 times the jacket radius.

IT REQUIRES LONG TERM PROTECTION

Fiber optics cable is manufactured in two configurations: tightly buffered and loose tube. Both configurations process signals in the same manner. The differences in the configurations have to do with the way the glass is protected within the jacket. All fiber optic cable has a core and a cladding protection on the glass core inside the jacket. Tightly buffered and loose fill tube cable provide protection, but the protection may not be sufficient when either cable is installed in cable trays. Fiber optic cable should ideally be installed inside an additional protective sleeve. A typical type of protective sleeving is called interduct. This interduct protects the fiber optics cable from being damaged by other cables when they are added to the cable tray at a later time. There is an additional benefit of using interduct. Interduct helps identify fiber in a densely packed cable tray because of its design and color. The fiber optic cable has a level of protection in and of itself, but heavy cables being pulled over the fiber can cause cable burns or small fractures in the cable and more.

One way to assure that these negatives are minimized is by using qualified installers. A typical electrical contractor who has never installed a fiber optics job is not a good choice. There are usually qualified installers in the telecommunication industry. Besides using a qualified installer, you should utilize a piece of test equipment called an Optical Time Domain Refectometer, OTDR. This equipment will transmit and receive a reflected light pulse down a fiber optic cable and plot the signal strength of the light. The plot will be available on the OTDR display and will show any variations or discontinuities at the exact spot (in feet or meters) in the length of cable to enable appropriate repairs to be made. The discontinuities can be caused by damage to the cable or splice points. The total loss in the cable is then known and should be recorded for documentation purposes. The cable can be checked at a later date and compared with the earlier sample to assure that there is no change in the fiber or the connections. As standard practice, all newly installed fiber optic cables should be checked with an OTDR prior to acceptance.

We have spent a large amount of time addressing fiber in video applications, but fiber can be used with the security alarm system, the access control system, and so on. The concepts of fiber apply to many security applications. There are different interface boxes that can connect to fiber to virtually any format available to copper. The correct selection of fiber or copper and the strengths and weaknesses apply to many functional pieces of equipment that report to the SCC. Fiber optic cable or copper wire can also be part of the company Intranet or lead to the Internet. The signals being sent over fiber and cable discussed earlier in this chapter assumed analog video; the basic discussion also applies to an IP communication scheme, because many of the physical properties of copper and fiber still apply.

There are other video transmission methods that we do not have time to discuss such as microwave, radio frequency (rf) or slow scan. Chapter 8 addresses the wireless considerations for video transmitting. Slow scan is either 64 or 128 bit transition available over the telephone line. Often the salesman selling this equipment will call up a camera that shows excellent video of a fairly stable view. When there is a great deal of activity the number of pixels that are changing will stress this transmitting technique. The important thing to remember is that there is no perfect transmission medium. The correct choice will be driven by each individual application, but care must be taken to assure that the display and recording equipment receive the best signal possible.

At the SCC, the video should be properly displayed, processed and recorded. The video that is presented to the SCC operator should be only the video information necessary to properly perform the job and not a wall of monitors. This is discussed in Chapter 11. A large number of monitors displaying cameras are an ineffective way to design an SCC. The operators become oblivious to the displays and miss important events. The best approach is to provide several monitors that will display video based upon some type of activation. This might be an area where no one should be and when a motion detector is activated the video switcher and the camera covering that area display on the monitor. After a predetermined amount of time, the alarm monitor would no longer display video. This is one of the benefits of intelligent video systems. The video is processed by software that evaluates activity within the scene, displays and may provide an alarm when predetermined activities are present. The software can determine where a vehicle or people are in an area and/or where vehicles or people are not permitted. The software can detect activities that are suspicious such as someone loitering in an area, or hiding behind a wall or carrying something that could be of concern or leaving an object and walking away. Intelligent video allows the normal video activities to proceed without being displayed, but when predefined suspicious activities are noticed, the operator is notified. This approach removes the need for monitors constantly displaying information that no one is watching. Tests have been performed to see how long someone can watch a monitor and be effective. The time is about 20 minutes. If the SCC operators want to view what is being recorded, a few additional monitors can be incorporated. The other approach is to record video in the historic-review mode. This approach is used to resolve problems after the fact. For example, a car is stolen from the parking lot and the recorder receiving the camera or cameras covering the area can be reviewed. It is possible to incorporate all the video display techniques above in the same SCC. Depending upon the view of the cameras, different display approaches can be utilized.

This brings us to the type of video recorders used in the SCC. The old Video Tape Recorder (VTR) is dying a slow death. The recorders require tapes to store the video, cleaning and adjustments of heads and capstans and periodic maintenance including the replacement of expensive playback and record heads. Tapes must be stored and reused, because some level of history should be maintained on any video system. This requires someone to change the tapes and verify that the recorders are operating properly. A history period of between two weeks and a month are typically required. The video recorder ideally should be activated based upon a trigger such as a badge read or motion detector to minimize the number of tapes needed to document a given period of time; however, this is not always done. A time lapse VCR that is on a mode longer than 72 hours per tape will not provide limited quality video and the taped information is of little value. One reason is the field of view of the camera. The smaller the field of view the more likely it is that the recorder will not capture activity. Since typical videotape will store two hours of real time video, a time-lapse recorder set for 72 hours will record 1/36 of the time. If more than one camera is being recorded, the time between recording information is even slower for a given camera. This allows several seconds of information to be missed between recorded fields. If the activity is in and out of the field of view within those several seconds then there is no recording of the activity. Even if the recorder does record one field of information, it is very unlikely that the quality of the recorded field has enough detail to be of much benefit. It is important to assure that tapes are changed regularly on a scheduled basis. Many companies record for one day (24 hr mode on their time lapse recorders) and then replace the tapes. In this way, the tapes are changed every day and it is easy to find the correct tape that recorded a given camera on a given day.

The problem with this approach is that there must be 31 tapes for each VCR (a camera or a group of cameras) to provide one month of history. Often the recorders will utilize a video splitter, which places several cameras on the same recorder to reduce the number of recorders. These are handy and efficient; however, with efficiency comes drawbacks, as with anything else. For example, a quad splitter allows the VCR to record four cameras at once. With four cameras on the same monitor the same 525 lines are being utilized, which means that the resolution is reduced by half vertically, because only half the monitor screen is being used. This can be a problem if the video is needed in court due to the loss of detail.

With a Digital Video Recorder (DVR), many of these problems disappear. Additionally, tapes no longer need to be changed, heads no longer need to be cleaned, and scheduled maintenance no longer needs to be performed. Even viewing the reordered information is no longer necessary; the DVR normally has an output to a monitor. This output will let you know that the DVR is on and operational. If there is video on the monitor being fed by the DVR, the DVR is operational. As with any technology there is not a perfect solution. DVRs require more thought and setup than the traditional VTR. For example, the number of cameras connected to the DVR and the activity viewed by each camera will affect the amount of record time consumed over a given period of time. The best way to address this issue is to utilize the motion detection capability built into the DVR. Unlike the VTR, a DVR records video constantly and when motion is detected the DVR not only records the motion, but can go back a predefined period of time and record what happened prior to the alarm. For example, the DVR might be set up to record pre-alarm video for 10 seconds and post-alarm video for 30 seconds. In this way, it is possible to connect a camera to every input on the multiple inputs DVR and still keep a month's worth of data while maintaining a high quality of recorded video. When the data needs to be reviewed, if the approximate time to be viewed is known, the time can be requested and the DVR starts at the desired time without requesting a large amount of unnecessary data to be viewed as required by a VTR. The use of DVR and other digitizing techniques will continue. The present move is toward a Network Video Recorder (NVR). In truth, there is no actual video recorded; it is digital data stored on a type of computer storage device/devices.

There are several other items that could be part of the video function within a typical SCC. One of these is a switcher. Switchers have been available for years to allow different cameras to be recorded on a "tour" and switched to a monitor. Large matrix switchers are available that will switch many cameras to many different monitors. The matrix switchers are purchased based upon the number of inputs (cameras) and the number of outputs (monitors). The matrix switcher also has an RS232 input port that connects the switcher with other computer driven security functions, such as a security alarm server. This allows alarms to automatically call up cameras to be displayed on a selected monitor. Matrix video switchers allow the SCC operator to view cameras manually via a keyboard or automatically when alarms occur or a badge reader is utilized. This is part of the integration process that allows operations to perform what must be performed automatically. This is discussed in great detail in Chapter 15. Many video switchers can also switch audio via an "audio follower" technique, which would allow a person pushing an assistance button in the field to automatically be connected with the SCC operator on an intercom and viewed via a camera by the operator.

The video function is one area that must be carefully thought through before installing cameras. There are two concerns that are seldom thought through when installing a video system. The first concern is liabilities. If cameras are placed in parking lots to protect employees, contractors and visitors, then the camera should always be working properly. You are opening yourself and your company up to liability issues if you have established a feeling and expectation of safety because there are cameras in the parking lot, when these cameras are not operational or being viewed and an incident occurs. Additionally, the use of "fake" cameras (cameras that look operational but are not) should be evaluated in light of possible liabilities. The other side of liability concerns would apply to placement of cameras within a facility. There are public and private areas within your company. Employees, contractors and visitors have an expectation of privacy in those areas considered private. Care must be taken to assure that trust is not violated or liabilities incurred by poor camera placement, such as in dressing or restrooms.

The final area of concern is maintenance. This was mentioned in respect to liabilities, but it is more than that. The video function, more than any other functional area in electronic security, appears to have the potential to suffer from lack of maintenance. Part of the problem is that everyone likes cameras. They add spark to a security installation. Management thinks cameras are a good idea and they can make the SCC look impressive. The problem is that funding is established to purchase and install the cameras, but no one calculates the ongoing support and the increase in the maintenance budget that is necessary to keep the video system operating correctly with quality video in the SCC. This includes the cameras, monitors, switchers, VTR, DVR, NVR, and so on. Then the liability issues start when the SCC cannot assess what they need to assess. Because of poor quality video, the cameras may work OK during the day, but may not work at night. The list goes on and on. The moral of the story is to plan for the purchase, installation and maintenance aspects of video systems when the project is approved.

No chapter on video would be complete without a discussion on video compression. Various compression techniques are utilized to store and transport video in order to reduce the size of the data to minimize bandwidth requirements and/or the size of file storage needed. The various techniques all have strengths and weaknesses. The four primary compression techniques used today are JPEG, Wavelet, M-JPEG and MPEG-4. (There are others such as H.320, H.261, H.263, H.264, MPEG-1, MPEG-2 and Fractals.) All the compression techniques have advantages and disadvantages. For example, JPEG is an industry standard that works well when there is a great deal of activity. While MPEG compresses individual frames and records only the changes between frames. One item to consider is that MPEG is a standardized tool-set. Different manufacturers have implemented the compression technique differently, which can impact compatibility between the different components and software that make up the video system.

8

Wireless

Wireless equipment is literally located everywhere in the entire world. Manufacturers are spending a tremendous amount of money to advertise their wireless products to expand an already substantial market. Probably the most widely advertised wireless products in the United States are cell phones, satellite television, and wireless laptop personal computers. Cell phones are a prime example of the expanding capabilities a product can provide when a product is desirable and wireless. For example, the new cell phones can send and receive text, send pictures, surf the Internet, and allow for special call groups. As more and more products strive to become more "user friendly," they often expand into wireless for customer convenience. We are a society that wants convenience and services no matter where we are when we want to use them.

Wireless products have become so commonplace that customers are considering replacing products that have conventionally not been considered for wireless applications—for example, the residential telephone. Many consumers have eliminated the old standard hardwired residential telephone with wireless home units and some have gone totally to a cell phone. In fact, the government has required that a person who wants to replace an existing phone with a cell phone can retain his or her old residential phone number. (The hardwired phone number can be transferred to a cell phone making the switch even more desirable.) Even the lowly computer mouse and keyboard are wireless.

At the office and at home, wireless computer LAN/WAN links have become commonplace. Laptop personal computers and other products are being manufactured with a wireless communication protocol capability referred to as BlueTooth. This technology allows a computer, cell phone or other device to communicate with each other when they are equipped with the BlueTooth technology. The communication does not require initiation by a person, but is an automatic communication between different pieces of equipment. The protocols are standardized and self-initiating. Many people do not even know their laptop computer, cell phone and other electronic equipment is "BlueTooth ready." In fact, BlueTooth is the technology that allows cell phones to communicate with their wireless ear piece/microphones. In this chapter, we will address the fundamentals of wireless technology, applications and environmental issues that can affect the performance of wireless products.

In the world of Security, wireless communication provides several benefits, as well as potential security issues. The benefits of wireless include reduced wiring costs, quicker installation, access to remote, isolated locations, mobile reception/transmission, backup and convenience. These benefits have been enjoyed in some applications by Security for years. Security departments in the past have used radios and cell phones for verbal communication. Closed circuit television, access control and alarms have been transmitted via wireless from a remote location to the Security Control Center (SCC) for years. Transmitting from the SCC to a mobile receiver enhances response time and the officer's effectiveness. The information that could be made available to the officer includes video, alarm data, global positioning, and so on. This capability would be very difficult, if not impossible, without wireless. Wireless communication has also been used to provide a backup for security equipment to transmit alarm information if a phone line or hardwired communication line failed.

Even with these benefits, there have been and currently are increasing security compromises possible with wireless communication. Convenience always has a negative side for security. It is important for you to become familiar with wireless technology and its products to safeguard your company. Most security professionals are comfortable with running wire or fiber around their facilities to process security alarms, video, intercoms, and so on. They are accustomed to the use of physical copper cable, but the world of wireless seems a little uncertain and tenuous. Understanding the technology, products that are available, and security applications will allow you to properly utilize the technology as well as protect the companies' intellectual property, assets, and employees.

To better understand the technology, one must first understand that wireless communications use different frequencies to transmit information. The frequencies used will depend on limitations set by the Federal Communication Commission (FCC). The FCC governs and assigns frequencies for different applications and power levels in the United States. The FCC started assigning frequencies more than 60 years ago. The explosive growth of electronics over the last 60+ years means that the frequency bands and applications assigned to those bands are not obvious. For example, when television first started, the FCC assigned frequencies for channels 2 through 6. These frequencies are referred to as very high frequencies (VHF). At the time, 5 channels were considered more than enough for the emerging television market. The frequencies immediately above television channel 6 were assigned for commercial radio use. The frequencies in this assignment were for radio stations using Frequency Modulation (FM). Then, as technology expanded, there was a need for more television channels. The solution was to add frequencies above the FM radio band, which are now channels 7 through 13. This band of frequencies is referred to as high VHF. Starting with channel 14 the band is considered UHF or ultra high frequencies. Today there are 125 channels assigned for television use. The FCC can change the frequency allocations and often does. By 2009, channels 63, 64, 68 and 69 must be vacated by commercial companies to make way for these frequencies to be used by public safety agencies. There is also a deadline in the same year for commercial television to be broadcast only in a digital format. The television frequency segment is not sequential through the television band, which is common for many other product groups.

One of the interesting aspects of wireless products is that the frequencies they use are electromagnetic. Electromagnetic waves allow energy to be transferred from the air into an antenna. The antenna can be a wire tuned for a specific frequency or a more elaborate design. You may remember the old television antennas that were composed of many tuned elements mounted on a long bar. Now most people think of only a dish as their antenna. The dish focuses the signal into a receiver mounted a short distance from the center vortex of the dish. Frequencies are measured in cycles per second or hertz and start at 0 hertz or DC (Direct Current) and end at cosmic rays. The average person can hear low frequencies around 15 hertz. Hearing usually degrades after about 20,000 hertz or 20 kilohertz. Visible light is composed of much higher electromagnetic frequencies. The average person can see the electromagnetic frequencies between high infrared and low ultraviolet. At one end of visible light is what we see as blue and at the other end is what we see as red. At the high end of visible light is blue and it continues upward into ultraviolet, which cannot be seen. Once the frequencies go below the visible red portion of the spectrum into the infrared range the average person cannot see them either. Video cameras are different in sensitivity than the human eye and can see further into the red frequencies. The near infrared frequencies will activate the Charged Coupled Device (CCD) imaging chip in the camera. This property allows the use of infrared illuminators to provide nighttime video in dark areas where a person cannot see. (This is discussed in Chapter 7.)

Wireless technology products use the electromagnetic wave frequencies that humans cannot see or hear. (These frequencies are actually lower than the visible frequencies just discussed.) The part of the frequency spectrum used for wireless applications is referred to as RF (or radio frequency) and microwave. Radio frequencies, as previously mentioned, derived their name from frequency use with commercial radio (AM and FM). Microwave frequencies are those frequencies just above the UHF TV band and are what is used by satellite television today. Commercial television channels 14 through 125 are immediately above VHF and those frequencies are assigned to UHF applications. The frequencies used for security radio systems are typically in one of three bands: 150 mHz, 450 mHz, or 850 mHz and are still in the UHF band. One mHz is one million-hertz or one million cycles per second.

The frequencies in the private radio band used by security require a license due to higher output power. There is always a possibility other licensed users will use the same frequency causing interference to develop, even though FCC licenses provide some frequency spacing protection. There are, however, wireless systems available that do not require a license due to lower output power. These systems transmit in a frequency band and/or maximum power level that does not require a license. The FCC has made these exclusions possible. For example, no license is needed for a garage door opener, remote controls for televisions/stereos, proximity badge readers, children's walkie-talkies, pleasure/sports 2-way radios or model airplane controls. These frequencies and power levels are such that the transmitted distance is also limited. To minimize interference in these applications, different techniques are used. In the case of a garage door opener, a programmable dipswitch is used on the transmitter to code the data at different frequencies within the approved FCC band to be transmitted. It is important to remember that different frequencies have different FCC requirements and applications. The wireless manufacturer that produces a product that security would be using will document any need for a license and control both the frequency and the transmitter's output level.

As the FCC needs more spectrum for different applications, they assign frequencies based upon request from industry, government, law enforcement, and so on. (For more information, please visit the Web site of the National Telecommunications and Information Administration at http://www.ntia.doc.gov/osmhome/allochrt.pdf, or the publisher's Web site at books.elsevier.com/companion/ 0750679999.) The manufacturer that produces wireless products must comply with the FCC regulations in making a product and notifying customers of any licensing requirements. This means the manufacturers must properly design, test, and register their products with the FCC and must stamp or label their products accordingly; therefore, these products normally display an FCC compliance label. The security professional should select a wireless product based on the manufacturer's specifications, the environment in which it must operate, and the security measures needed to mitigate compromising the quality of the RF signal.

Along with a basic understanding of the FCC's role in frequency allocation and control, it is important to look at the properties of frequencies and their transmission. Lower frequencies will suffer signal attenuation from electrically conductive obstacles such as metal obstructions or other conductive surfaces. As frequencies move up the electromagnetic spectrum, the signal degrades when it comes in contact with a fairly nonconductive surface such as leaves on trees or vegetation. As the frequency increases, the need to assure the transmitter and receiver are directly in line with one another becomes more critical. In the microwave frequency range, the transmitter and receiver must be closely aligned or the signal is severely degraded or totally lost. Another property of electromagnetic waves is their induction into a conductor. This is the property that allows the wave to be received by an antenna. The electromagnetic wave causes a current to flow in the antenna, which contains the data that is to be extracted. This same property can cause current to flow in other conductors where the current is undesirable. For example, a semiconductor fabrication facility uses many complex and precise machines to manufacture computer chips. These machines are not well shielded from RF energy, so strict controls must exist on the amount and type of wireless equipment used in these facilities to prevent equipment failure or damage. A less dramatic, but similar problem occurs when a security officer's radio is keyed close to the electronic equipment that would reside in the SCC. The challenge for the security professional is to consider the environment that the equipment will operate within to assure proper signal transmission and minimize unwanted signal induction.

When a manufacturer provides specifications for their RF product, they will normally include a maximum distance that a signal can be sent between the transmitter and the receiver. This distance is always given for "clear air" or "free air." That means, under ideal conditions with no obstructions, the transmitter and receiver can be X number of feet or meters apart. One of the potential obstacles inside a building is the construction material used within. For example, metal studs are often used inside sheet rock walls of commercial buildings instead of the wood studs used in residential applications. Metal will affect the transmit/receive pattern in three ways. It may either block the transmission, absorb the transmission or it may disrupt the beam pattern of the transmission causing reflected signals. At a minimum the metal studs can limit the transmission distance the manufacturer states in their product literature. In the worst case, the combination of metal studs and foil-backed Sheetrock can block the receiver altogether. If additional metal is present, degradation to the signal is exacerbated. This situation would exist when transmitting through or within mechanical rooms: air handlers, HVAC ductwork, cable trays or other areas that contain large metal equipment. There are rooms that are specifically designed to shield RF energy. These rooms are called shield rooms and are built to either keep RF energy in or out. A computer room might be an example of a shield room.

If the transmitting equipment is outside the building, there are other potential obstacles. For example, weather can impact the transmitting distance. Air that contains a high percentage of water will attenuate the transmitter signal. The transmitted signal quality may be significantly reduced during heavy rain or fog. For example, microwave satellite television systems may experience "rain fade" during heavy thunderstorms. Lightning storms producing high ozone content in the signal path may also degrade signal quality. Even vegetation such as trees that are in the signal path may cause signal degradation based upon the frequencies transmitted. This is especially true of deciduous trees in the summertime when they leaf out. (The higher the frequency, the increased likelihood that fairly nonconductive surfaces, such as leaves, will degrade the wireless signal.)

The FCC controls frequencies and the power requirements for those frequencies to protect the public and assure compliance to standards. There are other groups that also define standards that apply to wireless. Some of these groups are International Organization for Standards, ISO; International Telegraph and Telephone Consultative Committee, CCITT; Institute of Electrical and Electronic Engineers, IEEE, Electronic Industries Alliance (EIA). One of these groups, IEEE, has developed the 802.11b standard that assures compatibility with wireless LAN/WAN applications. This standard addresses protocols to allow communication between different pieces of electronic equipment that would connect to a wireless LAN/WAN. This standard assures that manufacturers comply, but does not address the potential security issues such as wireless electronic eavesdropping. The standards are in place to assure compatibility between manufacturers not to guarantee the wireless product provides secure communications.

The security professional must be concerned about someone outside the company's private wireless LAN/WAN being able to gain unauthorized access to the network. With standards in place, it is possible to gain access to the network with nothing more than a laptop equipped with 802.11b hardware/software and a basic understanding of networks. Equipment can be easily purchased or free software obtained from the Internet that allows a person to "sniff" for a wireless LAN/WAN network. Once a wireless LAN/WAN is detected it can be fairly easy to gain access to an unprotected network. To protect against the possibility of eavesdropping on a wireless network, a Media Access (MAC) address can be utilized. The MAC address is a unique identifier assigned by the manufacturer of the PC. Each MAC should be registered as a legitimate system user. Another approach is to physically limit the RF signal from leaving the protected area by limiting the power of the RF signals and providing physical space between the RF transmitter and general public access. This approach requires RF signal testing; however, even with testing, environmental issues can change the signal pattern causing a security problem when the signal expands past the protected area. Encryption also provides some level of security.

To aid the security professional in selecting the correct wireless product for a specific application, the manufacturer will provide data sheets defining the details of their products. The specifications from different wireless manufacturers should be compared. There are standard categories and details the manufacturers provide. Wireless manufacturers will normally specify the following about their products:

1. Communication
2. Additional inherent security
3. Electrical requirements
4. Packaging
5. Environmental limits

COMMUNICATION

Communication covers several aspects of the products' ability to communicate. If the transmitter and receiver have relay inputs/outputs for alarm points, they will appear under this category. There is any number of applications for alarm information to be sent to an SCC via a wireless transmitter. For example, a wireless video system may incorporate a motion detector or door switch alarm to be sent to alert the operator in the SCC to view a remote video camera via a monitor in the SCC. If data is being sent, then the baud rate, transmission capability (duplex or simplex), and format will appear in this section. For wireless CCTV equipment, these parameters are not of major concern, as long as the product states that the video is real-time. The needed baud rate requires transmitting real-time "live" video, which is 30 frames of video per second. This is discussed in Chapter 7. A concern for the security professional is that the wireless video equipment does not reduce picture quality. The wireless receiver should provide supervision if a signal is lost. The supervision wireless security product should not be adversely affected by surrounding electronic equipment or 120 volt alternating current power lines, and should not adversely affect electronic equipment in the area. Additionally, the security professional should never use wireless CCTV to cover an area that he or she would not want to be rebroadcast over the Internet. Always assume that wireless transmissions can and will be seen and heard by someone outside of security's control unless robust encryption has been employed.

ADDITIONAL INHERENT SECURITY

Often wireless equipment has security incorporated into the product. This is especially true in data transmissions used for wireless access control and alarms. This type of wireless equipment may include encryption. The encryption might be a proprietary encryption technique of a reasonably large bit size (128-bit proprietary encryption might be utilized). Encryption is also available in wireless products from standardized sources such as the Defense Equipment Security (DES) or National Security Agency (NSA). This topic has been discussed in Chapter 2. Any encryption technique will add some level of additional protection. Sending data in the clear without some level of encryption/protection is not a prudent security practice.

ELECTRICAL REQUIREMENTS

Electrical requirements normally include the input electrical power needed to activate the equipment. This is often low voltage, such as

12 volts ac (alternating current) or 12 volts dc (direct current). The transmitter RF output power is also specified. The RF power rating will be the maximum power output in watts. (Often in milliwatts, 1 mw = .001 watt, for low power applications.) For example, an interior wireless access control system would have a maximum power output in the 100-milliwatt range. The device would cover a distance of about 300 feet in "clear air." The frequency used by the product is covered in this section. For the access control system example above, the frequency would normally be in the gigahertz, billion hertz, range. If frequency hopping, spread spectrum, is incorporated it will be covered in this section also.

Spread spectrum is another technique that is often used to enhance security and it may or may not include encryption. Spread spectrum requires many frequencies to send the data. The data might be sent on a given frequency on one transmission and a different frequency on the next transmission. Or packets of data are sent on one frequency and the next packet will be on another frequency randomly, but in sync with the de-encrypted receiver. The receiver is designed to stay synchronized with the transmitter frequency to assure reliable data transmission. This is an old technique that was developed during World War II. The advantage is that it is difficult to "jam" the transmission due to the constant frequency hopping. In contrast, many wireless transmissions are sent on a single specified frequency. For example, when using a security radio transmitter/repeater, the radio transmits on a designated frequency usually in the 150 megahertz, 450 megahertz or 850 megahertz range.

PACKAGING

This section covers the physical enclosure that houses the wireless equipment. The height, width, and depth are defined for both the transmitter and receiver. The weight is also listed in this section. If the transmitter/receiver is rack mountable, that will also be stated. Any special physical features will be included. It is important to note that packaging techniques become more critical as the frequencies increase. Both the placement of electronic components within the product and the packaging of the product itself are important for proper operation. In fact, component placement within high frequency electronic equipment is sometimes so critical that you can cause the equipment to not function as designed by simply bending one of the components (via its leads) within the circuit board.

ENVIRONMENTAL LIMITS

This section addresses the temperature within which the equipment will operate reliably. This is normally provided in degrees centigrade, C. For example, the temperature range for a transmitter that would operate inside conditioned space might be 0°–70°C. That would translate to 32°–154°F. This unit would not be appropriate for outside applications unless a heating element is added to compensate for below freezing conditions. The level of humidity is also addressed in this section. This will usually range from 0 to 95 percent relative humidity. Unless the equipment is very expensive the relative humidity level will not normally go to 100 percent. (Rain is considered to be 100 percent humidity.) To address exterior applications with the transmitter mentioned above, a National Electrical Manufacturers Association (NEMA) enclosure would be used to house the transmitter/receiver for protection against rain. NEMA 3R is the first enclosure listed to address rain. Typically a NEMA 4 enclosure would be used, which will withstand direct hose water. (For applications where the enclosure might be submerged a NEMA 6 enclosure should be used.) These enclosures are often designed to provide direct protection from the atmosphere as well as environmental enhancements such as cooling fans. This approach is similar to that utilized by CCTV camera housing. Normally cameras are not specified to operate in 100 percent humidity or extreme temperature ranges. The housing protects the CCTV camera and provides an environment for it to operate.

The primary advantages to wireless are

1. Reduced cost
2. Quick installation
3. Access to remote locations
4. Overcoming harsh or difficult wiring environments
5. Mobil reception and transmission
6. Backup

REDUCED COST

A wireless technology eliminates the labor and material needed to provide the same security function with hardwire systems. The wiring process is usually a major part of the cost of a security system (mostly labor costs and some material cost). When field wiring is difficult to install, a wireless system can be very cost effective. Field wiring usually includes conduit, cable trays, and plenum or coax cabling. For example, let's assume that a camera needs to be located in the center of a large existing parking lot to provide better security. If the camera is hardwired, coax, power cable and possibly conduit are needed and the access to the center of the parking area is required. To obtain access for the coax and power cable requires that the parking lot be saw cut, the coax/conduit installed, the cabling covered, and the parking lot resurfaced. Using the hardwire approach, this camera installation will be very expensive. Cost is not the only issue: there is the inconvenience to employees who are unable to use part of the lot while it is being cut and then resurfaced. With wireless the camera can be installed and a transmitter can send the signal back to the SCC assuming electrical power is supplied from the light pole or via solar power. In this case, the cost of a wireless transmitter and receiver is much cheaper than hardwiring a camera. Another example is the installation of a panic switch at a lobby receptionist's desk. Most of the time the lobby is considered a "show place" and security needs are considered after the lobby has been completed. The conduits are typically full leading to the receptionist's desk. There is no way to run wire except to chip up the new marble floor. Wireless provides the only cost effective solution in this example.

QUICK INSTALLATION

The residential security market has been installing wireless devices for years. The door sensors, motion detectors, keypads, and so on can be mounted and activated without the installer needing to worry about wire access to the devices. The installer can mount the device, set a code (similar to a garage door opener), and "sniff" the area for other RF transmitters on the same frequency and be finished with the installation fairly quickly. A residential wireless installer can complete a location in less than half the time required to do the same project with wire. There is some risk that interference from an RF source will develop in the future; however, if the location is properly "sniffed" for a reasonable period of time the odds are that future interference is unlikely.

ACCESS TO REMOTE LOCATIONS

There are many areas where security is needed, but remoteness prohibits being able to connect alarm lines, video, and so on without costs being totally prohibitive. For example, the oil business has remote pumping site stations that are miles away from phone and/or power lines. Usually these sites have generators that provide limited power, but in cases where generator/commercial power does not exist, solar is an option. The pumping site usually has gauges that must be read and checked periodically. Sometimes there is also a small building for storing supplies. Security coverage for this type of area could be handled easily with wireless technology. A wireless camera could be focused on the gauges and a microwave transmitter could send the RF information to a central location. The limiting factor for RF is the distance covered by a transmitter.

HARSH OR DIFFICULT WIRING ENVIRONMENTS

Wireless can be installed when few other options exist. When environmental issues or limitations are too difficult or costly to overcome, wireless can be an excellent solution. For example, a company located in a large metropolitan area purchases a building across the street from their existing building. Security needs to be added to the new building and reported to the SCC in the old building. It is not feasible to tunnel under the street to run cable between the buildings. One option would be to provide a transmitter in the new building side and the receiver on the original building side. Both devices can be located in building space facing each other and transmitted through a window or via the top of the roofs. There are other options that would work in this example, such as IP data transmission.

MOBIL RECEPTION AND TRANSMISSION

Any organization with mobile security officers has been using wireless technology for years. Radios, cell phones, and pagers are all wireless devices that have been part of most security organizations. There are, however, more sophisticated wireless applications available today to aid the mobile security officer. For example, alarms, maps, and video of the area can be transmitted to the mobile officer as he or she responds to alarms. The alarm and a site map showing the best way to reach the area can be sent to the officer. Additional video information from cameras in the area can also be transmitted to the officer allowing the officer to better assess any danger entering the area. This can be a "picture in picture" type display thus optimizing the information in an easy format for the officer's use. Global positioning (GPS), on the other hand, is a product that sends information from the mobile officer to the SCC. This allows the SCC to know the officer's exact location, which is helpful, when an officer is lost or is in trouble, as in an "officer down" situation.

BACKUP

The cell phone has been used as backup for telephone lines to send alarms to an SCC for years in the commercial/residential market, because of the ease of compromising the telephone line. Normally telephone lines enter the building in such a way as to allow physical access for an intruder to cut the phone lines. A cellular dialer connected to the alarm panel would allow alarms to be sent to the SCC using wireless technology when the phone lines are cut. In addition, the cellular dialer could provide emergency communication for the protected area. An example of a cellular backup on the commercial side would be the protection of a company's phone switch. When a company uses its own phone switch to provide phone service, the cell phone on a regular analog line can send alarm information if the phone switch loses power or if the switch fails.

With any technology, there are strong points and weak points. The strong points for wireless are reduced cost, quick installation, access to remote locations, overcoming harsh wiring environments, mobile reception and transmission and backup. There are three weak points of wireless. The first is proper selection of a product to operate in a given environment. This includes all potential product limitations, such as operating temperature range, distance of transmission, frequency interference, and so on. The second is proper protection for the signal from attack. This can be jamming, electronic eavesdropping, or corruption of the signal. The third is available power at the transmitting location to operate the security equipment and the wireless transmitter. (The power source can be solar in remote applications.) In many company applications, power is often available at the transmitter, and the savings is in the elimination of signal cabling run back to a data gathering area or the SCC. It is up to the Security professional to protect the company's intellectual property, assets and employees. Security and convenience are usually on the opposite side of the equation; however, wireless capability is an important tool available to you. Selecting the proper wireless equipment should be based on the manufacturer's specifications, the environment in which the equipment must operate, and a basic understanding of electromagnetic waves. The wireless application goal is not only providing solid reliable data transition, but also protecting the wireless system from outside attack.

9

Intercoms and Controls

The Security Control Center (SCC) could not operate properly without being able to communicate with personnel in the field and be able to remotely control various functions, such as gates, doors and intercoms. Intercoms and controls are basic to the SCC operation and yet are seldom talked about—possibly because the subject is somewhat low tech or may, at first, appear to be obvious; but nothing could be further from the truth. The truth is that few SCCs and the remote locations they communicate with are designed to optimize the operation for both the field user and the SCC operator. In this chapter, we will address typical systems and many of the common pitfalls that often occur with these security functions. It is important to consider that the goal of the SCC is to provide the same level of professionalism, as would be expected, if an officer were stationed at each remote location that the intercom and controls replaced. The advantage of the SCC handling as many issues as appropriate is to save money. A single operator in the SCC can perform the function of many officers at remote points. The savings generated by reducing officer count is recurring year after year. A solid design is critical to provide the SCC operator with effective

149

and functional controls to perform the various remote tasks around the site.

One of the first places to start our discussion is with an intercom. There are many different types on the market. Intercoms basically break down into groups based on the electronic approach used by the intercom manufacturer and the application. A typical intercom is designed to operate a remote intercom station using the speaker as a speaker as well as a microphone. This is referred to as a "talk back" speaker. The speaker in the field allows the SCC operator to talk to the person needing assistance and the person in the field uses the same speaker to communicate back to the SCC. This has been accomplished with a "push to talk" button. The button at the field end is often a momentary button that must stay depressed to allow the speaker to operate as a microphone. (The button electronically allows the speaker to become a microphone.) The SCC has a similar button to accomplish the same operation. Now the button is referred to as a "call" button to notify the SCC operator who actually controls the field speaker/microphone. These basic systems are designed around a defined impedance (static electrical resistance). Sometimes the impedance is 8 ohms (resistance) or 45 ohms depending upon the manufacturer. In this example, we will assume 8 ohms per station. The number of stations depends on the size of control panel or master station purchased to go into the SCC. Normally each remote station would be connected to one speaker in the field. If two speakers were required to be on a single station, two 16-ohm speakers in parallel is the same as one 8-ohm, or two 4-ohm speakers in series are the same as one 8-ohm speaker. (This applies only if both speakers are activated at the same time.) Normally if two speakers are used for a location, the push to talk/call button on each speaker housing can bypass the other speaker allowing each speaker to be an 8-ohm speaker. When using the push to talk button, the actual switch inside the unit places a 600-ohm resistor in line with the 8-ohm speaker. 600 ohms is the standard impedance for a speaker when used as a microphone with a call button. The switching of the speaker is accomplished in the SCC master intercom station. One of the problems with using the speaker as both a speaker and microphone is the quality of the speaker itself. One difference in speakers already mentioned is the number of ohms that the speakers use. A 45-ohm speaker is normally a better quality speaker than an 8-ohm speaker. This is because of the difference in the speaker coil windings and the size of the magnet associated with the cone speaker. Generally speaking, the 45-ohm speaker can be driven harder providing more volume. Less expensive speakers will be capable of less than ½ a watt of power. Higher quality intercom speakers will be capable of several watts— up to about 6 watts. Time and weather cause deterioration of the speaker cone, and this will affect the quality of sound coming out of the speaker. This problem is exacerbated when the speaker is also used as a microphone. The quality of even a new speaker can be poor when used as a speaker. When the speaker is used as a microphone, the sound quality will typically be worse. The better the speaker is to start with the better it will function as a microphone. There are two aspects to this quality: one is the 8 ohms versus 45 ohms; a second is the materials used to make the speaker. This includes the cone materials, the coil windings and the magnet size. Polypropylene is used on the better speaker cones to reduce damage due to deterioration. These vary between manufacturers within a given impedance range. To add to the dilemma, the different speaker material gets worse at different rates as the speaker cone degrades over time.

Speaker quality and power rating are not the only issue to consider. There are several other issues such as the intercom housing construction. Some manufacturers seal the speaker so that it can be submerged in water for several days without it failing. They can add a buffer plate inside the housing to help protect the speaker from intentional damage. In areas where vandalism is very likely, there are several precautions that can be taken, including using stainless steel housing and buffer plates. The speaker cones need to be protected from being jabbed with some type of object. This can be accomplished with the speaker holes in the housing and buffer plate holes being staggered as well as other techniques. For less serious applications, a stainless steel wire mesh can be part of the housing to protect the speaker. The size of the speaker is also important. If the speaker is smaller than 2.5 inches, the overall audio quality will suffer. A 3- or 4-inch speaker is a solid approach. A 5-inch speaker might be necessary in some security applications.

A cone speaker/microphone is for the most part nondirectional. Unlike a directional microphone designed to cancel out unwanted noise, the speaker is nondirectional, so it will tend to pick up all the background noise that is in the field. The operator in the SCC will hear the background noise causing a distraction and possibly covering up the person's voice in the field. Hearing the person in the field at the SCC can be especially difficult if there is a large amount of traffic or the person requesting assistance is sitting in a noisy vehicle such as a running diesel truck or if they are on a motorcycle. Electronic filtering is available to help minimize the background noise.

A quality intercom system might use a separate speaker and microphone in the field as well as the SCC. There could still be a push to talk or call button that would connect the speaker in one position and the microphone in the other. This would improve the overall communication from the field back to the SCC and vice versa. The quality of the speaker and microphone would still be important in overall system clarity. There will always be some degrading over time, particularly in the field units. The field speaker and microphone should be in a quality housing that protects them from the elements. By just taking the step to add a separate microphone with an environmentally protected housing can improve the overall voice quality at both ends of the conversation.

The next type of intercom system is one that processes audio on top of a voltage. These systems are normally 25 volts or 70 volts root-mean squared (RMS). (RMS is the effective value of an alternating voltage.) The audio signal from the person's voice actually rides on the 25- or 70-volt RMS signal. Most commercial voice-enunciated fire systems use this concept. It allows the wire connecting the remote station to the SCC to be a smaller gauge (minimum of 18 gauge per National Fire Protection Agency (NFPA) for fire systems), yet still running a long distance. (There is very little resistive loss in the wiring between the field and the SCC with these systems.) The speakers and microphone also tend to be of good quality, which enhances communication. Nothing is worse than trying to talk to someone and not be able to hear them or vice versa. A cell phone is a good example. How may times have you tried to talk with someone who is fading in and out, or there is so much background noise that it is almost impossible to hear what they are saying? The very worst case is if both of you are on cell phones, which means that there is no way to know who is doing the fading. People have become so accustomed to this problem that they usually yell into the cell phone in an attempt to improve communication.

The quality of the housing itself, as mentioned earlier in this chapter, is important also. A plastic housing will work in certain applications, but these applications may be limited in a company environment. Generally speaking, interior applications are probably the best for plastic housings. Most of the time cast aluminum or steel or stainless steel is much better outside. There are several reasons for a steel, stainless or aluminum housing, including the fact that plastic is often affected by ultraviolet (UV) light, which tends to dull the shine or turn the plastic yellow and make it brittle. There are obvious concerns for vandalism, but even in environments where there is not a concern for vandalism, plastic may not be the best choice. Steel can rust when the paint is damaged. Stainless steel holds up extremely well, but it is expensive. In fact, the buffer plate inside the housing mentioned earlier in the discussion on vandalism may be stainless or it may be steel to cut costs.

Physical damage can also occur from people, vehicles, and so on. Part of a solid intercom design includes the proper mounting of the field intercom station. The housing should be at the proper level for vehicle traffic as has already been discussed. There are locations that are better for personnel use. For example, if an intercom is needed by an exterior door to allow people to contact the SCC when there is some type of problem, the speaker and the push to talk/call button needs to be ergonomically placed. Someone who cannot gain access through a badge reader they normally use might require access via an intercom. In this case, the push to talk/call button needs to be clearly marked and the intercom should be slightly to the side of the entry to allow the person needing help to be out of the walkway for other people utilizing the badge reader. The intercom speaker/microphone might be about 8 feet above ground level pointed slightly down toward the person who would use the intercom. See Figure 9.1. In this way, some of the background noise will typically be avoided and vandalism minimized. Another option is to incorporate a handset and have it mounted about 42 to 48 inches above the ground. This approach provides more of a home telephone atmosphere and better noise control, but also allows easy access for vandalism.

Another example is associated with intercom placement in the field and adding electronic filters to minimize vehicle background noise. The field intercom should be placed so that the intended user has direct easy access to the device. This means that if there is a gate

Figure 9.1 Elevated intercom.

entrance, the intercom must be high enough for a person driving a truck and low enough for someone else driving a sports car. (It is better if the entrances for large commercial trucks are separate from the general employee vehicle access.) Or possibly two separate intercom stations, set at two different heights, placed at the combined entrance. That could include an intercom, badge reader and Closed Circuit Television (CCTV) connected to the SCC. See Figure 9.2. To minimize the need for someone to use the intercom, the entrances should be automated as much as possible. The entry control could incorporate Radio Frequency Identification (RFID) to speed up the gate entry, or at least a badge reader. If RFID is utilized, it is a good idea, if possible, to use the same protocol as the company badge. If this is not possible, then some access control systems will require two separate database entries and there need to be identifiers as to which technology applies to a given credential number.

The potential problem with RFID car tags is that employees will always want more than one. They will want one for their car and one for their spouse's car; they will forget the tag and leave it in the car when it is at the shop; the list goes on and on. This will

Figure 9.2   Gate entry control.

happen even when you have designed an RFID tag that will attach to the windshield or hang from the rear view mirror and can be easily removed. (It can also be stolen, if you make it too easy to remove or go to another (nonemployee) person if the vehicle is sold.) (See Figure 9.3—the tag is the round disk above the inspection sticker.) There can be electronic interference with some vehicles that causes the tag not to operate properly. This brings us back to the problem at hand—the need for an intercom. The goal of a well-designed automated entry/exit system is to minimize the need for an intercom. An intercom should be incorporated at the entrance to handle unusual situations, not the norm. (My suggestion is where possible include CCTV with all intercoms.)

   After considering electronic, physical construction and installation technique differences, one problem that often develops with intercom systems is the lack of consistency. The intercom equipment that is available on the market can be part of other functional security equipment. For example, some video switching systems also include intercom capability. What can happen is that cameras are added and the additional cameras are purchased with a switcher that also has intercom capability. Then, the next project includes the purchase of

Figure 9.3   RFID tag.

equipment with a separate intercom. Very often the two intercom systems are not compatible. Over time, the continuing equipment additions find the SCC operator with multiple intercom boxes and no overall integrated solution. Audio, like the other functional systems in the SCC, must be integrated and incorporate a consistent philosophy that must be followed, even when the philosophy means that more money must be spent to stay consistent.

Emergency intercom equipment is also sold on the security market. These products may actually be an intercom or they might be radios or telephones. Normally they are available either as part of a pole or mounted in a box. They include lights, emergency/panic button, intercom and alarm. A light indicates their presence at night and emergency lights activate when the emergency/panic button is activated which makes it obvious where the emergency is occurring. The poles are often used in parking lots or campus type environments; the box units are normally used in parking garages. Any time emergency communication appliances such as the emergency poles are used, it is critical that they be maintained, and properly marked if they are out of service.

Another area that does not receive the attention that it deserves is controls. For the SCC operator to be effective, he or she must be able to provide assistance to personnel in the field via controls. Many controls are inherent in the functional security components discussed in this book—for example, the electronic access control system. If an employee at a revolving door contacts the SCC operator via an intercom to gain access into the building, that access can be granted through software commands in the access control system. The software command files can activate a relay contact in the field panel, which in turn starts the revolving door turning through an access grant command. The example assumes that there is a procedure to allow the operator to manually "grant access" to an employee when certain criteria have been met. This situation should also include a CCTV camera to verify the identity of the employee requesting access. Validation is required by the SCC operator to assure that the person is who they say they are and that the person is a valid, active employee/contractor. Depending upon the processes of your company this may or may not be a possibility, but it does illustrate a control function that is available without any special hardware in the SCC console.

Another example is the use of software commands to secure an area from the SCC. When government security areas are closed and secured, they normally incorporate a way for the first person coming into the area to deactivate the alarms. At the end of the day, the last person to leave would activate the alarms. This is often accomplished with a keypad that turns the alarm system "on" and "off" within the area itself. At a predefined period of time, after the area should be closed and secured, an automated report can be run that tells the operator if an area has been left on access. If left on access, the SCC operator will contact the custodian of the area to verify whether someone is still at work. If there is no response, the custodian is contacted at home. Most of the time, the custodian does not want to drive back to the building to secure the area. They will request that the SCC operator electronically secure the area for them. This can be accomplished at the SCC via a software command file in the security alarm system.

Separate command hardware and software are often designed into the SCC. Gate controls, elevator recall controls, Emergency Notification Systems, and so on must be part of the SCC operator's domain. The controls are typically a simple switch that connects via hardwire to the item that they control. The switches should ideally be grouped together and packaged into a single control panel. This is part of the discussion in Chapter 10 that deals with the SCC design. The control panel must be ergonomically laid out and easy for the operator to use. The controls for gates and elevator recall, for example, can also be incorporated into a keyboard and the control activated by software command files as mentioned in the earlier examples. This approach, however, requires software programming, available relays in the field panels, and an icon on the SCC operator's monitor or some other scheme for the various command functions to be easily recognized by the SCC operator to allow them to perform their tasks.

When incorporating controls in the SCC, there are issues that must be considered associated with the actual operation in the field. For example, when gate controls are incorporated, is SCC control required for entry and exit? Normally the SCC control is limited to access into an area via the gate control and exiting is automated. A loop of wire is often installed in concrete or asphalt on the inside of the protected area adjacent to the gate allowing vehicle egress. The loop, in turn, is connected to a gate controller. When some amount of metal (a vehicle) is detected over the loop, the detector activates a relay in the gate controller, which in turn activates the gate motor, thus opening the gate. City traffic engineers use this approach to control traffic lights. For this approach to work properly and reliably, the loop detector must be placed far enough back from the gate to allow a vehicle to activate the loop without having to touch the gate itself. There also must be an automatic control to close the gate; sometimes an electronic timer is used. When the time elapses the vehicle should have driven through the gate. This is often the way gate controls operate; however, there are reasons that the vehicle might stop part way through the gate, clear of the loop, but not clear of the gate. In this case, the gate could accidentally close on the vehicle. To avoid this potential problem, a beam detector should be added to or near the gateposts that would detect a stationary vehicle in the way of the gate.

Up to this point our discussion has primarily been focused on rolling vehicle gates; however, arm gates can have the same issues. When gates are used at shipping entrances, the truckers are normally well acquainted with the operation of the gates and the process is fairly smooth. Employee entrances can be different. For example, an arm gate that rises when access is granted must also have a beam detector associated with the arm control. There must also be obvious visual acknowledgment when access is accepted or denied. If not, the gate arms will come down on the next car following the person who successfully presented his or her badge or other access grand mechanism. This can result in damaged paint, vehicle bodies, or worse. They might be in a hurry and think that they received an access grant. This points to some of the physiological differences between trucker and employee entrances as well as the difference in gate control mechanisms (sliding gates versus gate arms).

In applications that require high security, pop up bollards, pointed car tire shedders, or ramps are utilized. Extreme care must be taken when incorporating these types of controls. There is often an officer post or station/kiosk associated with these types of applications. The controls are usually in the officer's station/kiosk. At issue is accidental activation. These devices can provide security that is difficult to duplicate using other means; however, they can cause major damage. The accidental activation of these devices will cause embarrassment, liabilities and personal injury or, worse, death. The control within the security officer's station/kiosk must be easy and quick to activate in an emergency, yet difficult to activate by accident. See Figure 9.4. One variation of this approach that I have seen used on an open campus environment incorporates pop up bollards that are left in the up position to prevent access into the area. When emergency response vehicles need to get close to the buildings the bollards are retracted to allow that access. This is basically a reversed security application design. The retraction of the bollards can be automatically accomplished by incorporating the same electronics in the bollard control system as the city engineers utilize at intersections to allow fire trucks and other emergency vehicles to change intersection red traffic lights to green. A manual backup control could also reside in the SCC or officer's shack to allow these devices to be placed into their normal position.

Another control function that is used for security in multistory buildings is elevator recall. The control of the elevators can be in several possible locations; one is the SCC. The SCC can be an

Figure 9.4   Officer activated controls.

effective location, if the workload is such that the operators have time to monitor the area access to the elevators to be able to activate the controls when needed. The other requirement is associated with the fact that cameras or direct viewing of the area from the SCC is required to assure the desired results. A lobby is another possible location for the elevator recall controls. The lobby receptionist has a view of the area and normally has time to activate the recall. One possible objection with the lobby control is that there may be some levels of vulnerability to the controls themselves by having them reside within a public space. There are a couple of options to consider if the controls are not only in the lobby. The lobby operator could be supplied with a panic button (should be required as a minimum security standard) that will notify the SCC operators of a potential problem in the lobby. The SCC operator could then, based upon the panic alarm, activate the elevator recall controls. The other is to have recall controls in the lobby and the SCC with override control in the SCC.

Intercom and control functions are very important to a company's security program. These functions provide assistance and security support to individuals throughout the facility. By using these functions real dollars can be saved while providing a value added service to employees, customers, contractors and visitors. Proper placement, quality intercom equipment, and integrated controls in the SCC will greatly enhance the likelihood of obtaining the desired results. That is, with quality equipment and a solid design, it is possible to reduce the number of physical security officers stationed at various locations while providing the same level of service with SCC personnel.

10

Security Control Center

Most security professionals think of alarm, access control and CCTV systems first when securing a facility. These electronic security functions are very important, as is the integration of these functions, but the operator in the Security Control Center (SCC) will ultimately determine the success of any electronic security system installation. No matter how well the security functions were designed and implemented, the operators will make the financial investment of any security project appear or not appear to be a good investment. There are human factors to consider when designing security systems to, for instance, reduce nuisance alarms, which have been discussed in Chapter 4. To aid the operators in being successful, it is critical that a serious effort be made to consider the entire SCC operation when designing or adding new functions to an SCC. This chapter will focus on designing an SCC that will provide an efficient, relaxing, quiet and effective environment for the SCC operator/operators. There are human factors, space planning, ergonomics and communication issues that must be considered when designing an SCC. Space planning is often not considered in the initial design of the SCC. Typically, the SCC is shoe-horned into unused space in the facility, often space that no one else wants. The best approach is to allow enough space allocated between two adjacent areas for the SCC. One area is for the operator/operators and the other is for all the necessary electronic equipment needed to support the operators. A wall as shown in Figure 10.1 should separate the two areas. The figure shows the field-wiring coming into the equipment room side of the SCC, going to a wall where electrical connections are to be performed. [These connections can be 66 block type connects (as in Figure 4.2), for alarm and access control functions. The phone company uses these connecting blocks for small gauge wire connections. CCTV would terminate into coax type connectors.] Then the field terminations are routed to the equipment cabinets, where the electronic interfaces reside. From there, the cables are routed into the consoles inside the operator's side of the SCC space. This approach provides several advantages. First, the equipment that does not require operator access or adjustments is out of their side of the SCC. Second, the noise generated by this equipment is not in the operator's area. Third, when technicians must repair or test equipment, the technicians are not making noise or interfering with the operators in the SCC. Fourth, the temperature can be controlled differently in the operator's side versus the electronic equipment side which typically will run five to ten degrees cooler. This allows different

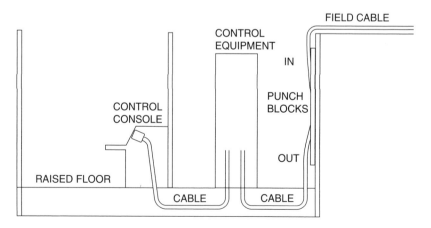

Figure 10.1 Operator and equipment sides.

operators to set the temperature in the room as desired without any concern for the heat generating equipment in the next room. (Electronic equipment normally lasts longer and operates more efficiently at a lower temperature than at a higher temperature.) Last, the physical wiring breaks from the field, into and out of the punch blocks and cabinet on the equipment side of the SCC, which provides easy access points for the technicians to perform tests needed to repair the system and its various functional components.

When multiple operators are in the SCC at the same time, walkway and any needed file space must be considered. No matter how diligently you try to automate and develop a paperless control center, some file space and writing surfaces are necessary. Ample space must be provided for the operator to move as needed to gain access to all the electronic systems, file space, and so on. If possible, the walls that provide a boundary around the operator's area should be irregular in shape. Walls that have some irregularity add interest and provide a desired psychological impact to the room. Windows and wall covering should also be considered. Windows provide a visual access to the outside world and eliminate the feeling of being closed in. For UL SCCs, windows may present an issue depending on which SCC listing is required and which floor of the building the SCC resides on. For example, some UL listings require the console monitors to be visually blocked from someone looking into the SCC and the perimeter of the SCC must match the structural integrity of the building, if the SCC is on the first floor and on an outside wall. Wall covering can provide both visual interest and sound absorption. Often murals, fabric, and/or pictures are used on the walls to reduce the feeling of confinement.

The SCC should be designed in similar fashion to a typical data center, because a larger electronic security system typically will become a small data center. (The security data center processes access control badge reads and alarms.) This design should include such items as a raised carpeted floor in the operator's area. A raised floor allows the cabling in both the operator's and equipment sides of the SCC to be out of sight and easily changed. The equipment side of the SCC might have either a carpeted or a tile-raised floor. There should be an Uninterruptible Power Supply (UPS) in the equipment side of the SCC. An emergency generator should connect to the UPS to provide additional primary electrical alternating current (ac) power backup capacity. The generator is normally located outside the building in close proximity to the SCC. The UPS will provide immediate power requirements for the electronics when power is lost and the generator will provide for a long-term power outage via an automatic power transfer switch. The UPS should contain an electronic filter for the AC used to power the SCC equipment. This is typically accomplished by charging the backup batteries in the UPS and inverting (making the battery direct current (dc) into ac) the battery dc current into ac, required by the SCC equipment. This approach isolates the ac house power used to charge the batteries from the ac power needed by the SCC equipment thus providing a filter or isolation from power spikes, etc. By isolating the power spikes, electronic noise and brownouts that cause problems for processing types of electronic equipment, many problems will be avoided. In addition, the electronic equipment will operate more effectively, have fewer breakdowns, and total failures due to electrical power problems will be unlikely. This type of UPS is referred to as an "online" UPS. The UPS should be sized to last about fifteen minutes when there is a generator backup. There are special requirements such as testing and battery calculations that should be checked if the SCC is UL certified.

It is a good idea to make all electronic connections in the operator's side of the SCC as connectorized as possible. This will allow a technician to remove and install equipment in a timely fashion, preventing unnecessary downtimes during these interruptions in the SCC. Many pieces of electronic equipment already incorporate connectors which allow for ease of removal. For those pieces of equipment that do not have connectors, a pigtail with a connector or connectors can be fabricated to allow easy removal and replacement of equipment. The primary focus for the SCC design should be the operators and making an environment that facilitates the tasks they need to perform.

Lighting is another important human factor that should be considered when designing an SCC. The equipment side of the SCC should have adequate lighting to allow a technician to perform all needed tasks. On the operator's side of the SCC, different lighting techniques can totally change the appearance and mood of the SCC. Normally a combination of fluorescent and incandescent lighting is desirable. Lighting fixture placement and shielding should be incorporated to prevent glare on the computer and video monitors. Indirect lighting can be a very effective approach. An incandescent light provides a "warmer" feeling and includes a spectrum of lighting that more closely represents sunlight, so these lights should also be part of the SCC design. They can be used to highlight paintings or wall murals. Providing controls for the lighting provides two important functions: (1) the operators can turn on or off the fluorescent lighting and dim or brighten the incandescent lighting and (2) there is a physiological need for the person (operator) to be able to control the environment.

The operator should be able to adjust the temperature and it should be uniformly distributed across the operator's side of the SCC: no cold or hot spots by windows, no drafts from natural air convection in the room or from the Heating, Ventilation, and Air Conditioning (HVAC). (A well-designed SCC will not require electric heaters under the console for some operators.) Other environmental areas that should be considered in the SCC design include (1) humidity, (2) airflow and (3) noise. The humidity should be maintained at a range that prevents static electricity issues that cause problems for the operators as well as the electronic equipment. Humidity must also be controlled to prevent a muggy feeling for the operators. The velocity of the airflow needed to heat and cool the operator's side of the SCC should be minimized so that the air is not noticeably different when the HVAC is on or off. Noise from equipment in the operator's side of the SCC should be as low as possible. By incorporating a separate side of the SCC for most of the equipment, the noise level should already be greatly reduced.

Noise level is an important, yet somewhat abstract, topic; however, it is very important when providing the desired level of comfort for the operator. For example, if you have been around small children all day, you are aware of the impact noise has upon your ability to concentrate and feel relaxed. To better understand noise and the level of noise, it is important to understand the way sound is measured. As already discussed in Chapter 5, sound is measured in decibels (db). The important thing to remember is that for every 3 db increase in sound level there is an increase of twice as much noise. A quiet room might be in the 40 to 45 db level. A phone ringing, depending upon the type, can be in the 75 db range. Many SCCs without much activity are in the 80 to 90 db range during normal operations. This high level of noise will create high levels of fatigue and the operators may not even know why they are stressed out. An SCC design should include acoustic tiles or sound deadening approaches for the ceiling, carpet on the floors and even fabric or panels on the walls. Every source of noise must be evaluated and appropriate steps taken to minimize that noise. One example of a noise source that can easily be removed is an alarm printer. Even in well-designed and automated SCCs the operators often want an alarm printer because it provides a sense of comfort by allowing the operator to visually be able to review an alarm they have acknowledged. (The operators can double check the printed alarm that is no longer available on the alarm monitor.) To reduce the printer noise and still provide a printer line type display, software is available that displays the alarms just as they would appear on the printer, but displays the information on an alarm monitor. With this approach, the operators can still double check and acknowledge an alarm without a noisy printer residing in the SCC.

The console design is one of the most critical aspects in determining the operator's efficiency. There are many electronic security functions that must be incorporated into the operator's console. Among the functions in a typical SCC are: (1) security alarms, (2) fire alarms, (3) access control, (4) radios, pagers, desk phones and/or cell phones, (5) CCTV, (6) fire pump controls, (7) intercoms, (8) public address and/or emergency systems, (9) building environmental sensors, (10) energy management, (11) computers connected to the company's LAN/WAN and (12) commercial TV for weather and news broadcasts. The best approach is to install the security functions that are used most directly in front of the operator. The area closest to the operator is often referred to as the primary area. The next area, which is a little farther away, is the secondary area and the farthest reach, but still in front and to the side of the operator, is referred to as the reference area. These area names provide some insight as to which electronic functions should reside in each area. For example, operation of the security alarm system needs to be within easy reach and visual view without requiring the operator's body to turn or use excessive head movement. Electronic security functions that are used often, but not as often as the functions directly in front of the operator, should be to the side, but still in the primary area. The functions that are used less would radiate farther away from the operator first in front of the operator and then from side to side. The goal is to place functions as close to the operator as possible that are constantly being used. An example of typical functions that would be close but on the side of an operator might be the intercom, telephone and radio functions.

The actual background used on the various server/computer monitors should also be considered to minimize eyestrain. This issue would impact the ease of reading text and the size of the text. Colors might be used to enhance an operator's awareness of an important situation. For example, a fire alarm might be presented in red on the monitor, or a red flashing symbol could be incorporated. Seventeen-inch flat screen monitors work well by providing displays that are easily read by the operator. The ability to change the background for each operator would allow them to have more control over their environment and create an individual display that allows them to operate more efficiently.

There are four ways to integrate electronic security functions and make the operator's console more efficient and easier to operate. First, integrate functions in the field panel to allow the operator to operate a single server that processes multiple functions, such as alarms and access control. Second, interconnect these different functions in the field or in the equipment side of the SCC to allow the operator to use one piece of equipment, such as security alarms and building automation systems. Third, physically combine equipment into the console and share an input and an output. This might include audio equipment, such as telephone, intercom, and radios sharing microphone and speaker. Fourth, physically clump similar functions together such as gate controls and other switches that control equipment into one location in the console, but leave each functional piece of equipment intact. This concept is covered in greater detail in Chapter 15.

Equipment failure is an area that causes frustration for the operator. Failures in the field require attention to minimize stress and phone calls to the SCC. Failures in the SCC itself can cause a major disruption. The electronic security functions discussed in the design of an SCC are all important and need to be operational at all times. The loss of any one of these items needs to be considered and a backup or a backup plan is needed if a function fails. The backup evaluation of the SCC as a total entity should include not only the security systems/functions, but also the heating, cooling, lighting and electrical. The electrical backup has been discussed and would also assist lighting, heating and cooling backup; however, these utilities require a backup plan for each item. For example, the security electronics in the SCC will not continue to operate when the cooling fails in the middle of the summer in the southern part of the United States. If the control center needs to be UL certified, additional backup and construction details must be considered and installed.

The actual design of the console cabinets is best left to the console manufacturers, although custom console cabinets can be built and are at times necessary so that they fit into a given space. The design concepts for custom consoles could be a book unto itself. For example, there are considerations that must be taken into account regarding viewing angles, height of work surface, depth of counter tops, edge protection of counter tops, writing surfaces, file space, chair height, toe guards, and so on. Then there are requirements for airflow to prevent failures associated with equipment that develops heat, such as monitors. Tables and charts are available from the American Institute of Architects (AIA) that provide this type of information. The data is based on a given percentage of the United States population. The problem is that all the operators will not fall into these demographics. The very best approach is to purchase a commercially available console that has included all the standardized dimensions and as many manual or motorized adjustments as possible. The operator's chair is a key ergonomic consideration and should be an item that is quickly adjustable and comfortable with lumbar support, and so on. This is an area where extra money should be spent to provide a top quality piece of furniture, due to the fact that an operator will spend hours each workday sitting in it.

The actual interface that the operator must use to operate the various functional electronic security pieces of equipment is also important. Most operators today have the basic typing and computer skills needed to properly operate electronic computer systems. Thanks to Microsoft and Apple computers, most operators are used to using icons and logical processes for operating computers in general, which allows them to move into the security system environment fairly easily. Track balls, ergonomic keyboards, wrist support items (to prevent carpal tunnel syndrome) and Graphical User Interface (GUI) interfaces should be incorporated as appropriate for the console. The operator's interface to various functions should be intuitive, easy to operate and nonfatiguing.

Color is another consideration for the SCC—an area that is often overlooked. Most security professionals are aware of the importance of color and the psychological impacts that it has upon us. The awareness may be only subconscious, but examples are everywhere. Can you imagine attending a school for six to eight hours a day looking at red chalk boards with blue writing? An example of the importance of color and our subconscious perception of tranquility or desirability is obvious in items as mundane as house colors. A given house may sit on the market for months with no buyers showing interest. By painting the house inside and out with a well-planned color scheme, the same house appears to be totally different and may sell quickly. The same is true for the SCC. A well-planned color scheme will impact the operators and can enhance their effectiveness. Consider what happens when you look at a painting. Different colors develop different moods and darker colors tend to recede and lighter colors tend to come forward. The actual details of the painting affect you, but the colors are what develop the real impact and emotion of a painting. The color itself will affect the SCC operator's mood as well. Greens and blues are relaxing colors while reds and oranges are lively high-energy colors. An example of a possible color scheme for an SCC is a blue-gray color that might be used for a carpet and a soft blue on the SCC walls with the operator's console being a variation of blues or warm browns. When choosing contrasting colors to highlight a function or an area, the color chosen should be at the opposite sides of the color wheel shown in Figure 10.2. For example, yellow and violet would be contrasting colors. The reason for covering this topic is not to make you an interior designer, but to make you more creative in your choice of color schemes in your SCC.

After addressing the issues listed above, it is important to consider the actual tasks being performed in the SCC. Step back and objectively evaluate the goals for the SCC. It may already be accomplishing many tasks successfully, but operators may be spending precious time on tasks that are not really important to the Security department. For example, the security alarm function is an important

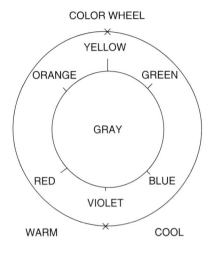

Figure 10.2 The color wheel.

security requirement; however, the SCC operators may be spending time handling an unusual amount of nuisance alarms. The source of the nuisance alarms must be determined and resolved. The resolution may be electronic or administrative, but the nuisance must be resolved to allow the operators to concentrate on more important tasks. Otherwise the entire alarm function becomes ineffective, due to the "cry wolf" syndrome that always develops with nuisance alarms. The goal is to have a workload that is associated with "real" issues, is as consistent as possible, and minimizes stress. There will always be stressful situations, but to develop stress due to the sheer volume of nuisance alarms is counterproductive and will cause other operator errors and can lead to operator burnout. Simple steps such as removing clutter from the work surface can also minimize stress. Several functions have been added over the years in many SCCs. The new equipment was simply stuck into any available space and a new keyboard or mouse added to allow the operator to interface with the new equipment. Often the new equipment is an addition to the same equipment that is already in the SCC, but not capable of handling the new requirements. For example, an alarm system is purchased and over time it becomes obsolete. A new alarm system is purchased, but to save cost the old alarm system is left in place. If there are multiple keyboards, mouse controls, and so on spread across the work surface either the electronics should be combined into a single system or a server switch should be added to utilize a single keyboard for multiple servers/computers. To expect an operator to be effective when the work surface is cluttered with equipment is unrealistic.

To aid in the understanding of unnecessary work being performed in the SCC, the operators should be interviewed and quizzed about the SCC operations. If there is an existing SCC, the operators should also be observed on all shifts to be sure all issues are addressed. They do not always remember all the issues and concerns during the interview process. They should be observed and possibly videotaped to study the way their work is performed and the motions required to accomplish that work. The incorrect placement of equipment in the console, the difficulty in performing a task, the availability of needed documentation, and the amount of time spent on given tasks all become clear.

The perception of the operator is important. To better understand their perspective, questions must be asked.

1. What is your job?
2. What prevents you from being effective in your job?
3. What can be done to help you accomplish your job?
4. What works well for you in the control center?
5. What works poorly for you in the control center?
6. What are the complaints you receive from employees?
7. What is the most frustrating thing you do?
8. What is the most enjoyable?
9. What would you change?
10. How would you change it?
11. What tasks are unnecessary or redundant?

Ongoing maintenance will be a large part of the system's cost after the initial installation and the warranty lapses. To minimize disruptions to the operator and unnecessary cost associated with maintenance, the systems must be properly installed and they must be installed with performing future maintenance in mind, as discussed earlier. A system that requires constant maintenance causes problems for the operators. The operators lose confidence in the system, when they constantly report the same problems to be repaired. The operators are often the ones that receive complaints when the equipment is not working. A malfunction report process must be developed that will aid the operators in bringing maintenance issues to a resolution. This requires an electronic system that documents when the malfunction was reported, when it was repaired and what was repaired. An efficient control center must have employees who are trained in the techniques of communication, and trained to remain calm when confronted with stressful situations. There are many training classes available for this purpose. Often this training is not specified to be for SCC operators. Many other groups within a company might provide training that is similar to that needed in the SCC, such as the technical support and response centers' telephone etiquette. Because most of the SCC operators' communications are not face-to-face, they must be able to exert authority through the tones in their voices. Checklists should be available to assure that proper questions are asked and proper information is relayed. Computerized checklists should be available for all types of situations (different types of health emergencies, bomb threats, disasters, etc.) and the check lists should be easy for the operator to complete. (Icons or simply typing in a block on the computer screen will assure ease and speed for gathering the essential information.)

To provide an effective malfunction report, some understanding of basic electronics is necessary. To operate and understand the operation of the various pieces of equipment, training is critical to the success of the SCC. When new equipment and software are installed, the operators, data entry personnel, and maintenance personnel need to understand the system. Training also promotes "buy in" for the new equipment. As discussed earlier, the goal of any new system is to allow the operators to be effective in their jobs. You cannot be very effective no matter how outstanding the systems are when quality training is not provided. Training means real "classroom" type training and should include videotaping the training to be used as a refresher course at a later date or to help train new operators. The lack of training is an area of major dissatisfaction with a new system, thus dooming the project, because the control center operators may not operate the system properly.

The importance of training and checklists cannot be overemphasized, but there is another side of an effective communication process that can be equally important. This portion of the process includes all of the electronic devices that aid employees in communicating. The frequency range of the equipment used in the SCC is important. The human voice produces frequencies from about 60 Hz to 3,500 Hz. A speaker, amplifier, and microphone (speaker) that cover these frequencies are the most desirable. The distance from the user to the microphone (speaker) must be considered to assure reasonable audio is heard in the SCC. There can also be an issue of privacy in the field where special hardware, such as a handset, should be used. This allows someone to use the intercom at a door, for example, without feeling they are being put on the spot in front of a crowd of people. This is discussed in Chapter 9.

The issue of operator effectiveness using intercoms will be realized, if the areas to be covered incorporate an extensive design effort. For the intercom equipment, it is important that the receiving audio in the control center is constant from each remote intercom speaker. At the user side, the level should be slightly above ambient noise levels to assure the employee/contractor/visitor/customer can properly hear the SCC operator. The adjustments in levels from different remote speakers should not be obvious to the operator (although the capability to change audio levels should be available to the operator). If multiple operators are in the control center, the intercom system must work in a master/master process. This allows the operator to talk to one individual and then switch and talk to another while a second operator helps the first individual.

Technology and various system capabilities are part of the options that must be considered in designing or updating an existing SCC. The mistake that is often made is that these two areas are the starting points rather than beginning with the functional security requirements and integrating those requirements into an ergonomically designed SCC. Technology and system capabilities are ways to solve problems and enhance an electronic security program. These areas are important and can be very complex. Fully evaluating these options requires a knowledgeable electronic security expert, who may exist within the company or may need to be hired as part of the design team. If there is technical expertise needed in the company, Appendix D provides some ideas on skill sets and knowledge base for various levels of personnel. Appendix E provides some hiring techniques.

No matter how well the SCC is planned, there is no way to be able to accurately estimate its expanded responsibility five years in the future. Security systems always expand and in turn strain the control center's existing equipment and operator. Expansion capability must be left in the SCC equipment room and at the field end in the electronic field panel. As the systems' requirements increase, the processing equipment in the SCC will need to expand or be replaced. Requirements will change and electronic security functions will expand, so proper planning is critical. Figure 10.3 is an SCC that has expanded responsibilities and has turned into an ineffective cluttered mess. Designing an SCC that just barely allows enough space to handle today's requirements is a major mistake. Allowing expansion room is very important. It is not necessary to allow more than 20 or 30 percent empty space, because even though new equipment must eventually be added, it normally requires less space than the old equipment. In addition, if you, as the security professional, must request additional funding to expand or move your SCC a few years after installation, management may look for a new security manager.

Figure 10.3   An ineffective SCC.

There are almost limitless variations and options that different manufacturers can presently supply. These must all be considered as options for an integrated SCC. The focal point must not be technology nor the latest fad, but the overall company and Security department priorities. These priorities may include easy movement between sites and within each facility for employees while effectively controlling access. When the functional requirements are prioritized and there is an understanding of why goals are not presently being met efficiently, the design can be developed that takes into consideration the SCC operator/operators. The way the systems function, their capabilities, and their technology becomes a way of reaching the integration goal. With these pieces of information in place, an efficient ergonomic SCC can be designed. The performance of the SCC operators is the key ingredient that separates an excellent SCC from the mediocre. The ease of the systems' operations and the fluidity of the operator's motions is a product of the level of integration that has been accomplished. Care must be taken to assure the proper amount of activity during each shift in the SCC. A comfortable environment during first shift when there is usually a great deal of activity will produce a sleepy, bored operator during third shift. The design of an SCC is not a mathematical problem that can be solved by plugging numbers into an equation. The result needed for a well-designed SCC is not science, but rather an art form. There is no single solution. It is based upon company culture, functional requirements, and objectives for the security department, integrating the various electronic security functions and properly weighing your SCC options.

11

Database Management

Development of a security alarm and an access control system for a large facility requires tremendous effort. This effort starts with a list of functional requirements that are translated into a system of alarm and access points. A solidly designed system must be developed and carefully controlled through conception to acceptance. The proper steps that must be taken to ensure an effective security system may take months to complete. The system may incorporate thousands of alarm points and hundreds of badge readers, which will affect all employees in the facility on a daily basis. To assure minimal disruption, a database containing all the alarm points, badge readers, approved access levels and badges must be accurate, well maintained and protected from corruption. This chapter will address the early decisions that affect the system and their impact on the alarm/access control database and the many aspects of protection needed to secure a reliable database.

It is important to review the concept of using and controlling badges, addressed in Chapters 1 and 2. A badge usually contains an image of the employee, employee name, company name, possibly a logo, an access technology and sometimes other detailed information about the employee or contractor. Their access level is stored in the database. A completed badge is the same as a key to the facility and must be handled and protected like a key. If the badge is lost or stolen, it must be reported in a timely manner. It is the employee's responsibility to control the badge, properly care for it, and wear it at all times when at the facility. The actual badge stock used to manufacture the badge must be safeguarded to assure that it is not stolen or otherwise compromised. Several techniques covered in Chapter 2 will minimize the possibility of counterfeiting the badge.

There are several badge technology options available, but four are widely used in the United States. The most common is the magnetic stripe, because it is fairly reliable, inexpensive, easily programmed, and widely used outside of the security industry; however, being easily programmed can be a potential security concern. Weigand is the second widely used technology. It is immune to most environmental issues and is not field programmable. It is also reliable and very difficult to simulate or copy. The third widely used access control technology is proximity. This technology offers "hands free" access, reliability and readers that can be hidden from view. The fourth technology is actually the second type of "hands free" technology. The fourth type is the contact-less smart card. This is the up-and-coming technology, because it incorporates electronic processing and data storage. All these technologies have their advantages and disadvantages. The technology chosen will, to some extent, affect the badge numbering scheme in the database. There is no perfect technology, so the decision becomes a matter of trade-offs, discussed in more detail in Chapter 2.

Each of these technologies incorporates a protocol which is one of the critical issues to address regarding badges and the database. A protocol is simply a set of binary digits set in a pattern that allows the badge reader interface to understand the data on the badge. Protocols allow communication between electronic devices and people. As an example, English is the human protocol used in this book, and for communication to take place between two or more people, they both must understand the same language and agree to use it. In this case, a badge and the access control system must use and understand the same language or protocol. The badge protocol incorporates a predefined clumping of binary bits that assign the critical data in the badge. For example, there are normally several bits of data to define a company, a physical site within the company, an employee credential number, and parity bits. The actual employee credential number contained on the badge is assigned to specific areas of access within the company for that given employee. A typical 37 binary bit magnetic stripe protocol uses a specific pattern. The company code might use 8 binary bits, the site code uses 6 binary bits, the employee credential number uses 21 binary bites, and parity uses 2 binary bits. This is discussed in more detail in Chapter 2. The definition of the bit patterns allows a badge reader and its interface and/or field panel to determine if a badge will grant access at a given portal. Badges that do not match the protocol are rejected. Even badges that do match the protocol may be rejected if the employee credential number in the badge protocol does not match the employee badge credential number in the security system database.

Managing and protecting the security system database is a major challenge because it deals with the human interface. Several areas of concern are:

1. Data entry
2. Alarm and badge reader definition
3. Passwords
4. Viruses and worms
5. Backups
6. System redundancy
7. Physical protection
8. Private network/wiring
9. Encryption
10. Training

DATA ENTRY

Data must be properly and correctly input into the database. There are issues with the security alarm database and the access control database. Let's look at several access control and alarm database issues. Normal credential number data entry problems are discovered in a relatively short time because the new badge does not grant the employee access into the facility or a specific area. Many more subtle issues, however, will not be as obvious. For example, when a new badge is given to an employee because the badge has been lost or stolen, the old badge number must be removed from the database. If the old badge data is not removed, two things can happen: an unauthorized person could find the badge and use it to gain access, and the database will become clogged with useless badge numbers, which is difficult and time consuming to correct at a later date. Security alarm database inputs require accuracy and ongoing modifications. The initial data input should be based upon a standardized input form developed for the particular manufacturer's product, including detailed information as to the definition of the alarm point. For example, the zone on the field panel circuit board, number of the field panel, panel communication loop, and so on must be required data fields on the form. There must be an alarm descriptor, location and response information. If the descriptor lists response personnel, then this data must be accurate and it must be kept up to date. As personnel and phone numbers change, the data must be updated which can be a challenge, particularly if the alarmed areas include classified government projects. These areas have access lists that must be constantly updated.

The identifier used in the database to separate one John Smith from another John Smith must also be considered. In the past, unique identifiers have been Social Security numbers which are unique and easy to incorporate into the database. The main concern with this practice is that of identity theft. The database might be compromised via a network attack or theft of the server/computer on which the data resides. There are several possible safeguards. One is to encrypt the Social Security number so that it is difficult to decipher, but the level of encryption required to assure the level of protection needed is a moving target. The encryption level that was OK two years ago is no longer acceptable. (The requirement is for the encryption to be up-to-date and robust.) Another approach is to physically prevent the theft of the computer where the database resides keeping the server/computer in an area of formidable protection. One such area is a 24-hours per day, 7-days a week (24/7) Security Control Center (SCC) operation. If the database ties to the network, a robust firewall must also be incorporated. The least painful approach to solving this problem is to remove Social Security numbers all together. Social Security numbers are not the only unique designator for employees. Most companies generate employee numbers for payroll that can be used which are much less sensitive than Social Security numbers. Contractors can still be a problem based upon the fact that they often are not given an employee-type identification number. To address this issue, another approach must be taken for contractors. One such approach might be to use a birthday plus initials or some other variation, such as a modification of their badge credential number.

ALARM AND BADGE READER DEFINITION

The definition of access and access levels is a source of many potential problems. The badge access levels are similar to the old key entry systems. For example, a key might be given to an employee to open his or her office door; the manager of the area might have a key that allows access to his or her office as well as the employee's office; the facility manager might have a key that would allow access to the above areas plus mechanical rooms, the front door and telephone closets. As the access key's use expands to more and more keyways it is referred to as a master key. This concept can grow and grow into grandmaster keys then to great grandmaster keys and even to great great grandmaster keys. Access control systems often utilize this same technique. Badge readers allow access to general areas, restricted areas, and sensitive areas. All employees are able to use readers in the general access areas and possibly some restricted or sensitive areas. In this way, the reader accepts everyone in general access and those that have special access areas, so it is inclusive. In this analogy, a badge that would gain access throughout all readers would be considered the great grandmaster badge.

The other technique used in badge control is to develop an exception list. The exceptions are the badge readers that the employee can use. For areas where only certain groups within the company have access, there are readers that exclude most badge holders. The sensitive areas that would exclude most company employees would be areas such as research labs, cashier areas, and so on. In other words, the badge for a given employee would only work at a list of exception doors and all other doors are excluded. This technique is the opposite approach of the grandmaster key concept. Whether to use the inclusive or exception approach must be decided during system installation and must be maintained by the system administrator. (The system administrator in most security and access control systems is not what Information Technology (IT) personnel think of as a system administrator. Security uses the term to address the person who oversees and is responsible for the general operation of the systems. IT uses the term to address the person who has total control of the network/database/computer configuration and controls passwords, access to the system and any maintenance performed on the system.) Either the inclusion or exception approach requires documentation, planning and proper data entry to assure the desired operation and data integrity.

To reduce the number of possible variations with either the inclusive or exclusive approach, groups of employees that compose a variation are grouped together. For example, all employees that can only gain access to the main entry points and to the fitness center, for example, might be grouped together. A group that had access to the main entry points, the fitness center and a research lab might be combined together as another group. In this way, groups or classes of access can be changed instead of each individual in the group requiring a change. With this approach, there will still be some unique groups that may contain only one individual. Even with groups being used to define access to badge readers, the process can still become very cumbersome in a large access control system. It is not unusual for these large systems to have hundreds of groups. As readers are added, the approach is to either exclude some groups from using the readers or include groups that use the readers. Keeping the database accurate requires astute administrative controls as well as careful review of the groupings or classes.

PASSWORDS

The database should have passwords to protect it and the database should be segregated into levels of authorization. Passwords allow only certain security personnel to have access to certain areas in the computer/server software. For example, data entry must have password protection and it is best that the smallest number of individuals possible have access especially to higher levels of programming authority. It is best if only one person does the data entry, because the data will be consistent; however, due to system size, vacation and sick time more than one individual must be utilized. Obviously some level of backup will be required, but having a small group enter the data minimizes errors and assures consistency. Standards must be developed that assure that data is entered in a consistent manner. Data entry is a critical part of protecting the database, and care should be incorporated in selecting the proper person or persons for this job. (The sensitivity of the data in the database should be taken into account when deciding whether to use an employee or contractor for data entry.) Some member or members of Security management should audit the database, audit security personnel who have access, and review data entries on a regular basis. For Security management to be effective in checking the database, it is important that they are well trained on the system. There must also be a policy and safeguards for inputting, updating, controlling and distributing passwords.

One of the major problems with limiting access and assuring security personnel that need and/or have access is obvious when reviewing the policy for temporary badges. Many locations among the company's facilities must be able to enter temporary badges into the access control system. The SCC, lobbies, and badge rooms are often capable of inputting temporary badges for employees who lose or forget their badges. This normally requires the person doing the data entry to "call up" the employee's record in the security database, input the temporary badge, and deactivate the regular badge. This temporary badge must be removed when the employee returns with the old badge. The old badge must be reactivated or, if it is not available, a new permanent replacement badge must be manufactured and loaded into the database. Keeping the database clean and uncluttered with temporary, lost, and unused badges is a major task. The badges of employees who have left the company should be removed as soon as possible after they leave. The situation is exacerbated when it includes contractors. Contractors normally come and go at a faster rate than employees. It is a good idea to limit the "life cycle" of a contractor's badge; a year is normally a reasonable time frame. After a year, the contractor might use the same badge, but the contractor must be reactivated in the database or the badge will no longer allow access. If left unchecked, the number of entries in the database will far exceed the number of employees and contractors in the company.

The password used by each data entry person must be unique and it should be difficult for someone else to guess. The length of the password is normally definable in the security system software and should ideally be at least six to eight alphanumeric characters that would include capital letters and characters (#, *, etc.). The password should be changed on a regular interval—at least once a year. (If a private security network/wiring is utilized, the interval between changing passwords does not need to be as frequent as passwords that would be used on a company's LAN/WAN, because a small number of employees are involved.) Keeping passwords up-to-date, reviewing access levels, verifying individual passwords that are being used, and reviewing the database's integrity are important tasks that should be performed regularly. Security management must take an active role in reviewing the status of the database and associated procedures. It is not what is expected, but what is inspected that counts.

VIRUSES AND WORMS

The introduction of viruses and worms into databases has become commonplace. Ten years ago, few security systems had experienced viruses, but this is no longer true. As mentioned earlier, viruses can be introduced via the company LAN/WAN as well as other physical connections to the nonsecurity world. Viruses have become so commonplace that new terminology is emerging such as "malware" (or malicious software). Instant Messaging (IM) is very popular because it provides flexibility, speed and ease of communication, but it is also very vulnerable to attacks because of its flexibility. Attacks are not limited to personal computers (PC). They now include cell phones and other processor-based electronics and will only increase and become more sophisticated. To protect the security system database from unwanted electronic intruders requires that no software be introduced into the security network without the Security management's approval. A problem that may develop is the installation of software that a data entry person or SCC operator brings into the company and loads onto the security system. The introduction of this unapproved software may not be malicious. It can be as mundane as software to play games during slow periods in the day; however, the negative impact is the same if it contains a virus or worm. To prevent this type of unwanted software from being loaded onto the security system, the server/computer can be physically moved or the disk, PS2 and CD drives can be blocked off. Some software options provide control to the various input devices on the server/computer through the operating system software such as the different versions of Windows. There are even easier to use and more effective third-party software programs to provide this type of software protection. If the security system is connected to the company LAN/WAN, the potential of an electronic infection expands, and if connected to the Internet, viruses and worms can come from literally anywhere. Antivirus software is a must in these situations because the software searches for "signatures" that match known viruses. The problem with this solution is that antivirus software is reactive; that is, the software patches are sent out to customers after a virus attack has taken place. Another issue is that the antivirus software sometimes makes the security system software run more slowly.

BACKUP

Backing up the database is also a critical process to properly protect the security system. Backups should be performed daily on large systems because many changes are made to the database on a daily basis. The backup can reside on a disk drive or can be loaded to tape. On a weekly basis, the data should be spooled off the tape drive and stored in a physical combination safe close to or within the SCC. A month's worth of tapes should be available at any one time in the safe. The next week the newest tape should replace the oldest tape. The oldest tape should be stored offsite in a secure area. One week storage tape from each month should be stored so that backups can be made as needed to resolve corrupted data files. Backups are kept for several reasons: a computer crash, documentation, employee/contractor investigation, and file corruption. For these reasons, there must be several levels of backup available. The requirements will vary depending upon a specific application. Often, an alarm and access control history is needed for an extended period of time—possibly a year. If the company is a government contractor or the SCC is UL certified, alarm data must be kept for one year.

SYSTEM REDUNDANCY

Even with backing up the database, there is still a remaining weak link—the security system itself. Deciding which parts of the security system must be made redundant is a topic that would require a dedicated chapter. For the time being, it is important to cover a few key issues. A disaster management/business continuity plan should be in place to address various levels of system redundancy for outages. The very worst case of loss would be a total loss of the SCC, but there are lesser levels of loss that should be planned for. Cost and the development of realistic problems that could occur will drive the redundancy plan. It may be that, with minimal expense, most situations can be mitigated to an acceptable level. The level of loss that is acceptable will affect the final plan for the money needed to protect the system against such loss. The cost will also be driven by the system architecture as well as level and method of protection.

Protecting the data transmission lines, the field panels, and database is accomplished by:

1. Physical protection
2. Private network/wiring
3. Encryption

PHYSICAL PROTECTION

The purpose of physical protection is to prevent access and detect unauthorized surreptitious access. Protection can be in the form of conduit, sealed cable trays, locked rooms, and alarms that indicate potential tampering or unauthorized access. Alarms for the electronic field panels would include tamper switches on the panels themselves and motion detectors and door alarms in the protected area. The server/computer is normally located within the SCC and is protected by alarms and sometimes a badge reader. The SCC is normally occupied 24 hours a day 7 days a week. If UL certification is involved, then visitor logs and other protection are required.

PRIVATE NETWORKS/WIRING

Today, many field panels are capable of several types of transmissions. For example, a panel that uses RS485 will by definition have dedicated wiring back to the server/computer. In contrast, a field panel that uses a LAN network and has a TCP/IP address may or may not be on a restricted private security network. It is best if the network is restricted to security applications only. The IT department typically prefers a separate network to minimize any impact on bandwidth; however, these systems are often connected to the company LAN, so security is sharing the LAN with other groups inside the company. A firewall can provide some protection from penetration initiated on the Internet, but hacking from outside the company is always a possible problem. There are still potential threats from within the company as far as gaining access to the field panels or the actual data contained in the database. Providing physical protection, as previously discussed, will add a level of protection, but internal hacking is still possible. Internal hacking is becoming more of a problem due to employee dissatisfaction and because of the difficulties of protecting against an insider threat. In addition to internal hackers gaining access or causing "denial of access" problems with the security system, there is an additional problem of viruses on the company network. This has been discussed already in this chapter. If the network or transmission system is restricted to security use only and is a closed system, viruses are more easily controlled.

ENCRYPTION

Encryption is often used in conjunction with both physical protection and private network/wiring. Encryption is critical when field panels reside on a company LAN/WAN or if there are government requirements for Department of Defense Closed Areas that must be met. Encryption is a technique that changes the data before it is transmitted and returns it to its original form just after it is received. In its simplest form, adding a random number to the transmitted data and then subtracting the same random number from the received data accomplishes encryption. There are many algorithms that are used to encrypt data. Four well known algorithms are: 1) Skipjack utilizes 80 bits 2) Data Encryption Standard uses 56 bits 3) Triple DES utilizes 168 bits 4) Advanced Encryption utilizes up to 256 bits. Encryption protects data while in transit, because it is disguised via the addition and subtraction of a random number. This approach may not; however, protect the data in the database, central processor, or the field panel. Special software is available that encrypts data at rest in the database.

Protecting the data transmission via private security networks and encryption, as well as providing physical protection of the field, does not fully protect the database in the central server/ computer processor. For instance, there will be requests for access to the database from groups inside and outside the Security department when there is an enterprise security-wide system. For example, the Human Resource (HR) department or a department manager may request pictures of employees, which reside in the database as JPEG files. If this data is provided electronically via connections to the security database, all the precautions previously discussed must be followed.

Another possible request from HR might be to use the badge as part of a time and attendance system. These system databases could be separate or they could interconnect the Security and HR workstations/computers. If they are together, the HR time and attendance computer system must physically connect to the security computer/server. This connectivity poses two potential problems: one is the physical cabling/network issue that has been discussed. The second problem is that another hacking/virus point has been provided. If electronic connections to the security database are made, then all the precautions mentioned above must be in place as well as a one-way data transfer from Security to HR.

If the databases are not physically connected, HR will want to know the badge protocol so that they can use the badge for time and attendance but remain separated electronically. Although it is generally not thought so, the badge protocol is one of the most sensitive security areas to protect and is at the very heart of what makes the access control database secure. The protocol should be a well-guarded secret. In this scenario, there are other approaches to solve the "time and attendance" problem without giving up the badge protocol to HR or the IT departments. As previously discussed, the badge contains a series of data bits, but the way the bits are grouped (protocol) is the sensitive information, so the HR/IT personnel can be provided the total number of bits including any parity information. In this way, the entire badge bit pattern can be read as a unique credential number without providing the actual protocol. This process allows the badge to work in both systems and still keep the protocol secure. The only problem with this approach is that each badge must be loaded into the HR database individually unless a protocol converter is written and a file transfer is used.

TRAINING

Training is needed for anyone who has any level of password approval to modify the database in any way. As mentioned earlier, there are often different levels of authorization a given password will allow. A real life example is the easiest way to show the impact of poor training and how it can affect the database when the user has only minimal authorization. A large company was in the process of transitioning from one badge technology to another. The first step in the transition was to provide a multitechnology badge for employees and contractors. In this way, when everyone had received a multitechnology badge, the readers could then be replaced with the new technology readers. This required that all employees and contractors have a multitechnology badge so that either the old or new technology reader could be used until the conversion was complete. Since there were too many readers to change, it was necessary for the conversion to be completed on a building-by-building basis. The training problem was with the lobby receptionist who had a password that allowed him or her to supply employees or contractors with temporary badges if they arrived at work without a badge. There were checks and balances in place to assure that the individual requesting the badge was approved to be on site and was indeed that person. The process was for the lobby receptionist to call up the individual's record in the database and replace the badge credential number with the credential number on the temporary badge. The receptionist replaced the credential number with the first database record that was displayed on his or her workstation, not checking to see if the credential number was for the old or new technology. By replacing many of the badge holder's new technology credentials with the old technology used in the temporary badge, the new technology credential number was lost from the database. When the conversion of the actual readers was to start, it was discovered that many of the employees and contractors could not access the building via the new technology reader because of the way temporary badges were processed in the lobbies.

In this chapter, we have considered the alarm and access control system as a complete security system to help explain the necessary precautions needed to manage the database. There are other databases in other security equipment that will apply to the issues addressed in this chapter. Some of those databases include functional security components such as video switchers, audio switchers, and digital video recorders, and LAN/WAN routers. The database used in all these systems is the heart that provides lifeblood to an electronics security system. All the databases must be properly maintained, updated and protected. Protecting a security system's databases is not a simple process. There are many aspects that must be considered. These aspects include the physical protection of field panels, transmission lines, server/computer, interconnections with nonsecurity computers and the personnel who interface with the database. The approach taken to protect the security system should consider the company culture and the complexity of the system. There will be requests to share information between groups within a company. Sharing JPEG files of employees/contractors, connecting the HR database with the access control system and sharing access control databases between sites within the company, to name a few. This makes protecting the database's integrity more important than ever before. The extent to which data is shared and the approach taken to share the data must be carefully considered. Every link to the database is a possible link to a hostile environment.

12

System Configuration Control

It has been a couple of months since the ribbon cutting ceremony for the new Security Control Center (SCC). The company president and upper management were very impressed with your project. You oversaw it from conception to completion. A great deal of study, effort, and teamwork went into the project. One major reason for its great success was everyone's desire to accomplish what was best for the company. The project began when upper management requested additional security as part of building a new research center. The existing system was out-of-date technologically, and lacked the necessary capacity for a new building. Your group became part of a team composed of an architect, a facilities department representative, a legal representative, upper management, and an outside security consultant. The team performed a risk assessment study and developed functional requirements, while evaluating the parking lot, building access, building alarms, and appropriate closed circuit television (CCTV) coverage. Various types of card access technology were also evaluated. The goal was to provide high security while allowing ease of operation for employees. Color and style of equipment, physical hardware configurations, and the placement of each device were weighed to maximize desired results. Cameras were evaluated for aesthetics, placement, viewing angle as well as resolution detail. At the beginning of the evaluation, it became obvious that the existing system would not be able to handle the new building. It was decided that the building project must also include a new SCC. The SCC would be housed in an existing administration building. Cabling would need to be added between the new research center and the administration building. The team faced many challenges when evaluating the operation of the original SCC. In overcoming these concerns, it was necessary to evaluate many new products. An operator from the existing SCC was added to the team to enhance the operational perspective of the new system. A plan was developed that would allow the existing system to operate while the new SCC was under construction. By the time the operators were sitting at the new SCC consoles, systems were running like a fine tuned race car. The planning, teamwork, and effort had paid off. Team members were pleased, operators were excited and interested in the new system after training, and upper management was satisfied. The consultant had done a good job providing options and opinions. Everyone was satisfied that the project went well and now all can return to their various primary job-related activities.

A couple of months have passed and some new security requirements have just come across your desk. Another research area needs to be added and caged storage areas at the dock must be secured to protect new high-dollar equipment that the company plans to use in the new research area. The question of who modifies the security system must be decided. Modifications are needed for alarms and badge readers that will control the new areas. The issues at this point become those of the correct personnel to perform this work, which includes adding badge readers, alarms, and CCTV. The devices must be physically mounted and connected to the various security equipment. There are needed modifications to the database to accept the new alarms and badge readers. The CCTV system will require software definitions to the video switcher and the motion detection software in the Digital Video Recorder (DVR) must be input. This scenario is typical of the problems encountered following a system purchase and installation. The manufacturer and/or contractor installs the system and programs it to function as specified by you. Even when everything to this point was correctly installed and the system functions as planned, there will be modifications and changes that must be incorporated. This situation is typical and the time frame between completing a major project and changes are not far apart. Problems occur when there are adjustments, modifications, or unique applications that were not planned for, even when an effective job was done in the initial stages. This is when it is critical that there was proper training, accurate as-built drawings provided, and a system layout that considered future expansion needs. System management is one of the keys for a successful, ongoing security program. The plan must address present needs and plan for the inevitable future requirements that are totally unknown when the project is initially finished. This is the point where proper management of the functional security subsystems becomes important. There are many subsystems or functions that compose a security system in the SCC. These are discussed in great detail in Chapters 1, 4, 5 and 11. One of these functions is the access control/badge reader system. In this chapter, we will investigate ways to control the security system configuration and real life issues that must be considered. For the purposes of this chapter, the discussion will be limited to some of the typical security system functions that require system configuration control. We will start this discussion with the access control system, which must be continuously managed. Proper system management is more dependent upon the specific security access control philosophy and manufacture's limitations than it is dependent upon the technology used in the system.

The approach used to manage the access control function includes details that should have started with the design, such as defining reader numbers. Reader numbers are defined by the electronic field panel that they connect to. As discussed in Chapter 2, the actual connection on the circuit board, where the reader connects, defines the last part of the numbering scheme. The first part of the number is driven by the electronic field panel itself. The actual panel number is either defined by software or by dipswitches in the field panel that are set to a number. These panels can be numbered based upon a location in a building or a floor in a high rise building. Blanks, or nonassigned numbers, would typically be left in an attempt to add readers and field panels to a given building at a later date. The new readers will then follow a given plan that allows you to know by reader number in which building or part of a building the reader is located. The problem is that no matter what the initial logical plan to define field panels, future numbering conflicts are inevitable. It is unusual for a numbering scheme to last for a long period of time, as originally laid out. The problem occurs with the unexpected growth that accompanies an access control function. For example, initially the access control portals for the building might all be connected to the same electronic field panel. As time goes by, the convenience of the access control system versus the use of keys promotes requests to add badge readers. It is not uncommon to start with a certain number of badge readers for access control and grow to ten times the original number in a few years. The growth often does not stop even at that point. It continues at a lower rate, but a rate that is almost impossible to plan for in the initial design.

Another possibility is that the building might be divided into four quadrants and all readers in a given quadrant connect to that quadrant's field panel. The planned numbering scheme might be field panels with numbers starting with 100 and running through 104 to cover the east quadrant. This plan allows for five electronic field panels in each quadrant, but panel 100 is the only panel installed initially. That means the system can be five times larger than when it was first installed. In this example, all the badge readers on the south end of the building are connected to the same field panel, and so on. After a period of time, a new reader is to be added in an area within the east quadrant, but there is no more space in field panel 100 to connect the new reader. Using a quadrant standard would allow the numbering scheme for the new east quadrant field panel to be 101. There is, however, space on field panel 105 in the south quadrant. The question becomes, do you install a new east quadrant field panel for the reader or use the existing south quadrant field panel and save money? The final decision will be based either upon the numbering scheme standard or saving cost and disregarding the quadrant numbering scheme. What will normally happen is that the reader will be connected to the closest field panel that has available space, in this case the existing south quadrant field panel 105. The badge reader number will no longer reflect the fact that it is in the east quadrant of the building.

It is not effective to constantly change numbering schemes to adjust for the expansion which will inevitably take place. To explain the problems with constantly adjusting numbering schemes, we can expand on the previous example. Assume all five field panels in a given quadrant were totally loaded with badge readers. That means that there are twenty field panels in the building. Now assume that another badge reader must be added to the east quadrant and there is no available space on the field panels in the building. The logical solution is to install another field panel in the east quadrant. To follow a logical numbering scheme, the next sequential number for the east quadrant field panel is 105; however, 105 already exists in the south quadrant along with field panels 106, 107, 108 and 109. In this case, the numbers would need to be changed from the existing numbering scheme of 100 to 104 up to 100 to 109 in the east quadrant. The south quadrant would need to change from 110 through 119. The other quadrants would also need to be changed to allow for expansion and still have a numbering scheme that defines the quadrant. The best approach to avoid continually changing a numbering scheme is not to confine expansion by predefining blocks of numbers for field panels, but to use a reader numbering scheme that is easy for the Security department to identify, because they need to know the reader numbers. For example, labels can be placed on each badge reader to show a number. If someone has trouble using a reader or wants to report a defective reader, they can let the physical security group know by referring to the reader number on the label. The numbers may not fit a clean predefined scheme, but the users only need a number to describe the reader, the system administrator only needs a unique number and the repair technician only needs as-built drawings. The number on the badge reader label can be a number that is cross referenced in a computer look-up table to define the reader by the system hardware point to which it is attached. With the as-built drawings, repairs can be made quickly and any change in wiring should be updated on the drawings.

This numbering approach can also apply to security alarms. The alarm points are defined by the loop that they connect to in the circuit board located in the field panel. The panel number is combined with the loop number designating a sensor number. The same labeling scheme can apply to emergency exit doors, government classified area alarms, loading dock doors and access doors such as a roof hatch. (Roof hatch and loading doors should be labeled, because they must be bypassed (turned off) at times to perform company related work.) For example, a facility department technician needs to go on the building roof to repair a roof leak. The facility technician can call the SCC operator and provide the identification number attached to the roof hatch access over the phone and take responsibility for the door being open. The SCC operator would then bypass the door alarm. When the roof repair is complete the facility department technician then calls the SCC operator to resecure the alarm, because work has been completed. By having the alarm number on the doorjamb, everyone involved knows exactly which alarm should be bypassed and reactivated. This approach works well when there is not a problem with aesthetics. The labels should be high quality, printed and kept up-to-date.

Part of system configuration control is the development of a philosophy for each security function that reports to the SCC. It is very important that a plan be in place to provide guidelines for the inevitable questions related to the philosophy that will be asked. Questions about an application of access control, for example, would be: Should all restricted access be controlled with badge readers? Should they connect to the central access control system that reports to the SCC? If this approach is taken, then many requests will be made to eliminate the conventional door key and replace it with a badge reader. The philosophy would also require that a badge reader that controls a restricted area, such as a government classified area, be connected to the central access control system. The philosophy would greatly increase the number of badge readers and the data input needed to keep the electronic access up-to-date. Someone must input the various closed area lists into the database. (Typically the list will change often.) This requires an area custodian to approve the additions and deletions. The approved list must then be sent to the Security department data entry person, possibly a system administrator, because every time there is a change, the database must be modified. Documentation should be filed to provide an audit trail of changes requested, who made the request, and when they were requested.

This philosophy of a centralized access control system does have advantages. The main advantage is that all readers are on a single access control system, which allows badge database changes to be made only once. If the philosophy were to keep only building perimeter and critical areas on the primary access control system, then several area access control systems would be allowed to exist. This philosophy would allow certain restricted areas (government classified) to have a stand-alone badge reader system. By having stand-alone systems, the data entry workload shifts to the stand-alone area and away from the data entry personnel associated with the primary building access control system. On the other hand, multiple stand-alone systems would exist and require multiple data entry for someone who needed access to several of the stand-alone systems, thus requiring multiple database entries every time someone forgets a badge or changes badges. In some classified areas, this can be beneficial, because the access control database can be considered to be classified. If this is the case, there are benefits in shifting this responsibility and data entry to the affected area access control computer. Another issue that must be considered in the philosophy is if certain groups or subgroups should have automatic access to all or most areas. For example, if physical security must have access to the area, their badges can be added either to the central server/computer database or to many stand-alone badge reader systems. If stand-alone systems are used, it is important that security be part of the planning process.

It is important that the same badge reader technology and badges be used in separate stand-alone systems as well as the primary access control system. The system should be approved by security management and a means of access needs to be provided for physical security personnel for after-hour emergencies and/or alarm response. One way to do this is to add security officers' badge numbers to the separate stand-alone access control databases. A second approach could be the use of a special alarmed lock box by the door of the stand-alone badge reader system containing a key for security to gain access into the area. This is similar to what is often used by the local fire department who need access to a building when there is an after-hours fire alarm. The stand-alone badge reader system approach transfers all the administration of the stand-alone system's database management to the owner of the area. The negative side to this approach is the dedicated administrative support necessary to handle the constant changes at a single location. Another negative aspect is the added cost for an access control computer to manage the local systems. It is possible to run other programs on the access control computer to minimize cost; however, problems usually arise due to daily operation, software issues, or throughput, which make sharing a computer to perform office related tasks undesirable.

Philosophies do not always remain constant. There are philosophies that were incorporated into the design and must be reevaluated over time. These decisions may have been correct at the design stage; however, as time passes, the decision may not be the best fit for the security needs today. One of those philosophies is dealing with changes in the workplace. Different groups of people that were allowed to use the badge access system may require modifications to their access levels as well as their access during the day. Obviously employees utilize access control via badge readers; however, there are always decisions about others who will need access, for example, the cleaning or maintenance crews that may be outsourced. Often today even the Security officers are contracted. There are nonemployee delivery people who come to the facility daily. As outsourcing continues to be a way of life in corporate America, the access of nonemployees will become more critical and access for these special situations will vary by time of day and areas, generating many variations of access that must be controlled. Keeping control of employees and nonemployees by area of the building or buildings and time-of-day is part of the system configuration control process.

Another philosophy for system configuration control is the level of control and access documentation needed from a system. One example of this process could be the need for access control on both sides of an exterior door where employees and contractors would be required to use a badge reader coming into an area as well as leaving the area. Another philosophy would be requiring a badge reader to enter an area while egress is "free." This approach could be accomplished by using a motion detector or electrified crash bar hardware to allow the flexibility of free egress. Both philosophies have advantages and disadvantages and there is not a solution that will fit every environment or every company. There could also be building life safety code issues that must be considered which would vary based upon the type of occupancy. For example, buildings that house hazardous chemicals or large numbers of people have specific limitations as to various access control techniques and the actual hardware used. Sometimes a combination of these two philosophies is used. In critical areas and perimeter doors, both entry and exit might require a reader, but for access into an IT department hub or phone closets, a reader is required to enter only. Whatever the philosophy, it should be consistent if system configuration control is to be handled properly. In large companies, it is desirable for all sites within the company to be as standardized as possible.

Security alarms should also be standardized under a philosophy to assure system configuration control. The type of sensors and the applications for those sensors should be standardized. For example, in a lobby where there is a receptionist during normal business hours there might be door sensors and badge readers on the doors entering the lobby from outside. There might be a panic switch at the receptionist's desk, and a key switch at the desk to disable and enable the lobby alarms and badge readers. In this configuration, the lobby can be locked down by the receptionists when they leave at night and be opened when they arrive in the morning. This approach eliminates the need for timed openings and closings which often cause problems in two ways. First, the receptionist might run late in the morning and the lobby would be opened by the timed event leaving the building unsecure. Second, it eliminates issues with time changes such as "daylight savings time" or holidays. If someone forgets to change the system time clock or adjust for holidays, then there are security issues. The security alarm function, access control function and CCTV function should all have a standardized philosophy to aid in system configuration control.

Another example for proper alarm system configuration control is the way that inactive alarms are handled. Often, particularly in government classified areas, the space use changes and many of the alarms that are in the area may not be necessary for the new occupants. If there is a reasonable chance that the area will, in the future, again require all the alarms that it now has, system configuration control must be put into place. The alarms should not be allowed to report back to the SCC and there is no advantage in physically removing the alarms, when they will be needed in the future. One system configuration control might be to place end-of-line resistors across the sensor loops back at the field panel, place a paper tag on the resistored loops with a note and make changes to the server/computer database descriptors indicating that the sensors are "temporarily out of service." It is more cost effective to maintain an area at a higher security level and place sensors temporarily out of service than to remove the sensors and wiring only to replace them again in the future.

In addition to philosophy as a system configuration control method, there are issues associated with managing the architecture and database. We have discussed some of the architecture numbering issues, but we have not discussed the database system configuration control. These issues will be impacted by a given manufacturer; however, generally the issues are:

1. Software modifications
2. Software system upgrades
3. Database administration
4. System configuration

SOFTWARE MODIFICATIONS

This is an extremely broad topic; however, there are many practical problems that will require software modifications. We will address a few examples of modifications in this chapter. A modification may be required because of the way the system handles some functions. For example, reports can always be a problem. It seems that the "canned" data provided by the standard system configuration straight from the manufacturer is never quite what is needed. Sometimes a field or fields need to be added to the database to provide the desired report. This requires software modification to some extent. The level of modification will depend upon the flexibility and type of software used by the system. Another possible software modification is the need for one security function to "talk" to another function. If the software does not already exist, then special application-specific software must be written. This will be discussed in more detail later in this chapter.

SOFTWARE SYSTEMS UPGRADES

The uniqueness of a particular installation can cause problems unforeseen by the manufacturer when they developed their product for market. As changes are made by the manufacturer to overcome problems or "bugs in the software" at some customer's location, these changes are provided to other customers usually at no cost, as a system upgrade. There are also changes that are required when upgrading the server/computer operating system. If the system uses an operating software package such as Windows NT or 2000, upgrades are frequently made available by Microsoft to satisfy nonsecurity applications in the wider consumer electronics market. (Microsoft refers to these as "service packs.") These upgrades or service packs are seldom evaluated specifically for security market applications. When these upgrades are incorporated into a security product, they may cause unplanned consequences unknown to the manufacturer. This is particularly true when the application software is proprietary. All upgrades should be carefully evaluated. It is important that you understand exactly what the upgrade is supposed to correct or what additional features it will provide. It is not normally wise to upgrade a large security system every time the manufacturer introduces a new software upgrade. It is normally a good practice to let the upgrade be used by others before you incorporate them into your system.

The best way to mitigate problems associated with upgrades is to hire or have access to a programmer or a trusted IT person who can facilitate upgrades. A potential problem using an IT person is that IT is an early adaptor, which means that they want the latest and greatest. This approach may cause you serious frustration and potential embarrassment when an upgrade causes a series of unplanned consequences. It is not normally recommended that a company be a "Beta test site" for a security product, unless you have time and upper management support for the inevitable system problems. Often with large systems, a computer room support person/staff is developed to handle such situations. The person/staff can also handle the testing and repair of servers/computers, peripherals, and so on, and they can help evaluate system problems. If it is possible, it is always a good idea to use a mock-up area to test software upgrades prior to incorporation into the "online" production system. In testing, the mock-up system must be capable of simulating the existing load being handled by the online system, requiring programming expertise be available to the Security department, which is a luxury not many companies will provide.

DATABASE ADMINISTRATION

Badges, readers and alarms are always being added or removed. When these changes are made, personnel must update the databases as previously discussed. These changes must be timely and correct. Usually an employee within the Security department is designated to handle this function, but as the system grows, more people are needed to keep up with the changes. One system terminal may be located in the badge assignment area, another needed within the security area and more in lobbies. The complexity of the system starts to grow as multiple terminals and operators are needed to incorporate the additions, deletions and modifications to the database. When these changes are made, maintenance to assure the integrity of the database is critical. A "spot check" approach becomes necessary to assure reliable data, as well as consistent access lists and alarm descriptors. The impact of this effort depends on the philosophies discussed earlier. Standards must exist that cover exactly the way data is to be entered, requiring training and very detailed standardized formats. This is discussed in detail in Chapter 11.

SYSTEM CONFIGURATION

System configuration is another area that evolves over time, especially on larger systems. The communication loops that connect the electronic field panels to the SCC server/computer can become overloaded. A good example of this occurs when a loop connecting field panels is processing too many badge readers at a given time. The load on communication loops which service more badge readers than another loop can be reduced by moving readers to a less loaded loop. By redistributing the load the badge processing will speed up. Making a change to the various loops requires two efforts. First, the existing documentation should be in place to understand exactly what loops are connected to which field panels. Second, changing communication loops requires personnel with the knowledge and understanding to evaluate loop response configurations. Even the addressing scheme of the electronic field panels requires some system overview, which is seldom fully considered when a new system is installed.

System configuration control requires an understanding of the various components and software that comprise the system. This applies to the level of openness of the architecture. If the system is full of proprietary hardware and software, then there are several limits related to what can be changed and how that change can take place within the system. Open architecture is another area where manufacturers claim to provide security electronic products of the very latest design and provide the best product for the end user. As with the term "integration," "open architecture" is used very loosely throughout the security industry. The concept of being "open" implies that the system architecture is totally exposed with no hidden or proprietary aspects. If you use the strict definition of "open architecture," it is virtually impossible to purchase an "open" security system. The term is usually used in reference to the system's operating system software; however, the terms can just as easily address the application software and the hardware side of the system as well. In the past, many aspects of a system's software were proprietary application and proprietary database management software. The reasons the security industry started with proprietary systems are the same reasons that many other industries started in similar fashion. One major reason was the lack of electronic and software standards which has caused the security industry to be slow in developing an open environment at any level. Standards within security have developed a tremendous amount of emotion for those in favor, as well as those against standards. Standards being called for range anywhere from total open architecture to Computer Aided Design (CAD) symbols. So this is an area that requires definition in order to set boundaries for any discussion. In this chapter, the discussion will apply to the standards that are directly applicable to system architecture such as Windows NT. The Windows NT standard has affected communication protocols, database management software, and so on. When one evaluates business environments where standards have developed, it helps to understand the impact of a standard such as Windows NT. In most environments, standards of some type develop over time to force a more open and interchangeable system. The companies and users that ultimately established Windows NT over OS/2 had little to do with the security industry. Some of the standards in security systems are being forced by groups outside of the security market. For example, the federal government is pushing internal standards, which will impact the security industry.

By establishing a software standard, the end user benefits in several ways. First, over time the software becomes "bulletproof." In other words, the software becomes very reliable and stable, because many different groups are using it and they have helped find the problems. Second, the software has been upgraded to incorporate many enhancements. These enhancements can be added at minimal or no cost to the end user. Special needs have been requested from many different customers and the benefits of these requests become available to all users. Third, the software sets the protocols for other manufacturers to use, which ensures communication. Forcing the communication between manufacturers is a real benefit to the end user. For an example, consider the PC and a printer from the commercial PC market. A printer can be purchased from many manufacturers. When establishing communications the PC is configured for printer model number xxx. From that time on, the PC will communicate with the printer. In the past in the security market, the communication between different manufacturers' products was typically costly and cumbersome to incorporate. Making the various manufacturers' products communicate often required an integration company to write special application software or drivers.

Hardware also must meet the open architecture requirement to allow a system to be open. If you follow the hardware system from the SCC into the field, you can better examine the hardware claims for open architecture. The computer, keyboard, monitor, printer, and mouse located within the SCC are interchangeable between manufacturers (with appropriate software drivers) and therefore are considered open architecture. (One possible exception is a UL approved system that requires specific circuit boards to be used to match the approved configuration.) As you move from the SCC to the field, the first piece of hardware you come to is a field panel. The field panel communicates with the computer based on information sent to it by the security sensors, keypads or badge readers. The field panel hardware is proprietary in the sense that a field panel from one manufacturer cannot normally be replaced with a field panel from another manufacturer. The main reason the field panels cannot be interchanged is because electronic field panels have a proprietary protocol used to communicate with the server/computer in the SCC. The security alarm sensors and some badge readers in the field are compatible with any other security systems manufacturer's product.

There is concern for proper system configuration control even with a top quality installation and well-planned approach. There are many aspects of a security system that must be managed. Philosophies and configuration of standardized equipment must be developed to assure consistency. There are limitations to the manufacturer's equipment, changing software needs, database issues and system evolution that must be managed in the light of changing system configurations. In successfully developing the system configuration control of a security system, time, energy, standards, philosophies and support budgets are needed. The management concept itself is simple to state, but the implementation can be difficult. There are often forces that impact a philosophy that are not known when the plan is first put into operation. Care must be taken to prevent a system's administration viewpoint from overriding the practicalities of an ever-expanding system. Successful system configuration control requires vision and flexibility.

13

Process Automation

Automation is the first step in a three-step process that will greatly enhance any electronic security system. The three steps are automation, integration and consolidation. Chapters 15 and 16 address each of the remaining steps. To automate requires that each security function be studied and evaluated to find ways to make it automatic to whatever degree possible. In this chapter, we will start in the field looking for ways to automate tasks. Then the automation effort must shift to the Security Control Center (SCC) to evaluate ways to automate activities in the SCC. The goal of automation is to enhance the operation of security from both the SCC operator and the employee/contractor/visitor/customer user's standpoint. This sounds like a fairly simple task, but it is not as intuitive as it first sounds. Some aspects of automation will come naturally and others will require out-of-the-box thinking. Automation is defined in Webster's dictionary as "a machine or control mechanism that is designed to follow automatically a pre-determined sequence of operation or respond to encoded instructions." To address this goal we will start in the field and work our way back to the SCC. Figure 13.1 shows some of the various

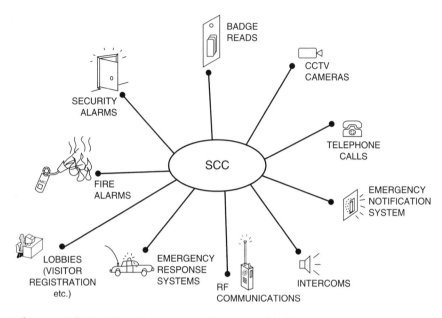

Figure 13.1 Functions reporting to an SCC.

security functions that report to the SCC. Figure 13.2 shows an automated SCC operator area.

There are many applications that can be automated in the field. We will cover several examples, but it will be impossible to address every possible application for automation in this book. My goal is to provide several examples that will start the creative juices flowing so that you can find ways to automate various functions at your company. Security design is not an engineering discipline where you plug in the information and the output is the only correct answer. It is more of an art form where creativity is needed. The final form will be different at different companies and in different environments. The company culture will impact your specific automation processes, as well as budgets and key concerns at your company. Recurring budgetary cost over time should reduce with a solid design that includes automation but it usually takes money to save money.

In our first example, we will look into automating controlled car parking areas. An automated gate often controls these areas.

Figure 13.2 Operator area.

Usually a gate arm is raised and lowered to allow access to or egress from the parking area. Parking access should be as automated as possible, so that the SCC is not involved and the employee/contractor has control of the process. To give the employee/contractor control of the process, they will need to be able to manage the entry and exit themselves. This means that there should be an access control device; it could be a badge reader or an Radio Frequency Identification (RFID) reader or both. The advantage of the RFID reader is that there is a longer "read" range so the employee/contractor entering the area can do so at a reasonable speed, because the gate arm will lift before they are actually there if the reader is correctly positioned. This keeps traffic flowing into the parking area. There needs to be a visual indicator that shows that the access control device (in this case the RFID tag) was read and access has been granted. Many times a red and green light similar to a traffic signal are added to the gate control or mounted close by to let the employee/contractor know that they have been granted access. Additional support equipment is needed in case the employee/contractor is not granted access; a video camera to view the employee/contractor if visual identification is needed; and an intercom to contact the SCC for assistance must be installed also. Ideally if RFID tags are used, then a badge reader can be at the gate control to allow employee/contractors who forgot their tags or if the RFID reader is not working to gain access. If the assistance button at the gate is depressed, the intercom and camera should activate. If the badge reader is not used and the person has access to the parking area, the gate arm will lift and there is no need to contact the SCC operator. Although the badge reader is not automatic in the literal sense, it does prevent the SCC operator's involvement and provides the employee/customer control of the situation. These features are discussed in more detail in Chapter 9. It is an automated approach to have a "full" sign that illuminates when the parking area is full. This saves the employee/contractor time and gas trying to find a spot in a full parking area, especially if the parking area cannot be seen as they pull up. A parking garage is a good example of an area that needs a "full" sign. If possible, it would be desirable to indicate where there are empty parking slots when the parking area is nearly full. There needs to be plenty of access off the main street before the employee/contractor encounters the gate control.

For locations that use an officer at the entry, some of the same functionality still applies. First, the officer shacks need to be protected from oncoming traffic. RFID tags can still be used to speed up traffic flow. An RFID tag on a vehicle that is granted access could activate a light that both the driver and officer could see (a red light indicating that there is no tag or that the tag is not authorized). There must be traffic lanes that allow for parking, so that vehicles can be stopped if necessary and be out of the traffic. Panic buttons should be inside the shack as well as a radio frequency (RF) panic button on the officer. There must be automatic Closed Circuit Television (CCTV) callup in the SCC if a panic button is activated. It is a good idea to utilize a specific CCTV camera that will read the license plates on the back of the vehicles and automatically record each plate. If an RFID tag is used the tag number could be recorded on the same video as the license plate camera. An additional CCTV camera should view the driver and front of the car. Both CCTV images should be automatically linked and recorded in the SCC.

Another automation example deals with CCTV alarm coverage providing display and recording. CCTV coverage should always be part of the exterior alarm system, particularly if the system includes outdoor sensors. These sensors are susceptible to nuisance alarms due to animals and weather. Any alarm received from an outdoor sensor should automatically activate a camera on the monitor in the SCC. The camera should properly cover the outdoor sensor's zone with quality video that will allow the operator to at least detect or possibly, depending upon the requirements, recognize the intruder. The video should also be recorded for retrieval later. Video should be part of any intercom system. When someone pushes an assistance button, the camera associated with that intercom should be activated. Then the SCC operator can see the person needing assistance via the CCTV camera and the intercom. An assistance button can be activated or the intercom button can activate the request for assistance. In this example, both the intercom and CCTV camera should be automatically activated when the assistance button is depressed and the SCC operator acknowledges the assistance button alarm. The video and audio associated with the assistance/intercom button should be automatically recorded for retrieval later.

Intelligent video is a good way to automate video and eliminate the requirement for the SCC operator to watch the monitors. The length of time that a person can watch a monitor is only about 20 minutes, after that the alertness of the operator dissipates quickly. Intelligent video allows the SCC operator to perform other tasks while the CCTV cameras are being checked by software looking for predefined situations to occur. When these situations are observed by the camera and processed by the software, the system notifies the operator via an alarm and provides the video on a monitor for the operator. This can be very effective in many different situations. For instance, in a public area where there is a great deal of people and vehicle traffic, the intelligent video system is watching for someone loitering or groups of people gathering and moving together, such as a gang. Another possibility for an intelligent video alarm is an area with some level of activity such as a hallway, where the software could be looking for someone leaving a package. The SCC operator does not need to watch the monitor all day for this to happen; the intelligent video system software can do the work for the operator. If the situation did occur, the operator would be notified via an alarm and the video would automatically be displayed when the alarm is acknowledged.

Another automation approach is a badge reader that is placed at the health center or at the HR office area. When an employee arrives to receive help, the badge could be read and various forms could be automatically filled out on a monitor screen for the health center or HR personnel. The results or any additional information could be added to the screen and the information stored electronically to show who visited and when and why. This automated system would allow an employee to use their badge to call up general information about them. This information could reside in the security database, or the security database could send the person's name and employee number to the HR database and the information needed for the monitor forms would be sent to the monitor from the HR database. The security database would be used to verify and request information for that specific person, but the actual data could be sent to the health center monitor from a different database.

Revolving doors or turnstiles are products that provide portal automation for access control. For example, a security officer might be used to control the portal or a "mantrap" might be to control access. In the case of a mantrap, some identification is typically shown to the SCC operator via CCTV. The identification (badge) is viewable and the person or people in the mantrap are viewable via another camera. After the identification and personnel in the mantrap is verified, the SCC operator allowed access. If the mantrap is utilized for entry and exit, then the SCC operator is involved in both processes requiring a tremendous amount of time. A revolving door can automate the process and reduce the load on the SCC operator or operators. There might be high security requirements for this type of control, but for most applications, installing a revolving door provides the needed automation and reduces security officer cost associated with manning a portal.

Revolving doors and turnstiles can be added to the building perimeter, a fence line, or as access to an interior area. The choice between the two products is primarily a choice of aesthetics. The revolving door typically provides a less industrial appearance. There are optical turnstiles available that may or may not have a partition of some type. The partitions can be glass, which provide security and a professional appearance and are often used in areas where a large number of people must be processed and where there is an aesthetic requirement. Optical turnstiles allow a few security officers to watch many people gain access into a facility and they provide a light or audible if a badge is not properly read or access is not allowed. These automation techniques are discussed in Chapter 1.

Any security function in the field should be carefully studied to find ways to automate its operation for the benefit of the user in the field and the SCC operator. The operation and documentation should all be automated to the largest extent possible to allow the user in the field to obtain the help needed and the SCC operator to perform tasks effectively and automatically document what happened. There is always a need to retrace an SCC operator's response or an officer's activity. Documentation being automatically linked to events as much as possible allows ease of information retrieval and assurance that the situation has been properly documented. Manual documentation after the fact is typically poor documentation. Complete manual documentation is always a problem during the crisis, because everyone is trying to get the situation resolved. During the crisis, details may be fairly clear, but later that day or the next day, the mind is not as certain as to what transpired.

There are several ways to assist the automatic documentation. One of these is to use an automated time stamp. All electronic functions in the SCC should be automatically linked with a standardized time clock. Nothing is more irritating than reviewing the alarm log, CCTV coverage, and the intercom/telephone recorder trying to reconstruct a situation to evaluate how well a response was handled and having each function use a different time stamp. There are also liabilities that must be mitigated by being able to verify the length of time different aspects of a response required. For example, when an employee has a heart attack: How long did it take to call an ambulance? How long did it take the officer to arrive at the scene? When did qualified first responders arrive? Was the victim given any medication? If so, what time? There are any number of questions that will come out of this type of situation. If you are relying on various time clocks in the different pieces of functional equipment, then there is no way to have accurate time information, because each piece of equipment will have a different time on its internal clock. The only way to avoid this type of situation is to have all clocks in synchronization with a standard clock. An easy way to accomplish this task is with a timing module that links to the atomic clock radio station (WWVB) located at the National Institute of Standards and Technology's facility in Boulder, Colonado. The radio station provides a timing standard and can automatically sets the clocks in all the pieces of functional security components. This way, when the alarm log is checked against the video recorder and any other system component, the time provided by each device will be tied to the same time standard. Speaking of synchronizing the internal electronic clocks, this should include changing to daylight savings when needed. Holidays and special shutdown periods should also be part of this automatic updating. What often happens is a holiday occurs during the week when no one is there. Some of the software control programming already in place has been forgotten, because the holiday was not programmed until someone discovers a security breach. For example, a lobby might be software programmed through the security alarm system to unlock at a certain time in the morning during the workweek. The automated door release time was chosen because the officer would be at the lobby post by the scheduled time and the company would be open for business. The problem is that on the weekday holiday the doors will still "unlock" because no one remembered to change the software control program. Now the lobby is open and there is no one available to correct the problem. An in-house person must be called to come in on a holiday or an alarm company must provide the technical support to reprogram the system or an officer must be at the post all day. If the alarm company has the same holiday, you get stuck with a higher bill and slower response for them when they do respond. This situation is totally unnecessary, if at the first of the year each holiday is planned for with the needed system software command programming. Any automated function can be just as negative as it can be beneficial when proper planning has not been incorporated.

Another type of automated documentation deals with response to alarms. Many times critical alarms activate and some detailed word document is needed to describe the response. If your SCC must meet UL standards, then this response documentation must be included with the alarms. Such issues include the alarm time, which is normally a time stamp generated automatically by the security alarm system, the time the officer was requested to respond, as well as when they arrived. The findings of the officer must also be documented along with notifications of the area custodian and/or a repair technician. This documented information can be part of the security alarm system and input by the SCC operator directly. There can be prompts that automatically display on the screen to help the operator remember to fill in each required response. Automating reports for the SCC operators is another way of eliminating unnecessary work. Normally standard reports that you want your SCC operators to supply might be on a daily basis or after an incident. There is no need to run the report by requesting the various fields in the database needed to run the reports. The report format can be predefined and be an icon on the computer that the SCC operator can activate by providing the time frame or possibly an alarm number. The various standard reports should simply be icons that can be activated and a minimum of data to get the report running. They can even be routed to a printer in the area where the report needs to be sent, thus eliminating operator effort to get the report to a certain location.

Various response documents that the SCC operator must fill out should be available on a computer screen activated by activating an icon. For example, there are certain questions that should be asked during a bomb threat. That form should be displayed by an icon to allow the SCC operators to complete it as they are talking over the telephone to the person making the threat. This way the threat is documented without relying on the SCC operator's scribbled notes and also assures that all the information is gathered. Normally during theses types of situations there is a great deal of stress that usually results in information being missed. This way the information is all covered, in a document and ready to send to management.

Another area of automation for the SCC operator is automatic alarm notifications. When an alarm is received at the SCC, there is information associated with the alarm such as the alarm's location (possibly directions to the alarm), the response and employee contact for the alarm. If the alarm is a typical security alarm, the contact will be a responding officer. In this case, the operator could click on an icon and activate the radio or cell phone of the responding officer. If the alarm is a computer room temperature alarm, the operator could click on an icon and call the custodian of the computer room or someone in the Facilities department. If the alarm were a fire alarm, that icon would call the local fire department, and so on.

Integration is another way to automate functions. The integration process allows different security functions to operate as one and is covered in Chapter 15. In this chapter, we are concerned with automation; so I will not go into any more detail about integration, except to use an example for integrating the fire and access control/security functions in a semiconductor facility. We will look at the automation that is possible through the integration process. In a semiconductor manufacturing facility, there are many requirements and regulations to meet in order to comply with uniform building and fire codes. These facilities are typically classified as H6 by building code, defined in the Uniform Building Code (UBC). The "H" portion of the designator specifies that the facility houses hazardous materials. The "6" designates the quantity of hazardous material within the facility. The Uniform Building Code (UBC) specifies the details of construction as well as the types of fire and safety systems that are required. In an H6 facility, sprinkler system water flow, fire pull and smoke detector activations are required and must provide an automatic evacuation. The fire alarm, according to National Fire Protection Agency (NFPA) must arrive in the SCC within 90 seconds. The evacuation annunciation devices require both the use of voice and strobe lights and must cover an entire area within physical firebreaks. The proper function of the fire system is key to the protection of personnel and the facility. A loss of a modern semiconductor chip manufacturing fabrication facility could easily be in excess of $1 billion. Even nuisance alarms causing evacuations usually result in losses of thousands of dollars per minute. The fire system is a major focal point to detect problems early and minimize losses in the materials being processed as well as the physical building. The fire alarm system also often interconnects or "integrates" with the safety system that controls chemical flow into the facility per H6 requirements. A fire alarm will trigger a control/safety system that in turn will cut off the flow of flammable chemicals to reduce further damages. (The communication between the fire and safety system is usually more complex with bidirectional data and the associated software handshaking protocols.) Nuisance alarms from the fire alarm system impact building occupants via evacuation and production via loss of personnel and chemicals. The fire alarm system is a critical piece of a semiconductor fabrication plant (FAB).

On the other hand, the access control systems are usually rudimentary in a semiconductor FAB. There are few portals for access and the facility has built-in pressurized containment areas to minimize the introduction of particles that could affect the production of chips. The containment areas are used for changing shoes, putting on shoe coverings and smocking-up and can function as natural security barriers. In addition, these facilities usually have only one lobby entrance, dock entrance, and emergency exits. These facilities are built for manufacturing a product, which occupies the majority of the physical space, so the importance of an access control/security system is minimal compared to the fire system, thus producing little desire to purchase a manufactured integrated single product for both fire and access control/security. There are options to the combination system that would allow for the integration of fire and access control/security, most of which include the integration at the field end of the fire system. The access control/security system, as well as the fire alarm system often controls the door release hardware. Security normally requests fail-secure hardware on the doors. Fire systems require fail-safe hardware on the doors. In fact, the entire existence of fail-safe hardware is due to fire code requirements. (Smoke and water flow within a newer facility is required by fire code to provide release of controlled doors.) Fail-safe electromagnetic locks, strikes, and crash bars are released via an output from a fire panel (covered in Chapter 5). To integrate the fire and access control systems in the field requires the sharing of information by interconnecting the field hardware. Connecting output relays from the fire panel to the door release hardware used by the access control/security system can accomplish this by hardwiring the two panels to the same electronic door release. This approach allows the fire system to automatically override the access control system during a fire alarm. During normal operation the output relay in the access control system will release the door after reading an authorized badge.

The fire system can send a signal to the access control/security system to bypass the door alarm during the fire or it can shunt the door alarm in the field to eliminate alarms from activating when emergency exits are used during evacuations. This automatic shunting of door alarms allows the SCC operators time to deal with the evacuation without being side-tracked by unshunted constant door alarms. The access control/security system can monitor any doors that are considered fire doors. These doors have an electromagnetic "hold open" device or devices which keeps the area open until there is a fire alarm. At that time, the electromagnetic device releases the doors which then shut to provide a fire barrier. If the access control/security system monitors these fire doors and only provides alarm information when the doors are closed, the SCC operator will be able to remember to send an officer to the doors to reopen them. If the fire panel is clear, the "hold open" devices will be reactivated—ready to hold the door or doors in an open position.

There are many ways to automate security functions for the SCC operator. Some ideas have been presented in this chapter. Automation should be at the field end to help the SCC operators and the employees/contractors who use the security systems. The automation process will be somewhat unique to a given company due to culture and the environment in which these systems must operate. The automation solution is a process that never ends because whenever new functionality is added, the automation process must be revaluated. There is no one answer for every company, but automation requires careful thought and imagination. It is not a scientific process even though it may require science to achieve the desired automation. The automation process is similar to the Quality/Six Sigma process. It is never complete because there are always opportunities to automate another component in the process.

14

Building Automation

There are two reasons for addressing this topic in a book devoted to electronic security functions. The first is that security may monitor building automation systems or those systems may be the primary system and security is integrated into the building automation system. Second, there is an interest in the industry to integrate various functions and building automation is part of that integration. In Europe, the intelligent building concept, which includes the integration of these two systems, has been pushed. There is a benefit to understanding how these systems work and how they are different from security systems electronically. Most Facilities or Property Management personnel have heard the common sales pitch "This is a great energy management system and security can be added at virtually no additional cost." This is the approach used for years by energy management manufacturers. Most security professionals have felt less than comfortable with a system that they consider extremely important and that the Facilities department considers a free "add on." In many companies, energy management and security have been segregated primarily because of different organizations being responsible for the two functions. In smaller companies,

221

and in many tenant building situations, the functions are combined and under one department although security may monitor both. The decision on whether energy management and security should be part of the same system is decided for the most part by who manages the facility, how their personnel report administratively and who controls the budget. In this chapter, we will address the electronic differences between the security and building automation systems as well as the differences between the Facilities and Security department philosophies.

There are, however, good reasons to combine building automation and security systems. As discussed above, one advantage in combining systems is cost reduction, which is achieved via common hardware and software. Another advantage is a common architecture with similar components within the architecture. Both functions are composed of many of the same subsystems. There are sensors that measure temperature, airflow and humidity in an energy management system while security alarm sensors measure motion, door status and tampers. The sensors in both systems connect to an electronic field panel, which collects the sensors' data and sends that data to a server/computer. The server/computer displays, processes, and logs the information. So in both energy management and security alarm systems, there are sensors, field panels, and a server/computer. It is obvious why some manufacturers have incorporated these two systems into an integrated product.

By integrating these two functions, there is a savings based upon the reduction of hardware and software. For example, purchasing a field panel for the security alarms and a field panel for the building automation function is unnecessary. Costs are also reduced by combining the server/computer. Different sensors connected to the same electronic field panel is a true integration. However, connecting different types of electronic signals into the same field panel requires different types of electronic interfaces within the field panel. This is usually accomplished with different electronic circuit boards within the field panel. This will be discussed in greater detail later in the chapter. The integrated field panel then communicates both functions, alarms and building signals to one centralized server/computer. Integration of functions is discussed in Chapter 15. Historically this type of integrated product has originated with manufacturers that started out in the building automation side of the industry. This basic architecture is also shared with access control systems, which are often also part of an integrated product that covers all three functions: building automation, security alarms and access control.

The reasons that security alarms and building automation, also referred to as energy management, have not been integrated by all manufacturers include differences in types of signals received, signals sent, software focus, and operator interfaces. The details of these differences in sensors, outputs and software can add up to major philosophy differences. The actual hardware used by building automation and security alarm systems is different at the sensor and signal level. Even though the sensors measure information and send it to the field panel, the information varies between the two functions. Security sensors are normally "closed" devices. When activated, they open the circuit and can be thought of as switches connected to the electronic field panels. This is discussed in greater detail in Chapter 4. Although security sensors often have a relay output that can be either normally open or normally closed, they are typically considered normally closed in the secure state. Security sensors are often referred to as digital devices because the sensor is either providing a closed switch or an open switch. The sensor has only two output states. Technically there is a current running through the sensor output that can vary slightly with wire distance and connection resistance, but the sensor is normally considered to be a digital device. Security sensors use an end-of-line supervisory resistor to assure the integrity of the circuit. This topic has been covered in greater detail in Chapter 4. The electronic field panel compares the current running through the sensor's circuit. When the switch activates, current flows only through R2. If the wire is cut, no current flows.

Fire sensors can use two, four, or six wires to accomplish line supervision. A two-wire circuit requires a more sophisticated communication technique where each sensor has its own address. Power and alarm information are sent on the same two wires. A four-wire configuration uses two wires to provide power and two wires for the alarm switch and end-of-line resistor. An activated smoke detector alarm will cause a short across the end-of-line resistor. To supervise the circuit, to be certain all smoke detectors are in the loop, a relay provides a path for the end-of-line resistor via an energized relay coil. If a smoke detector is removed, power will be lost to the smoke detectors farther downstream from the one removed. (See Figure 5.6.) The six-wire approach uses two wires for power, two for alarms, and two to monitor a relay that is added to the last sensor on the loop. If the wire is broken or cut, the relay de-energizes and provides a separate trouble alarm. This is discussed in greater detail in Chapter 5.

In the field, energy management systems are a combination of electronic and pneumatic components. An electronic sensor generates a current flow that represents what is being measured. For example, a temperature sensor will send a current that varies from four to twenty milliamps (4 ma to 20 ma). A 4 ma current flow will exist when the temperature is at or below the designed temperature range. A 20 ma current will flow when the sensor is at or above the high design temperature. A 50°F to 85°F sensor, which is typically used to measure areas within the building, will send 4 ma when the temperature is 50°F or below. This 4 ma to 20 ma signal is available in virtually any building automation sensor and is a common analog input into the field panel. This signal type is considered an analog input (AI), because the signal varies. The interface for this type of signal in the field panel would be on an AI circuit board.

If the input is a digital input (DI), it will only have two states similar to a security sensor. This type of input would be associated with a signal such as a fan is "running." When devices are turned "on" or "off" in a building automation system, a good design practice is to send feedback to the operator so he or she knows that the command was successful. This is often accomplished with the same relay that supplies the electrical power to the fan motor. When the command is sent to turn on the fan, the power going to the motor would activate a relay that sends a signal when the coil on the relay is energized. When the fan is commanded to be turned off then power is removed from the relay, causing the signal to go away, indicating that the fan is turned off. Two possible shortcomings using this approach are (1) if the wire is cut between the relay and the field panel, then the building automation system will indicate that the fan is turned off, when that may not be the case and (2) when electrical power is applied to the relay, there is no assurance that the fan is actually running. The fan motor might be damaged or the fan blade might be broken, and although power is applied, the fan may not be operating. The way to overcome this limitation is to incorporate an airflow switch similar to a water flow switch in a fire system. When the flow switch moves with the flow of air caused by the fan "coming on" the digital signal caused by the flow switch will indicate that the fan is actually running and creating airflow.

Outputs for building automation/energy management and security systems are also different. Security systems provide outputs that are either switch closures or a set voltage. Voltage is often provided for audible alarms, and switch closures are available to activate other devices. For example, when an emergency exit is opened it causes an alarm. The field panel might provide a 12 volt Direct Current (12VDC) power to a sounder to let area occupants know that the door has been opened or a relay in the field panel might be energized that allows current to flow to ground through the field panel and activate the same sounder. Energy management outputs can also be voltage or switch closures, as well as a current level. If a valve that controls the flow of hot water to an HVAC coil must be regulated, a current output is used. This type of output is referred to as an analog out (AO). (The circuit board in the electronic field panel that supplies the AO signal is referred to as an AO board.) A valve can be purchased as either a normally closed or normally open valve. The actual valve that controls the flow of hot water can be either fully opened or fully closed at 4 ma. At 20 ma, the other extreme of the valve would be reached. If the building automation system output is a switch/relay closure, then it is referred to as a digital output (DO) similar to the security system output.

Building automation/energy management systems use special software that does not exist in a security system. To make valves or dampers operate properly, some variation of an integral equation called Proportional/Integral/Derivative (PID) is usually used. The PID is a mathematical equation used to force a control (valve) in the direction of a predetermined set point in a linear manner. The software needed to perform this function is a major part of an energy management computer program. The equation accounts for differences in the set point and present condition and the rate of change needed to reach the set point. A less complicated way to control a valve used in some energy management systems is providing current output in steps. Each step puts the control closer to the set point. This approach requires a waiting period after each step verifying remaining differences between the control and the set point providing a time delay that allows the sensor feedback to the field panel to decide if another step is necessary. The advantage of a PID loop is that it allows the valve to be modulated based on a mathematical curve instead of switching step voltages or currents to reach a set point. The valve can be constantly changed electronically and updated toward the set point which provides smooth operations and accurate control. No matter which approach is used, these outputs are both totally alien to security systems.

The inputs and outputs described up to this point apply to those available in the electronic field panel. This unit is usually a fairly intelligent piece of hardware. The way in which security and energy management systems utilize the electronic field panel is very different. In a security system, the level of decision making varies tremendously from one manufacturer to the next. In energy management systems, the electronic field panel can be self-contained, making all decisions locally. The connection to the computer is for the operator's benefit, not necessarily for operation of the system. The operator can observe, send commands and make changes, but if the computer is not manned, the electronic field panel will process sensor information and control valves on its own without the server/computer or the operator. The operator uses the server/computer to provide manual directions to the energy management system or to check the systems operation by verifying temperatures, and so on in different areas. The server/computer is being monitored on an intermittent basis. On the other hand, a security systems operator in the Security Control Center (SCC) is monitoring alarms to provide response to those alarms. The computer section of the architecture is used for loading programs into the electronic field panel and for the operator's interaction with the system. In security systems, the operator is not optional but essential. Most security decisions are human-based and the human is relying on the computer to provide the alarm signal, descriptor information and the response instructions. The security signal must be acted upon by the operator. This is usually accomplished by directing additional personnel to respond to the alarm location. In energy management systems, the electronic field panel usually has RS232 or the newer standard Electronic Industries Association (EIA) 232 output capability. Some security field panels do provide an RS232 port primarily for testing and programming remote panels. The energy management system can also have an alarm activation that is processed in a similar way. This is, however, not the primary function of an energy management system. Its primary function is to modulate valves, start and stop motors or pumps, and make decisions on its own. The decisions are made without an operator's assistance.

The field panel is a point at which integration between the two functions can be accomplished without using the same electronic field panel. For example, the building automation system field panel might utilize a DO that connects to the security field panel. The DO could be activated in the building automation system when the temperature in a critical computer lab was out of tolerance. There might be two DOs, one for high temperature and one for low temperature, although the concern for computer labs is typically for temperatures becoming too high. The DOs would have a resistor or two resistors in the loop that connects them with the security field panel. In this way, the security field panel would have its required supervision and be able to monitor the building automation function and not be physically integrated in the same field panel. Since the security field panel requires supervised digital signals for an input, all physical connections between the two field panels must be from a DO in the building automation system to a loop input in the security field panel and an end-of-line resistor or resistors must be added for supervision. Supervision of security alarm field panels was discussed in Chapter 4. This type of integration falls under the heading of field interconnection and is discussed in Chapter 15. This is the most practical approach if some level of integration is desired and when a commercially combined system is not appropriate.

The third type of integration would be to connect the RS232 outputs from the servers/computers of the energy management system to the security system. This approach is the least desirable, because it requires special software and is seldom done. The simplicity of connecting the desired signals in the field is a clean choice and allows the Facilities and Security departments to be independent, but cooperative. If the Facilities technician needs to check temperatures or send commands to activate or deactivate mechanical systems in the building, he or she can go to the server or computer or workstation whenever needed. The SCC operators can monitor the security functions and if critical areas develop alarm situations, then they can do what they do best, which is monitor alarms and dispatch response personnel. Instead of calling a security officer, they would call the appropriate Facilities department personnel for response. In any large company, it is important for the SCC operators to monitor some building automation alarms, because they are available twenty-four hours a day, seven days a week. The approach used to integrate these two functions will depend upon organizational structure (Facilities and Security) and the way funding is handled by these two groups.

Although energy management and security systems have a common systems architecture, they have very different electronic interfaces as well as signals. This raises a question as to the benefit of having combined hardware. If a system manufacturer begins producing energy management equipment, their primary focus will be energy management. As already discussed, the thinking process for energy management and security are different. This problem would also exist if a manufacturer begins with the security business and moves into the energy management business. Wherever a manufacturer starts their product line will affect the product's primary purpose and quality. The combined systems tend to be excellent for the intended primary function but not as advanced at the secondary purpose. There is also the issue of having all your eggs in one basket. The more integrated a system, the greater the impact of a failure in that system.

The goal of an energy management system is to minimize energy costs. In many cases, most of the energy saving dollars are derived from turning off equipment when its operation is not needed. This is true for heating and air conditioning as well as lighting. This level of control can be easily handled by a security electronic field panel. Any energy function that could be controlled by a switch closure is an ideal candidate to be added to a security system. If the security system started and stopped the use of energy, then only the security system would be needed. An example might be a motion detector, keypad or badge reader that turns on lights and/or HVAC equipment. The benefit gained by monitoring and controlling switchable points may be all that is required. If, on the other hand, more elaborate controls are needed, then an energy management system should be used. Security systems are not designed to monitor or output 4 ma to 20 ma circuits. They also do

not have the built-in programming needed to provide the calculations for PID loops. When modulation of values or dampers is
required, then an energy system with 4 ma to 20 ma outputs is
required.

The personnel that interface with the two systems have a different focus. There is a difference in the way system operators are
used with security and energy management systems. Since most
of the energy management is done automatically, only out-of-
tolerance alarms would be presented to the server/computer. The
energy management system might send a signal to a pager that
would notify the appropriate Facilities department person of the
alarm. Their response could include the use of a remote worksta-
tion/terminal to electronically modify the cause of the alarm by
modulating valves to cool or heat the area. A security operator is
monitoring alarms and dispatching security officers to those alarms
on a twenty-four hours a day, seven days a week basis.

The decision to incorporate energy management and security
in the same physical system includes three key areas. The first factor to consider is the organizational structure of the company and
personnel requirements for monitoring, using and maintaining the
system. The monitoring and operation of the systems have been
discussed, but maintenance is an important aspect. Part of this
analysis must consider ongoing support. The vendors that repair
energy management systems are often different from the alarm
companies that support security systems. These two functions have
for the most part been provided by different technical groups. There
are commercial companies that support both systems; however,
their capabilities should be verified and be part of the evaluation.
The second area includes cost analysis and the complexity of the
energy management and security needs. Third, the functionality
needs of both systems must be weighed.

To this point, we have addressed sensors, electronic field
panels, server/computers and philosophies. There are several other
aspects of an integrated building automation/security system that
should be considered. Access control and Closed Circuit Television
(CCTV) are critical functions for security of the building. Both of
these functions are totally different from capabilities normally available in dedicated energy management systems such as a Programable
Logic Controller (PLC). Security systems have incorporated access

control in their electronic field panels because this function is critical to security applications. The CCTV interface between the cameras and the security alarm system is usually via an RS232 port to a video switcher. Interface software allows the security computer to communicate with the video switcher allowing alarms to activate and "call up" specific cameras. There are energy management systems that also provide these functions; however, this is not a standard.

There is no single answer as to the best approach for the handling of energy management and security functions. The solutions should be based on the following:

1. Complexity and size of the systems
2. The most cost effective approach considering personnel as well as equipment
3. Functionality needed
4. Company culture
5. System maintenance

With careful considerations of the above areas, energy management and security can exist in many configurations as already discussed. The solution will depend upon the real life environment you must work in. There are no universal solutions and no single correct answers. However, it is important for you to understand the electronic differences between the building automation and the security alarm systems, since there are several options as to the way these systems can operate and provide the same desired result. One last point is to understand the thinking differences between the Facilities and Security departments. I realize that in many companies, the Security group may report to the Facilities department or they may both report to the same managerial point in the organization or they may physically be the same person. For those of you who reside in an organization where there is a separation of the Security and Facilities departments, I will try to provide some insight as to a typical Facility department's thinking process. First, they are driven by cost constraints and tend to calculate all projects based upon a dollar amount per square foot. This approach works very well for the vast majority of what they do. They also are interested in the return on investment (ROI). If an air handler is changed, there might be an energy savings, due to a newer unit, that pays for the cost of the air handler over some period of time. In this example, the energy savings might be $4,000 per year and the air handler cost $12,000, thus providing an ROI of three years. Second, they can hire any painting contractor or mechanical or electrical company to do almost any task they may have. So they believe that one alarm company or any given alarm manufacturer is just as good as the next, just as Security assumes one air handler from Company X is just as good as an air handler from Company Y. Third, they do not believe that Security needs any specialty that requires a higher dollar per hour rate than another trade group that Facilities normally utilize. The cost per hour of a security tech from an alarm company will often be compared with an electrician's rate. This tends to make Facilities personnel think that security is over-priced and needs their help to provide the company with the most cost effective solution. Fourth, Facilities is measured by speed of installation, money savings and solving problems quickly. These measurements may not be the correct metrics to measure a Security department. Fifth, Facilities solves problems on an area by area or building by building basis. They do not normally address enterprise-wide electronic system solutions. Sixth, Facilities believes that they are much better qualified to manage and direct projects, which is true more often than not. Lastly, they believe that they are better qualified to pick the security system, and in some cases that system is a building automation system that can provide security at virtually no additional cost.

Building automation and energy management have been used interchangeably in this chapter. The two topics from my viewpoint are basically the same. Energy management is specifically designed to cut energy costs and incorporates other software programs such as load shedding to keep the consumption of energy as low as the company culture will allow. Building automation includes energy management, but has added functionality, such as parking garage controls. Security is also typically rolled up into building automation. A "smart" building is usually a combination of energy management, building automation and security. This concept is important and often impacts the SCC. There are many ways to interconnect/integrate these functions and some have been discussed in this chapter. The important concepts to gain from this chapter is to understand the basic differences in the building automation side and the security systems side. We also addressed the different philosophies of the Facilities department. This is important because Security must often work with Facilities to provide a total company-wide solution. Many times the Facilities department runs and manages the actual installation of security systems for the Security department.

15

Integration

Everyone is selling an integrated solution today. The word has become synonymous with a total enterprise solution. It is so overused that its meaning is often lost. To evaluate the importance of integrating security system functions, the first step is to define integration. According to the dictionary, integration is a way of forming a whole, or uniting one thing with another, or incorporating into a larger unit. In this chapter, we are going to focus on the integration of electronic security functionality. The integration will be addressed from a philosophy/technology standpoint. There are two concepts that are used to address this type of integration: (1) Integrating similar functions. For example, bringing multiple access control systems into a single database. This is mentioned in several chapters and Appendix A. (2) Integrating dissimilar functions. For example, combining or integrating security alarms, energy management, fire alarms and access control. This topic has also been mentioned in other chapters. Integrating similar or dissimilar functions might be accomplished in the field or in the Security Control Center (SCC).

Interconnecting devices/functions together, purchasing the electronics in an integrated package, purchasing special application-specific software or through physical placement within the SCC are all approaches to accomplish the integration task. The way you accomplish integration is not as important as the SCC operator seeing the different functionality as integrated. In the strict sense of the word, to integrate security functions means that the product of integration is seamless and packaged. Since there is not an absolutely perfectly integrated electronic security system covering all functionality available on the market, integration must be accomplished through whatever means possible.

When integrating similar functions, you might combine badge computer databases from several locations into a centralized server/computer database or remove several stand-alone systems and replace them with a centralized system. Data entry, as well as monitoring, could be performed at one location instead of several, thus providing more effective database management. This type of integration would encompass both hardware and specialty software. For example, the integration might be accomplished in the case of a centralized database by using a central server/computer that would receive and send data to all connected access control systems. See Appendix A for the pros and cons of this type of integration approach. To make such a system work, it would be necessary for the server to be able to convert the data to the proper protocol for each manufacturer's access control system that connects to the server. (As discussed in Chapter 2, each manufacturer has a proprietary protocol that provides communication between the field panels and the server/computer.)

Another example of combining similar functions would be combining audio functions in the SCC. These audio functions might include telephone, intercom or paging and radio systems. These functions could be electronically connected together at the SCC console or combine the controls of three different systems into an ergonomically effective console layout. The console layout philosophy would fall under the physical placement approach. This is discussed in Chapter 10. Proper physical placement would aid the SCC operator in using each audio function because of their close proximity, eliminating the need to answer the telephone and use an intercom at different ends of the console. The physical placement could be a benefit as an integration situation only, or an electronic integrated component could be added. In the example of integrating audio functions, the best approach is both physical placement along with electronic applications. The physical placement within the SCC operator's console has been discussed in detail in Chapter 10. The electronic integration portion might be to use the same microphone and speaker for all the audio systems. This can be accomplished with an earpiece similar to those used with cell phones. The exact solution will depend upon the best ergonomic approach for the SCC operator or operators. When combining dissimilar functions, many manufacturers have designed electronic field panels that process different electronic security functions, such as security alarms and badge readers. Other dissimilar functionality such as fire alarms and energy management could also be part of the same integrated manufacturer's package. (The field panels make the connection between the actual sensing devices and a server/ computer in the SCC.) Although the functions are dissimilar, it can be cost effective to have multiple functions collected in the same field panel. This eliminates the cost of separate systems and reduces hardware, labor, and wiring. The same end result can be reached by physically connecting inputs and outputs from the electronic field panels of dissimilar functions in the field. For example, the energy management system might provide a digital output to an input in the alarm field panel. The energy management system output might indicate that a computer room is getting too hot. The electronic security panel would receive the temperature alarm and notify the SCC operator of the alarm. This is discussed in greater detail in Chapter 14. If the dissimilar functions are connected in the field or within the same field panel, the functions are "integrated" as far as the SCC operator is concerned.

Software integration of dissimilar functions is obtained when programs allow data to be used in multiple functions. An example would be the use of an RS232 port on a video switcher connected to a serial port on the alarm computer/server. In this approach, when a specified alarm from the alarm field panel is received at the SCC server/computer, that information is modified to provide the needed protocol for the video switcher to "call up" a specific camera. In this way, the manual camera callup by the SCC operator has been replaced by an automated approach that integrates the security alarm system with the video switcher. This is discussed in Chapter 13. The integration of various functions through software can be "off the shelf" or custom application software. The video callup example is accomplished with off-the-shelf software, which is much cheaper than custom.

Integrating similar and dissimilar functions is more of an art form than a science. It takes scientific or technical knowledge to properly integrate functions; however, what functions and how those various functions are integrated is up to the security professional. One security professional might consider a given function critical to integrate; another might consider it unimportant. The basic problem with integration is that there is no "single way"' nor is there a single universal approach to integrate security functions electronically or conceptually. If a group of security professionals were gathered from different industries and asked to integrate a collection of functional systems to provide the ideal security scenario, there would be many different solutions because every industry has its own unique requirements that have evolved specifically for that industry. Because these requirements vary greatly across industries, there is no universal way to integrate the needed components to make an integrated system. For example, Factory Mutual (FM), an insurance carrier, requirements are very important to some industries; therefore, these industries would never think of combining fire and security alarms into one field panel. Since fire alarms may be more important in this situation than security alarms, the fire system would stand alone and be enunciated only through a separate fire panel even though a combined fire and security panel might be FM approved. This same group, however, might have no problems combining security alarms and badge readers in the same field panel. So the question "should someone integrate his or her system?" becomes "how is the best way to integrate the system based upon company culture, industry in which it resides, and any code or special requirements?"

With all of the obvious advantages of integration you might think that it is a perfect solution. There are, however, some negatives with integrating systems. Each item in the list below can be a positive or a negative consideration when integrating security functions. We will discuss the negatives listed below, but it is important to remember that each negative can also have a positive aspect.

1. Cost
2. Complexity
3. Skill level of repair technicians and SCC operators

4. Reliability
5. Impact of a failure
6. Redundancy
7. Custom hardware and software

COST

Cost can be a double-edged sword. Over the long run, it usually adds value and saves money to integrate security functions as in integrating fire and security alarms with badge readers in one system. Let's look at some specific issues with integrating security alarms and access control. This saving is achieved by reducing installation costs such as wire, labor, and multiple separate security and badge reader field panels and associated servers/computer. On the negative side, equipment usually costs more initially when functions are integrated. There is always a tradeoff for the number of alarm points and the number of badge readers that can be added to a single field panel. There are also numerical combinations of security alarms and badge readers that are defined when the field panel is purchased. The exact number of each will vary based upon the combination. For example, the reader side of the equipment is based upon multiples of 4. If a field panel is capable of 64 readers or 128 alarms, then when readers and alarms are combined the number of each is reduced. The field panel version purchased for 16 readers may only have 32 alarms available. If the number of either exceeds the single field panel's capacity, another panel must be added. When the additional panel is added, the new panel must contain the predefined number of readers and alarm points plus processing/interface circuit boards that allow for communication from the field panel and to the server/computer in the SCC, which adds cost.

COMPLEXITY

When hardware is interconnected or software is driving several functions, the system complexity increases significantly. This complexity impacts costs, reliability, and level of repair personnel's competence needed to keep the system functioning. For example, when a security alarm fails to activate a video monitor with the correct camera "callup," repair personnel have to determine where the problem lies. Is it with the alarm sensor, field panel, video matrix switcher, the server/computer or interconnecting software? The problem could be any of the electronic hardware, wiring or software in the field panel, video switcher, or server/computer. Repair and ongoing support has been mentioned in this book as a serious consideration. The success of any system will be driven more by a quality installation and repair support than by the actual equipment manufacturer.

SKILL LEVEL OF REPAIR TECHNICIANS AND SCC OPERATORS

The training and competence level of the repair personnel becomes very critical as the system becomes more and more integrated. No longer can the technician simply swap hardware hoping to find the problem. The cost to train competent, highly skilled people, in-house or not, must be considered as part of the complexity of integrating. Appendix D provides a possible list and competency levels for in-house technical personnel. Appendix E covers an interviewing overview. Large-scale systems, in my opinion, are difficult to maintain when there is not in-house expertise. Someone needs to understand the "big picture" and have the technical competence to oversee the system and resolve issues that arise. For example, when microprocessor-based field panels first came out, I had technicians that replaced field panels that "locked up" and corrected the problem with a new field panel. The real issue was power fluctuations and/or lightning causing the microprocessor to lock up or "crash." If they had just rebooted the existing field panel, the problem would have disappeared and the technicians would have saved a great deal of effort mounting the new field panel and rewiring it.

RELIABILITY

System reliability has the potential to drastically degrade with complexity. There are several areas that can be affected. Complex systems can exhibit "throughput" problems due to loading activity. For example, a field panel that processes security alarms and badge reads might become overloaded when there is heavy badge usage, and alarms may not be processed through to the SCC operator in a timely manner. This might cause critical alarms such as panic, life safety, emergency or Department of Defense (DoD) alarms to be delayed to the point of being unacceptably slow, thus adversely affecting required response times for these alarms. Another area that can degrade with complexity is component failures. It is more likely that a failure will occur as the system becomes more complex—more components would provide more points of failure. When a single failure does occur in a field panel that processes fire alarms, security alarms, and badges, all three systems might be down. It can also be argued that by having multiple field panels for the different functions, the added volume of hardware and software provides more points of failure due to the additional field panels. On the other hand, if a single failure occurs and each function resides in its own field panel, then only one function will be down. In the 60s and 70s, it was popular to own a console TV that contained a stereo record player, an AM/FM radio, and possibly a tape deck all in one piece of furniture. This concept was replaced by purchasing individual components that were interconnected to become a system because people realized that when one function failed in the console, the entire console had to be sent to the shop for repair leaving the customer without a TV, stereo player, an AM/FM radio and a tape deck—not just the one unit that failed.

IMPACT OF FAILURE

The impact of losing an integrated field panel has been discussed. The possibility of a system failure in the SCC, through the loss of a server/computer, must also be considered. Such a loss causes many security professionals to add backup server/computer systems in the SCC.

REDUNDANCY

Redundancy might be handled in several ways. The least expensive way to handle backup is to have a spare server/computer that can be switched, replacing the defective unit. The problem is assuring that the data on the replacement server contains the same up-to-date information as the failed server. Another approach is to have multiple computers mounted and ready to provide needed backup. The backup computer or computers might be online in a hot backup configuration or left offline ready to connect to the field panels. When failure occurs with the primary computer either wires must be moved between units or a switch can be incorporated to electronically change connections. In the case of a hot backup, automatic transfers will have occurred without human intervention. This is the most desirable approach, but it is also the most expensive.

Disaster management or business continuity emphasizes the importance of operability when there is a highly integrated complex security system. That is not to say that nonintegrated systems do not have a need for a disaster management plan; but as complexity increases, there is usually more reliance on the system; therefore, disaster management planning becomes a greater necessity. The need for redundancy is not only focused on the server/computer. As systems become more complex, it becomes necessary to have other critical functions in the SCC to be backed up. Power, temperature control equipment, lighting, field hardware, and communication wiring should be considered in your business continuity plan. In fact, you may want to have a backup for your SCC.

CUSTOM HARDWARE AND SOFTWARE

The last negative to address is the need for custom hardware and application-specific software. Many functions that a security professional would like to incorporate are not commercially available. The equipment manufacturers want to make products for general appeal so that their customer base is maximized. If special needs exist, the only options, at present, are to have the special function integrated through custom hardware and/or software. Customized functions can be accomplished through an agreement with the manufacturer, through a contractor, a security integrator or in some cases with the use of in-house staff. One note of caution is if a custom software package is needed, having the Information Technology (IT) department do the design work or become the sole source for the system specifications might not result in a software package you will be happy with. This is not to say that IT can't provide valuable information, but their perspective can be or often is substantially different from what is needed in security software. The IT or IT security department's perspective is typically not like the conventional "security" perspective and their interpretation of Email processing does not match well with conventional security processing needs. IT security is a cyber security focus, which addresses firewalls, antivirus and antispy software. If IT or a group outside is utilized to help with software development, a thorough, detailed succinct scope of work must be written. The Security department must develop the scope of work with guidance from the group providing the software code, be they IT, or an outside software firm. It is never easy to develop a scope of work that encompasses all the security needs, let alone avoid delays in implementation; and with extremely expensive modifications a quality scope of work is mandatory. The security professional must carefully think through the scope of work and minimize changes and the software-coding group must be controlled or the project will never end.

Now that we have discussed some of the issues and concerns regarding integration, it is important to think through how an integrated system should be optimized. Integrating functions in security is similar to having a company-wide quality thrust. The company may have a solid quality program, but the optimizing of the quality effort is never finished. Optimization for an integrated security system is similar. Consider the development of a race car. Every aspect of the racecar must be evaluated during the car's fabrication: constant fine-tuning the engine, adjusting the suspension, modifying the aerodynamics and assuring all components are in top condition after each race to maximize performance. The same is true for optimizing an integrated security system. Each component, function, that makes up the whole of the system and the SCC must be checked, adjusted, and modified for peak performance.

Webster defines optimized in the following terms: "to make perfect or effective or as functional as possible." It is impossible to make the system perfect, but it can be adjusted, fine tuned, and modified to be as effective and as functional as possible. To adjust the system properly, each aspect must be checked and the defects eliminated. The key is to get a jump-start on the "fine tuning" process as early in the integration project as possible by learning, understanding and stating the objectives as clearly and knowledgeably as possible.

For example, the constant nuisance alarms associated with an emergency exit must be corrected quickly. This situation has a couple of primary concerns. One concern is the "call wolf" syndrome. The SCC operators lose any desire to be concerned about alarms because they constantly appear in the SCC. (The console is "crying wolf" and the SCC operators will eventually ignore the alarms, even when the alarms are not nuisance alarms.) The other concern is adding a level of stress on the SCC operators just by the sheer volume of alarms. The actual cause of the alarms must be determined. A common cause of emergency exit alarms is the unauthorized use by employees. This abuse develops for the sake of convenience; employees crash out of the emergency exit to reduce their walking distance. In this example, it is important to decide if the door should be changed to a regular entrance or left for emergency use. If the door is changed to a regular entrance, it may become necessary to add sidewalks, remove exit signs, and so on to facilitate the use of the door. A second option would be to leave the door as an emergency exit. Then signs should be added to make it obvious that the SCC electronically monitors the doors. Even small breakaway ties might be placed on the crash bars as a psychological deterrent. To curb abuse, it may become necessary to enforce the use of the door as an emergency exit with upper management support and a security officer for a period of time. A combination of the two options is possible by adding badge readers and delay crash-bar hardware to the door. The delay crash-bar will allow emergency exiting after a short delay interval (usually about 15 seconds). The use of this capability depends upon the classification of the building (building codes) and the Fire Marshall (fire codes). Chapter 19 deals with code issues. During the delay interval, a horn would sound drawing attention to the person exiting. In an emergency, the horn would be expected, but during normal movement the badge reader would be utilized. The reader would provide immediate movement through the door while bypassing the horn and intrusion alarm. The main reason for using this approach is the lack of emergency exits within the building requiring a door to act as both a badge reader door and an emergency exit door. This is typically the least desirable option. It is usually better to have a portal as either a regular entrance/exit or as an alarmed (24-hour) emergency exit. One of the goals in optimizing is to eliminate nuisance alarms. Motion detectors are another source of potential nuisance alarms in the SCC. If alarms occur with no apparent cause, they must be studied until an adjustment to solve the problem is obvious. Heating, air conditioning equipment, or certain activities cause motion detector nuisance alarms that often occur at a certain time every day. Even moving heavy carts on the floor above ceiling mounted motion or glass-break detectors can cause these devices to activate. Banners and light weight signs hanging from the ceiling, moving around due to HVAC coming "on" and blowing them can trigger sensitive motion detectors, causing nuisance alarms. Rats and even larger insects close to the motion detector can also cause nuisance alarms. Modifying sensor type or their placement should eliminate most nuisance alarms. Chapter 6 addresses this topic in more detail.

Procedures can be just as effective as physical placement of sensors in reduction of nuisance alarms. Procedures must be in place to handle situations that are known to cause these alarms. For example, a secured doorway where material movement is processed must have a procedure. This procedure could include the use of a badge reader to control limited access or simply the use of a physical security policy. These physical security policies are needed when the use of a "doorway" is infrequent or will be kept open for an extended period of time. For example, if the doorway is on top of a building leading to the roof, and used for the installation and removal of equipment, a physical security policy would be used. This policy would typically include a phone call to the SCC and the alarm bypassed by the SCC with responsibility for the open door shifting to the personnel who requested the door be bypassed.

A dock is another area where a procedure needs to be used to transfer ownership of alarms from the SCC to the site of the alarms. The dock master should be able to receive all alarms and take responsibility for the security of the dock during business hours. In a typical security procedure, the dock master would take responsibility for the dock by contacting security and having them disable the alarms. Then at the end of the day, the dock master would notify security to reestablish alarm monitoring. To change this procedure to an automated/integrated process, an electronic verification of the dock master's presence would activate or deactivate the alarms in the field panel. This procedure can automatically be performed using a keypad, badge reader, or both. The control center could also have the capability of being notified electronically when the dock is not opened and closed within the standard time window. This is often referred to as an exception report.

The access control part of the fine-tuning process should include use of as many badge readers as possible to provide automatic access control. Manual access control activity in the SCC should be minimized. It is not desirable for the SCC operators to operate at peak workload during a normal workday, because during emergency situations, they will not be able to perform tasks causing delays for some critical process. This is discussed in Chapter 10. An employee badge is part of most access control systems and is often the method used to visually identify the employee. The employee badge can be used for many applications to automate/integrate access control. In addition, any areas such as the dock that previously required a phone call to the SCC for manual alarm control should use badge readers in automating this process. Other automation of access control would include elevator controls to certain areas, employee verification at the health center, as well as gate controls for loading docks.

The CCTV function might be fine-tuned in four ways. First, cameras should only be installed where there are long term plans to view/record them. Often cameras are installed with no thought of the long-term costs associated with their use. Cameras tend to be added even to the point that they become a maintenance burden. The second adjustment requires that the cameras be connected to the alarm and access control functions. In this way, the operator in the SCC does not need to view the camera by forcing it to be displayed on a given monitor. The alarm or badge reader would automatically activate the camera and display it on a predefined monitor. The camera request is automated and it is connected to an alarm event (security alarm, badge reader or an assistance button) that enhances the operators' ability to perform their activities. The third way is to use intelligent video. Intelligent video was discussed in Chapter 7. It allows the video system to analyze the information and automatically notify the SCC operator when the camera is viewing suspicious activity. The fourth and final fine-tuning is keeping the closed circuit components operating at their best. This requires repairs and maintenance when necessary, proper lighting, and correct camera placement.

Fine-tuning the audio systems is, for the most part, accomplished by adjusting two aspects of the system. One of the aspects is overall voice reproduction quality. It is important to reproduce good quality voice in the SCC as well as at the remote intercom speaker. This often requires the filtering of background noise. For example, if the intercom is located at a dock gate, it is important to filter any engine noise so that the driver can be clearly understood. The second area is volume control inside the SCC as well as the speaker in the field. The volume should be adjusted for a given operator and the noise level inside the SCC. The operator should hear every remote speaker at the same level. This eliminates the operator constantly adjusting audio levels every time a different intercom is activated. The remote speaker should have the audio properly set to provide good quality voice over the ambient background noise level at each location. This also eliminates the SCC operator's adjusting outputs for each remote location so that the person using the remote speaker can properly hear the operator.

After all fine-tuning functions and field issues have been accomplished, it is time to fine-tune and make adjustments within the SCC. The overall goal in the control center is to provide an effective environment for the operators. Issues that should be addressed include lighting, ambient noise levels, equipment placement, temperature, furniture, and other ergonomic concerns. Most of these areas should have been included in the system integration project, but often only the electronics functional portion is addressed. The operators must be part of the integration process because their performance is the measure of the system's success. The entire field adjustments previously discussed is for the benefit of the SCC operator. By eliminating nuisance alarms and unnecessary calls to the SCC, the operators can better focus on the important parts of their job.

To fine-tune the SCC it is first necessary to review the operator's concerns. Some of these concerns include

1. Equipment and software problems
2. Time management issues
3. Procedural difficulties
4. Temperature controls
5. Lighting issues

6. Comfortable seating
7. Ergonomic console issues
8. Stress generating procedures

After studying each concern by interviewing all operators, a solution will often become apparent. For example, the complaint might be that the operator must turn to the side and reach across the console to talk into the radio system. Moving the microphone to the center of the console by the alarm screen and adding a foot switch to activate the radio system could resolve this, or issuing each operator a personal ergonomic headset.

After evaluating operator concerns, the next level of fine-tuning requires direct observation of the operation within the SCC. It is necessary to observe the operator during various times of the day. It is often helpful to videotape the operator to assure that details are not missed. Several items will surface that did not show up during the interview stage. Often the fine-tuning at this level will include areas the operator accepts as part of the job or may not even be aware of. Some of the areas that could surface are

1. Access to and storage of supplies
2. Overall efficiency of the console
3. Processing of emergency response
4. Inconsistency of data descriptors
5. Lack of critical information
6. Areas in need of automation
7. Training needs
8. Inefficiencies of working with the response personnel
9. Non-value added tasks
10. Periods of no activity

When these areas are evaluated and adjustments are made, the performance of the operator or operators will increase. They will be more effective and they will be ready to handle stressful situations because the unnecessary and unconscious stresses have been removed. Another advantage to the company is that the SCC operator's time is not being wasted with unnecessary tasks, but rather is being utilized to its fullest. For example, operator time that was spent performing manual access to a door is now spent viewing areas in the building rather than using a physical guard. When a badge reader entrance door malfunctions, the operator often must verify authorized access and then manually release the door. The operator must perform this task until the door is repaired. If the operator does not know the procedure or does not have the authority to expedite repair, a great deal of time will be wasted and the operator's stress level will increase. When proper procedures are in place, the operator can directly contact repair personnel and spend the newfound time on other efforts.

Integration of security functionality, even with the negatives, is important for companies for two basic reasons. First, manpower is continuing to be reduced and costs are being closely scrutinized in most companies. Many integration techniques can save manpower. Second, integration allows the Security department to do their job efficiently, accurately and more consistently. The impacts of downsizing, quality thrust, Six Sigma and an efficient workflow are forcing Security department managers to closely evaluate how to improve operations through integration. Manufacturers are making integration easier to accomplish through interconnection of various pieces of equipment. This flexibility and interconnecting will be a continuing trend with manufacturers producing more integration into their products as the demand increases. As already mentioned, there is no concrete recipe for all security applications and there is no "ideal way" to integrate electronic security systems. The impact of integration will require an evaluation of the competence of the repair staff and the impact on the SCC operators. The approach taken will require evaluating the specific application and how best to solve the system and people problems of that application. As equipment and software continue to become available to enhance system integration, many new opportunities lie ahead for you to fine tune their operation and provide better security.

16

Consolidation

In the world of security, consolidation could refer to several different ideas ranging from combining equipment to gathering security personnel into a single location. In this chapter, consolidation applies to consolidating the various Security Control Centers (SCCs) across a company into a single location within that company. Consolidation in the security arena is the direction many major companies are heading. The possibility of saving costs by combining SCCs into a single location is a tempting plan in today's cost cutting environment. Continuing to support multiple SCCs, sometimes at different plant sites within the same city, is an expensive operation that can be combined to save equipment costs and reduce the personnel needed to operate the multiple control centers. The reduction of a single position, which is operated twenty-four hours a day/seven days a week, would be equivalent to reducing the head count of four plus operators or four operators with overtime. In larger control center operations, this reduction can easily amount to two daytime positions, two swing shift positions and one midnight position, totaling a reduction in personnel of ten or more operators. Depending upon the salaries and benefits, the savings can be three to five hundred thousand dollars annually.

Large companies are also evaluating whether or not to consolidate SCC operations on a much wider scale than within the same city or state. There is no reason control centers throughout the United States cannot be consolidated into one location. For years this has been the approach used by the commercial monitoring side of the business. They have found savings in consolidation, so it is only natural that companies that are not specifically in the security monitoring business would take the same approach. The commercial monitoring services have also taken the approach of standardizing data inputs, defining an alarm as an event that needs attention, and providing a descriptor, which provides the proper response to the alarm. It does not matter where the alarm comes from when phone numbers, responsible parties and responding authorities are provided in the consolidated SCC database.

A large corporation's SCC responds to alarms in the same way the consolidated commercial monitoring service responds to alarms. An alarm server/computer displays the alarm's location and provides response instructions that include any necessary contact numbers. Both a commercial monitoring service and a company should have database standards to assure information is consistent from one alarm to another. This is addressed in Chapter 12. There are differences, however. The company SCC tends to have more detail in the alarm location descriptor, because the descriptor describes the exact alarm location within a building for the benefit of the responding security officer who may have to use keys to gain access to the alarmed area. The company alarm types are limited in number based upon the type of industry that the company is in. For example, the types of alarms may differ between companies that process chemicals and an Insurance company. One company will be primarily concerned with toxic chemical spills and the other will primarily be concerned with security alarms and access to their Information Technology (IT) data center.

Even though there are cost benefits and improved standardization across the enterprise with consolidation, there are still some issues that should be considered. One obstacle that must be overcome by a company with multiple locations (that could be consolidated) is the "local is better" issue. The argument is based on the premise that no one can know the local site as well as the security personnel in the SCC at that site. So to properly respond to alarms, the SCC operator and the responding security officer must be familiar with the site. This argument can be overcome by addressing the SCC operator separate from the responding officer. The responding security officer will still respond at the local site; the SCC operator is the only change. It is important to use descriptors that assure enough detail that the responder at the local site will know exactly where the alarm has occurred based upon the descriptor in the database. For large corporations, the concerns of moving the local monitor can be minimized by properly addressing each local site concerns. Then with the support from upper management, based upon their desire to save cost, you can proceed with the consolidation plan. (The primary benefit for upper management is that there will be a substantial dollar savings.) These savings are in themselves justification to proceed with consolidation. The "local-is-better" argument at a plant site is typically more a turf protection issue than a legitimate argument, because the responding officer still resides at the local site. This issue does require diplomacy and time to overcome the local resistance that is bound to exist at a site losing an SCC. This diplomacy must be incorporated prior to consolidating. Referring back to the commercial monitoring business example, they monitor remote locations often across the entire United States. They overcame the local-is-best mentality years ago.

After the decision has been made to proceed with consolidation, many questions need to be resolved.

1. How much functionality will be consolidated?
2. How will functions be performed in the consolidated SCC?
3. How will the database be updated?
4. How will dispatch response be handled?
5. What technology will be used to perform the consolidation?

How much Functionality will be Consolidated?

In the earlier example of commercial monitoring services, the extent of consolidation was limited to alarms. Commercial monitoring services deal with residential, industrial and commercial clients.

Residential users typically have four to eight alarms that need to be monitored. Banks and other institutions have traditionally requested "opening/closing" reports. Openings record when the business is opened and closings show when the business is closed. Openings/closings reports "with-users" can also show which employee entered the numbers into the keypad to access or secure the alarm system. The same opening and closing reports are used in government areas and many locations within a company environment. This level of consolidation of these types of alarms is extremely simple and requires relatively inexpensive equipment. The digital dialer used in the control panel at the house or business field location and a digital receiver at the commercial monitoring service provides the total configuration of a typical commercial monitoring business. A digital receiver at the monitoring company decodes the information, which is usually a location code combined with an alarm or report code. An existing telephone line at the residence or business is often used. The monitoring company interfaces these phone lines through a toll free number to send the information back to the commercial monitoring service where it activates a lookup table that provides the operator with the alarm descriptor and any response instructions, usually the local police and fire departments and emergency contacts.

The consolidation of large company security alarm signals is similar. Alarms are collected in the field via a field panel that usually does some processing and sends the alarms to a server/ computer in the SCC. (This is discussed in detail in Chapter 4.) The alarm is sent via a direct wiring scheme or wireless, over the Internet or Intranet or a phone line. The method will depend upon the company's philosophy and any UL listings or government requirements that must be met. The alarm activates a lookup table in the server/ computer that provides the descriptor and response instructions. The alarms are processed via an operator who dispatches a security officer at the remote site and the alarm is recorded on the server/computer system printer and/or electronic mass data storage.

There are, however, differences between a commercial monitoring service and a consolidated SCC for a large company. In addition to alarms, the security field panels in a large company environment often processes badge readers. The field panel often has memory that can evaluate if an employee has access to a given area without involving the server/computer in the SCC. Typically field panels have some amount of memory (electronic storage capacity) whereby they can store a certain number of user badge credential numbers. In this way, the field panel can recognize a user that presents his or her badge to the reader for the "access grant" process to occur within a fraction of a second, because the appropriate employee information is not only stored in the security access control server/computer, but in the field panel, as well. The acceptance or denial of access is normally handled at the field panel and the result is then sent to the SCC server/computer history log database and documented on the printer. If the field panel does not list the employee requesting access as having access to a given area, some field panels will check with the server to see if the server will allow access. If access is allowed, the employee's access information is downloaded to the field panel and the door lock is released. If access is still denied, the request and denial is recorded in the history log database and on the printer. This is addressed in Chapter 1.

A company's SCC also typically monitors other electronic security functions, such as Closed Circuit Television (CCTV) intercoms, gate controls, energy management, and so on. There is more integrated functionality in the company SCC than in a commercial consolidated control center (Some consolidated commercial monitoring centers do utilize audio and/or CCTV to support the alarm information, due to the number of "sales" alarms that they receive.) In consolidated company SCC the additional security functions received would include CCTV cameras in the field that are connected to a multiplexer in the SCC that sends video to monitors via operator's control or automatically via integration with the security alarm system. This was covered in Chapter 15. All the security functions from each site and the integration of the security functions must be part of the consolidated SCC.

To consolidate an SCC with the functionalities addressed above, a careful study must be performed. The bottom line of that study is to determine what must be consolidated to provide reasonable service at the remote site. It is easy to simply move all functionality to a consolidated SCC without carefully evaluating each function and how it fits into a holistic solution. The basic concept of consolidation is to extend the functions of each remote SCC to a central company SCC, as if you were using an "extension cord" to the consolidated SCC. The "extension cord" can be the Internet, Intranet, or leased data lines such as a T1 line. A precaution of this approach is that all local functionality may not be needed when consolidating. Some functions could be accomplished in another way or be discontinued. The cost effective, as well as the responsible approach requires you to evaluate all activities and functionality presently performed at a remote site and then to make a decision as to whether the task should be continued locally, discontinued or consolidated. The initial expense to build the central consolidated SCC and interconnect the other SCCs will be substantial; however, when considering manpower alone, these initial costs can be recovered quickly. The Return On Investment (ROI) can easily sell this concept to upper management. The cost of the equipment required, digitizing all the SCC functions, and remoting them to a central consolidated SCC as well as any ongoing leased line monthly costs must be included in the ROI calculations.

On the other hand, it would be counterproductive, for example, to remote alarms and access control from a site and leave local site operations to process the other security functions just as they have in the past. For example, instead of leaving an intercom at an entrance that required an SCC operator to talk with the employee/contractor, a telephone could be mounted by the entrance. A nonsecurity person at the site could answer the telephone during the day. The nonsecurity person could page a roving guard to provide support to the person requesting assistance at the entrance. Another possibility is to have a roving guard with a cellular telephone who could receive the phone call directly from the entrance telephone. Either approach would eliminate the need for a consolidated SCC operator to sit at the other end of an intercom to process this type of request, but would add to local site requirements. If the local site did not want to be responsible for answering the call but wanted the task handled at the company consolidated SCC, that could be done also. The goal is to transfer as much of the local SCC type requirements as possible to the consolidated SCC. The solution developed for each site's security functions would depend on many factors. In the above example, the number of people at a given entrance requiring assistance would be one consideration. If very few employees/contractors typically needed assistance, then it might be better to let the local site handle the situation.

Other functions must be evaluated in the same way. Tasks that can be automated should be. Gate controls, for example, might be controlled via a badge reader instead of an intercom or telephone. The badge reader would allow employees who have access to the gate to process through without intervention from the site or a consolidated SCC. This method would also provide a history (inside the access control server/computer history log) of who requested passage through the gate and when. For nonemployees, it might be possible to issue special delivery badges, if the same people and/or companies tend to have a consistent need. This would leave the human intervention either at the remote site or the consolidated SCC to handle on an exceptions-only basis. That would include visitors, contractors or employees who do not have normal access to the gate that would request assistance. A receptionist or someone on the dock could handle the remainder of traffic or it could be handled at the consolidated SCC. Automating functions is discussed in Chapter 13.

The goal of evaluating each function is to decide if a specific function must be consolidated. The decision should be based upon available personnel to handle the function and the cost to send that function to the consolidated SCC. To make an informed decision requires creative thinking and removing yourself from the "business as usual" mode of thinking. Some functions that were being performed by Security may need to be eliminated altogether or shifted to another group. For example, after hours the SCC at a major U.S. company's site provided aspirins and bandages after normal business hours when the health center was closed. The solution was to install vending machines that had these types of items available and place the vending machines throughout the building. This was a function being provided by the Security department that did not provide "added value," but was an evolution of support provided because the site SCC was available after hours and everyone knew where the SCC was located. After all functions have been evaluated and solutions found for handling each of them, the next question should be considered.

How Will Functions Be Performed in the Consolidated SCC?

After the needed functions for consolidation have been determined for the remote sites, then the workload that will be added to the consolidated SCC must be evaluated. Obviously when the consolidated SCC has operators in place, the question becomes "which operator will handle what functions?" This seems fairly simple, but in reality is usually a more difficult problem. Each site that is consolidated will have some unique requirements. For example, a remote site might have a credit union or fitness center inside a controlled building. Nonemployees (a spouse) have access to the credit union or fitness center. To provide control of the movement of people without badges through the facility could be accomplished in several ways. If the controls are the responsibility of the consolidated control center, the electronics and associated "manpower" must be part of the consolidation plan. While alarm monitoring and access logging are typical requirements across the various consolidated sites, the volume of effort each security function provides will impact the SCC operator's workload.

These activities are easy to plan for, since each remote site is consolidated one at a time into the central SCC. Consolidated company SCC, often assign tasks to operators based upon the different functional areas that must be addressed. There might be operations that only handle alarms. Others might only deal with access control issues. Operators may not be able to cleanly segregate the function assignment based on the additional workload provided by a new consolidated site. For example, if an operator usually processes alarms at the consolidated SCC and that operator is presently fully loaded, the alarm monitoring function from the next new consolidated site would need to go to another existing operator who is performing a different task and had some available time. If this approach does not fit into the operational scheme, there are two other options. First, the addition of another operator might be necessary. Second, any other tasks that the operator is already processing, such as access control support, might be moved to another operator and an "alarm" operator could process the new consolidated site alarms.

In the example of a commercial monitoring business, the solution to this workload problem is much more obvious. Since all operators are doing basically the same tasks and the operators are busy, then another operator must be hired. In a large company environment with many distant and diverse operator functions, the distribution of workload is more difficult. The solution will depend totally on the workload at the consolidated control center as the remote site is connected. Proper planning for the consolidations must be considered, but their impact is not certain until they are funded for consolidation. Unfortunately funding can be cut off at any time in today's corporate environment and the impact of the additional workload in the consolidated control center can cause high operator turnover.

HOW WILL THE DATABASE BE UPDATED?

This is an area that is usually overlooked until after the consolidation of the first remote site. There are changes in the alarm system that will continue forever with alarms being added and alarms being removed. The database must be updated to reflect these changes on a timely basis. What usually develops is a centralized data entry group at the consolidated SCC to handle alarm database issues. Commercial monitoring businesses have utilized trained personnel at a central data entry location for several of the same reasons. The most compelling reason is compliance to standard formats for data input. Having consistent alarm numbering schemes, descriptor files, and response instructions for dispatch is a large part of how well the consolidated SCC operator or operators can perform and how effective they are. There are many ways to improve operator confidence and efficiency. Consistent data on the operator's screen is a must. To provide consistency requires a dedicated data entry group. This group must adhere to standards, develop standardized forms to be filled in by the technician installing the field equipment and require timely form request when alarms are installed and/or removed. Any changes in the descriptors or response instructions, such as contact personnel, must be kept up-to-date. Chapter 11 discusses database management in detail.

The access control function might be handled totally differently than the alarm approach just described. If access control badges are made and distributed at the remote site, then activating the badges and setting their authorization at different site readers could be accomplished at the remote location. The system architecture will affect the way that the access control data is entered. The entry of access information into the database still requires standards and spot checks be made by the consolidated SCC data entry group;

however, this function can be a very dynamic process that may require immediate and constant support. The remote site tends to provide the most personal service to its employees, contractors, customers and visitors and will want to have some control of the access for these individuals. If the capability of access control data entry is available at a remote site, it must be limited to only that remote site. If access were needed at a different remote site or the consolidated site, then the designated affected site would control their own access issues. The concept to keep in mind as far as access control via a badge technology should be the same as any visual requirements. For instance, if anyone in the company can go to another site and gain entry into that site by a simple visual check on the badge, the database or databases across the company should allow the same access electronically. Appendix A provides the pros and cons of a consolidated database and several options for that database.

How Will Dispatch Response Be Handled?

Consolidation of an SCC does not eliminate the need for a roving security officer. The need to dispatch upon an alarm is a requirement that must be adhered to whether the consolidated SCC is local or thousands of miles away. For this reason, it is critical to have some type of guard communication between the remote site and the consolidated SCC. This could be an alphanumeric display pager, cellular telephone or radio. If a proprietary radio network is used at a remote site it can be operated from the consolidated SCC, if the necessary equipment and network are in place. The decision of what type of communications will be used to dispatch will ultimately be made based on the bidirectional communication need, allowable delay times, and costs.

What Technology Will Be Used to Perform the Consolidation?

The technology questions will to some extent depend on the answers gained in question #1 (How much functionality will be consolidated?). If only alarms are being consolidated, a dedicated phone line with a dial backup could be used. If other functionalities, such as CCTV, gate controls, and intercoms must be consolidated, then a more extensive communication system such as T1 network or Internet or LAN/WAN must be utilized. A T1 line is basically a digital phone line that allows 1.5 M bit data transfer rates. (The 1.5 M bit bandwidth is composed of 24 blocks of 64 bites of data.) Alarm and most of the other functions can easily process all the data needed in 19.2 K bit rates. The big consumer of bandwidth is CCTV because it requires such a large portion of the communication bandwidth to send "real time" video. For example, usually the field of view for interior camera applications is fairly narrow and in a few seconds, it is possible for a person to pass through the field of view. If the data is not close to "real time," an individual can be in and out of the field of view before non-real-time video can be sent to the consolidated SCC. With compression techniques as well as some loss of video frames, a bandwidth of 384 K bits per second can be used in lieu of real-time video. The monitor displaying the video will show some jerkiness in movement, but this is minimal and will provide acceptable results.

Depending upon the total bandwidth needs, usually the entire T1 capability is not used to bring back a single remote site. The T1 is defined in 24 blocks or channels of 64-Kbit data groups. The blocks/channels are normally referred to as DSOs. For the 19.2 K alarm data, 1 DSO of 64 Kbits would be consumed. When using 384 K for video data, multiple 64 K DSOs will be consumed. (Part of each DSO is consumed by "overhead" that is used by the phone company to manage a T1 line. In reality, there is 56 Kbits available for you to use in each DSO.) This may leave more than half the T1 unused. There could be other groups within the company that would like to use some of the unneeded T1 space. Another option to reduce costs is to order a fractional T1 line. Any remaining blocks of 64 K that are unused may not have to be paid for if a fractional T1 is leased. Depending upon the number of needed 64 K blocks of a fractional T1, the cost savings may be determined. The problem is the cost for a fractional T1 system, if it is a large percentage of the total channels, can often be almost, or as expensive, as an entire T1. Another issue with T1 networks cost is the equipment needed to transmit and receive on the network. When an entire T1 is leased, the equipment usually resides with the company leasing the T1. This equipment is composed of multiplexers and demultiplexers as well as digitizing equipment and line cards that are assigned one of the 24 channels of data. In addition, there may be cost for the video compression and decompression hardware that is normally used to minimize bandwidth needs for CCTV. This is discussed in Chapter 7.

Another approach to sending video that allows less expensive network and equipment is Integrated Services Digital Network (ISDN). This approach is very widespread in Europe, but not widely used by security in the United States. An ISDN network operates at 64 Kbits and uses existing phone lines. The equipment is less complicated and usually belongs to the phone company. The capability is leased similar to T1 lease. (Charged by distance.) One obvious potential problem with ISDN for CCTV applications is the slower transfer rate. To minimize the impact of the slower rate, CCTV ISDN manufacturers utilize one of several approaches. They have high and low resolution displays that can be chosen with a scheme where the lower the resolution, the faster the update and the higher the resolution, the slower the update. They also only change areas or pixels on the display that have had movement since the last update. This minimizes the amount of data that needs to be sent. There are two options, a dual channel ISDN transfer capability that allows 128 K rates or a single channel ISDN that allows a 64 K rate.

The basis for LAN/WAN, Internet, and intranet networks is the Information Protocol (IP) option for data communication. There are many manufacturers that are making alarm, access control systems and cameras that can connect directly to the network without interface equipment. This option is often chosen because of the ease and cost effectiveness of the Internet. Larger companies usually have their own intranet that is already in place and security can use the existing infrastructure, thus saving money for the company. This has driven the convergence between security and the Information Technology (IT) department. I have already addressed some potential issues that should be considered if the desired direction is the company intranet and working with IT so we will not readdress those at this time. If the intranet or Internet is used for alarm and access control, it is important that the security communications be handled as a Virtual Private Network (VPN). It is also important that the data be encrypted. The encryption needs to be robust. This option is very viable for companies that want to consolidate control centers. With proper precautions and addressing any UL issues that might apply, IP networks can work very well to provide communications to a consolidated SCC.

When deciding on establishing a consolidated SCC, the first step is to build a business case for consolidating. This means that Return On Investment (ROI) must be calculated. Normally this is fairly straightforward, because the number of personnel reduced by removing a remote SCC provides an initial cost reduction and a recurring cost reduction year after year. The cost of the consolidated SCC will depend on several factors, such as if an existing SCC can be used, the amount of functionality that will be consolidated, and the number of operators that might need to be added. What functionality will be sent to the consolidated SCC from each remote site is a critical question that is a good starting point. After this question is answered, the design parameters are bounded to some extent. The communication technology solutions for each remote site will be decided by what functions must be consolidated: the bandwidth needed and cost constraints. We have discussed T1, ISDN and IP solutions; however, a technology or combination of technologies could be used. For example, to consolidate a small site, an ISDN could be used to send video and dedicated phone line or lines could be used to send security/fire alarms per code. Access Control could be handled by a single server/computer located at the remote site.

Consolidation is a part of life in corporate America today. A security professional must always be evaluating ways to reduce costs while maintaining or improving level of service. This demand for value added and reduction of cost requires a very careful evaluation of different options. Consolidation is definitely a strong option. Not only does it reduce ongoing costs, but also it tends to make security practices between sites more consistent. This is due to the same SCC operators monitoring different sites as well as eliminating unique tasks that may not be needed or at least not provided by security. This applies to the aspirin and bandage example discussed earlier in this chapter. Appendix B addresses a security audit. A security audit can be an effective way to standardize remote site security and understand any unique site practices. Thinking must be outside the normal boundaries if a consolidated SCC is to become a successful reality. Often, using a team of representatives from different areas within the company is a good way to facilitate this type of thinking. The team should include at least one representative from the local site to improve support for the project and provide information on unique issues that must be addressed. The design of the consolidated SCC is even more important than an SCC at a single site because there will normally be multiple operators and much more responsibility. Chapter 10 addresses design considerations for an SCC. As more sites are added to the consolidated SCC, the reliability of the security system becomes much more critical and downtime must be minimized. There needs to be a recovery plan or business continuity plan if a major disaster occurs at the consolidated SCC. This could be redundant hardware as well as a backup remote site monitoring capability. The successful consolidated SCC also requires a backup plan because all your eggs are in one basket. Consolidation is a good solution to today's pressures to reduce costs within the security department of large companies. The consolidated SCC requires careful planning to arrive at the desired result.

17
Maintenance and Testing

Security system maintenance and testing seems to be a topic that does not deserve a whole chapter. The topic appears to be straightforward and obvious. The typical approach for addressing maintenance issues is when something breaks—fix it. This is the manner in which many companies handle the maintenance of their security systems. You have heard such comments as "if it ain't broke, don't fix it." As far as testing, most companies do not spend the time or money to test their security systems unless required to do so by a customer such as the Department of Defense, the company's insurance carrier, or under-writers' laboritories (UL). Testing of fire systems is required at various intervals during the year by local codes and the NFPA. In our discussion in this chapter, we will address maintenance first and then the testing aspects. These functions are tied together, because testing often shows problems that must be addressed by repairing the equipment. Maintenance can be broken down into three areas: requested, preventive and predictive.

REQUESTED MAINTENANCE

Requested maintenance is the approach that is taken by the vast majority of Security departments—that is, the "fail-and-fix" mode

263

of maintenance. Preventive and predictive maintenance on security systems is not normally considered to be a cost effective approach; therefore, requested maintenance is the norm. Door sensors are an extremely reliable component of a security system and operate for hundreds of thousands of openings and closings and should only be fixed when broken, physically damaged or misaligned. To send technicians out to perform preventive or predictive maintenance on door sensors would appear to be a waste of time and money. The problem with door sensors is that it is not always possible to know when the equipment has failed. When a door sensor fails and the Security department does not know about it, there can be a security breach. For example, if the door sensor fails when the door is in the closed position, the security system will not show a failure. This happens when the contacts inside the door sensor relay stick together. There will be no alarm or trouble signal if the door sensor fails in the normally closed position. (This was discussed in Chapter 4.) This situation can easily occur when the building takes a lightning strike, or a near strike, and high voltage spikes throughout the building are coupled into the security wires fusing the contacts in the door switch together. When the sensor is on an emergency exit door that is normally not used, the problem will not surface until it is operated during an emergency and it is reported. To prevent security breaches of this type, it is important to know when equipment such as a door switch is broken and needs repair. To avoid problems such as this, a schedule can be developed that requires all door sensors to be tested. A yearly test is a good way to check for defective sensors on emergency doors. A security officer can proceed through a building activating all emergency door alarms once a year and checking with the Security Control Center (SCC) to be sure that the alarm was received and verify that the descriptor in the alarm database is correct. The yearly check can be expanded to include other security alarms, which allows the responding officer to better understand what alarms are in what location, which will then provide better officer response during a real alarm activation. Testing will be discussed in more detail later in this chapter.

Requested maintenance works well for problems in the security system where failures are known. The main issue here is to decide the source of the problem and not just the symptom. Several examples of this have been provided in other chapters, so for brevity we will discuss nuisance alarms coming from a sensor. Motion detectors can commonly display this problem. For example, a motion detector is reported as alarming X number of times during the night. The actual source of the problem could be incorrect placement of the motion detector and it is alarming because of motion that is not expected, such as banners and free-hanging lightweight signs waving when the HVAC comes on. If the motion detector is simply replaced, as the solution to the requested maintenance, then the repair effort was only looking at the symptom, not the solution. All maintenance should be performed with a holistic approach to a problem and not simply a swap out plan, which delays the actual repair and frustrates the SCC operators and responding officers.

Normally when a motion detector fails, it will fail in a state that prevents it from detecting motion and the only way to find that problem would be during a scheduled test. This situation is similar to the door sensor example where lightning fuses the sensor together. Testing must be scheduled to find these problems. There are hard failures that are easy to find and requested maintenance is the best way to solve them. To address issues of a hard failure, we must also consider examples of a camera that failed or a badge reader that stopped working. These problems can easily be repaired through a replacement process via requested maintenance. If a camera stops working, the solution is simple. Often the camera does not totally fail, but its performance starts to degrade and the requested maintenance does not occur until the picture quality is unacceptable. In the case of the badge reader failing, it can be replaced, but the impact to the employees/contractors of the company will be much greater than the early motion detector example. If a badge reader fails, it will most likely impact a large number of people, depending upon its location and usage.

The downsizing and tight budgets that are part of today's corporate right-size environment have also reduced maintenance to the fail-and-fix level even in cases where maintenance was expected and planned for in the budget. These added pressures cause management to evaluate the impact of the part of the security system that is inoperative and decide if their cost of repair is warranted. The length of downtime must be weighed against the costs of the needed repair, impact on security and the impact on employees/customers/visitors. When downtime is acceptable in an organization, the only type of maintenance needed is requested maintenance; however, there are problems with the requested-only maintenance approach.

One problem with this method is inconvenience. Failures never occur at a convenient time; often they occur after hours, on the weekends or holidays. These situations require a period of downtime until repair personnel are available or called in on over-time for the needed support. A second problem with the fail-and-fix method is that the failures seem to always follow Murphy's Law. When a card access system reader fails, it will be when a member of senior management is trying to use it. These situations often cause the Security department to appear unprofessional or unprepared and can develop a tremendous amount of stress for the SCC opera-tors. A third problem is the failure often occurs when other factors make it difficult to determine the exact cause of the problem. For example, during an access control system upgrade, a computer disk failure occurs causing tremendous confusion as to the source of the actual problem. The failed disk can cause corrupted data to be processed by the server/computer. The first conclusion of the repair technician might be that there is a problem with the software upgrades when, in reality, the failed disk is being "masked" by the new software upgrade that is in progress.

For the requested maintenance approach to be successful requires proper reporting, notification and documentation. The maintenance report must include all the critical detail needed for a technician to make a timely repair. This would include the details of the actual problem, its location, time of failure, a contact person, and any charge/cost accounting information, if required. At this point, there must be a decision as to the time frame in which the maintenance problem must be addressed. Can the repair wait until the next business day to be fixed at a normal hourly rate or must it be handled sooner? The normal options besides the next business day might include a one- or four-hour response. The decision as to the needed response time is normally driven by the seriousness of the failure and the dollar cost for a quick or after-hours response. Is the problem a must-fix immediately or a next-business-day problem? The cost associated with the repair will be affected by the required response time and whether a contract for maintenance is in place with an alarm company or other provider. A maintenance contract should address different response times and the associated costs as well as any holiday and after-hours premiums. The contract should address when the response time starts: Is it from the time the technician is called and starts toward the company site, or is it the time the technician must be on site ready to repair the problem? After all, the particular technician could live a few miles away or a hundred miles away.

The maintenance contract discussed above assumes that there is not an in-house group that handles maintenance issues. If there is a maintenance group in-house, the cost of a callout may or may not be an issue; however, the rest of the discussion still applies. A common callout problem is that the SCC operators do not normally like to make the decision to call the technician, much less decide how much of an emergency the maintenance issue is in the first place. It should be the responsibility of the SCC operator's supervisor to decide the need to call a technician and the timeliness required for the technician's response. In most large companies, a repair technician will be available during the daytime, but after-hours tends to be when such problems occur.

It is important that the SCC document the maintenance problem, who was notified and when the problem was addressed. For a UL certified area, any repairs must be addressed within a defined period of time. If there is a failure of the alarm system server in the SCC, it must be addressed and back online within one hour. Another reason to document the actual repairs that has not been discussed is for the operator's benefit. For example, a motion detector may send a large number of alarms into the SCC, but when the technician arrives, the motion detector appears to be operating correctly. The technician might test the motion detector's coverage and leave the area with no resolved repair. It is important that the technician complete a write-up on his or her findings, and that information should be readily available to the SCC operators. In this way, when the motion detector causes additional nuisance alarms in the future, the operator can verify that the motion detector has been checked and the new problem is not just caused by a lack of interest on the technician's part. Otherwise, the SCC operator will assume that the whole requested maintenance process of reporting alarms is just a waste of time.

It is important at this point to address the maintenance contract in more detail. The goal of such a contract is to define response times and set rates. There will be different hourly rates that must be defined and possibly different skill levels of the responding technicians. For each response time and technician level, an hourly rate must be stated. For a one-hour callout, the holiday hourly rate will typically be significantly different from a callout during normal business hours. The alarm company will often want the after-hours callouts to be for a minimum amount of time— typically four hours. That means if a technician is called out after hours, payment would be for four hours at a minimum even if the repair took only five minutes. For example, they might come to the site after hours and only need to reset a field panel to correct the problem. Another issue that the contract should address is travel time: Do you pay for the time it takes a technician to drive from home after hours to your site and the travel time for them to return to their home? All these types of issues should be covered (worked out ahead of time) and written in the contract. On the other hand, a one-hour callout rate might work well for you. This will typically run three to four times the normal hourly rate to cover problems that are similar to those in the rebooting of a field panel example. You may only pay the high hourly rate while the technician is onsite. This would save cost versus the four hour minimum type of contract. If preventive and/or predictive maintenance were incorporated, the contract would need to address not only hourly rates, but also material cost. The materials can be at a predetermined markup from wholesale or a percentage deduction from list price or a price can be established for commonly replaced items. When dealing with materials, the premiums that must be paid by the service provider for rush items must also be written into the contract/agreement or the service provider must keep items in stock. The other approach is to set a yearly rate that includes labor and material to perform certain stated maintenance.

A maintenance contract that would normally cover a new installation is not what has been discussed. When a new installation project is bid, there is often a maintenance contract that can be part of that bid. The maintenance contract is often a percentage of the project's installation cost. The amount often runs around 15 percent and takes effect after the normal warranty period ends (usually one year). This type of maintenance contract is normally purchased by the end user under the premise that they do not have to worry about support and repairs, because it will be taken care of for a monthly or yearly fee in the form of this type of maintenance contract. It provides some peace of mind and is similar to a warranty plan that can be purchased on a new automobile (for the next seven years or seventy-five thousand miles all repairs will be covered). As you know, those warranties may not cover all situations, and the same is true for this type of maintenance contract. The contract must be read carefully; if not, the results may be disappointing. This type of contract will cover some of the issues we have been discussing; however, the discussion was based on a "callout only" type of maintenance contract, not a contract driven by a percentage of the system installation cost. The alarm company will want a percentage type contract, but it is normally cheaper to set up a callout type of maintenance contract. No matter how the maintenance is paid for, the goal is to avoid the inconvenience, embarrassment, and confusion of failures that will occur with a requested maintenance-only plan. Alternative maintenance measures are needed. Manufacturers have developed extremely reliable products, but no matter the level of effort or quality, it is inevitable that products will fail over time. Even military hardware that must comply with rigid requirements of temperature and vibration still experience failure. To minimize failures, there are two other forms of maintenance that can be used: preventive and predictive.

PREVENTIVE MAINTENANCE

This approach incorporates a time-based system for maintenance and provides for routine maintenance of various security components. For example, if a VCR requires that the heads be cleaned every 2,000 hours and a schedule is set to clean the heads quarterly, then the maintenance is preventive. For preventive maintenance to be effective, each piece of equipment to be maintained must have documentation that includes any recommendations from manufacturers, generally accepted industry practices and history of failures, or Mean Time Between Failures (MTBF). These are all necessary to establish reasonable and cost effective time increments between maintenance efforts. Preventive maintenance is very effective for electromechanical systems or systems that must comply with certain regulations from insurance carriers, the government, some other regulatory group or by code.

Another variation of preventive maintenance is to replace components on a set time interval. It can be more cost effective to throw a correctly operating component away at a set time interval rather than have it fail in service. An example in another industry illustrates the efforts that have been made to quantify the preventive maintenance approach. The electrical industry has found it is cheaper to replace fluorescent lamps on a periodic basis than to handle the defective ballast caused from lack of lamp replacement. The ambient temperature of the area where the lighting fixture resides, the frequency of lamp replacements, and the rate of activation of the fixture will all affect the ballast failure time frame. A closer look at this approach helps us determine why this type of maintenance is cost effective.

Ballasts are a fairly expensive component in fluorescent lighting fixtures. By incorporating preventive maintenance on the lamps, the lifetime of the ballast can be doubled. This approach replaces cheaper components, the lamps, while saving the more expensive component, the ballast. Another way to save money is by buying a large quantity of lamps at a single time to reduce the cost per lamp. Fluorescent lamps are rated to last 15,000 to 20,000 hours. (The lumen level drops as the lamp ages.) If the lamps are replaced every 2 years, the lighting level remains satisfactory and the ballast can last as long as 10 years. To replace defective ballasts cost more money and inconvenience to the building occupant than simply replacing the bulbs on a fixed time interval.

Additionally, when ballast failures start, they will typically occur in the other fixtures in the same area fairly soon after the initial failure of the first ballast. Ballast failures often cause smoke, which disrupts the workplace and can cause an unnecessary building evacuation, which affects more employees than just those in the area where the ballast failed. Then another ballast will fail causing the above process to repeat itself. After several ballast repair trips to the same location, it becomes obvious it would have been better to replace all the lamps on a set time schedule instead of the numerous, more costly, and more disruptive replacement of ballasts.

Security systems have functions that would fit well into this type of preventive maintenance scenario. If we look at the functions that compose typical security systems, several areas could use preventive maintenance.

1. Fire alarms
2. Security alarms
3. CCTV system
4. Access control
5. Audio/Communication systems

The smoke detectors in the fire alarm system need to be cleaned yearly which can be easily accomplished via a preventive maintenance program. The number of smoke detectors is known and an hourly rate can be established per smoke detector and replacement detector cost can also be established. This will eliminate false alarms and allow you to meet NFPA 25 and NFPA 72 requirements. Security alarms do not fit well into a preventive maintenance program due to the reliability discussed earlier in this chapter. The exception would be exterior sensors such as fence alarms. The fence fabric should be tightened on a yearly basis and vegitation removed around the fence to prevent false alarms.

Another example for preventive maintenance is the CCTV system. Exterior CCTV housings often use a blower, which is needed to keep the camera cool in the summertime. An air filter associated with the fan needs cleaning on a preventive basis. The viewing window that the camera "sees" through must also be cleaned on a periodic basis. An example of preventive maintenance for access control systems would be associated with the many different types of portals that are used. Revolving doors and gate controls, for example, require lubrication, adjustment/testing of safety controls and component replacement on a periodic basis. Many of the failures within all of these functions can be effectively minimized or eliminated with preventive maintenance. Audio/communication systems, such as radio transmitters, can require a yearly maintenance plan to assure that they are operating within frequency and that they are radiating at the desired approved level. Even the radios themselves should utilize a deep cycle charger to extend the battery life. By deep cycling nickel cadmium batteries, they last longer and do not develop a memory. A memory causes the battery to charge to a certain point based upon repeated charges and short usage and will then operate only for a time period similar to the last time period. It is as though the battery has memorized how long it will last before recharging. Replacement batteries for radios are costly, and proper care/recharging will extend their usability.

When incorporating preventive maintenance, it is important to keep in mind the value and level of requested maintenance associated with each component. It is not cost effective to perform preventive maintenance on a VCR, for example, that has experienced several major failures in the last year. The cost of new equipment versus maintenance costs must always be weighed. When preventive maintenance is not used and requested maintenance is high, it may be cost effective to replace the VCR. To properly evaluate the level of maintenance performed on a preventive maintenance basis, a software program that documents all preventive, predictive, and requested maintenance is needed. The maintenance software program allows the technician to check on previous maintenance issues and automatically provides preventive and predictive maintenance notification for each component. This software requires proper data inputting at the start of the maintenance program and it must be continually updated with changes and any maintenance that is performed.

PREDICTIVE MAINTENANCE

Predictive maintenance is focused on the condition of equipment based on measurable data. This type of maintenance requires data defining normal operation and characteristics of components prior to operational failure. For example, if the current of a pump is being monitored, the predictive maintenance can be determined. As the pump reaches the point prior to replacement, the current needed to operate the pump increases. Higher than normal motor run current is usually caused by defective or dry bearings. (By monitoring the current, an alarm can be activated when the pump reaches a potential failure point based on the current it draws.) The high run current alarm for the pump will indicate it is time to lubricate or replace bearings. In this case, simple bearing maintenance when the alarm is received is much cheaper than pump replacement, not to mention any hidden costs due to downtime. In security systems, one obvious example from the list of security functions is fire alarm equipment. Fire panels manufactured in the recent past can monitor the sensitivity of the sensing element within each smoke detector.

As the smoke detectors get dirty, the current within the detector circuit starts approaching a fire alarm level. The panel monitors the smoke detector sensing obscuration and notifies the SCC operator, via the fire panel, that certain smoke detectors are dirty and need to be cleaned, thereby preventing false alarms and possibly building evacuations.

Predictive maintenance is probably the least used maintenance approach in electronic security. There are applications as shown above; however, the cost associated with and applications that fit with this type of maintenance are limited. Earlier we discussed the push to limit overhead budgets such as Security department budgets, which put pressure on all types of maintenance. If requested maintenance can be decided on a cost versus impact approach, then predictive maintenance must be driven by safety issues, regulations or employee/customer satisfaction. We have discussed smoke detector obscuration as being an example of safety predictive maintenance. Smoke detector obscuration would also apply to regulations. The Fire Marshall, the company insurance carrier and NFPA 25 and 72 require yearly cleaning of smoke detectors. But because the fire panel is verifying the level of obscuration or sensitivity of each detector, not all detectors must be cleaned each year. As far as an employee or customer predictive maintenance issue example, we can consider a temperature alarm for out-of-specs temperatures. A freezer in the company cafeteria that gets too warm can allow meat to spoil and possibly cause employees and contractors to get sick. A loss-of-alternating current (ac) alarm for the company data center might cause the data center to crash with many possible impacts on employees.

Now let's consider a few thoughts on maintenance in general. The level of maintenance a system requires will depend to a large extent on the quality of the installation. One way to minimize maintenance in the first place is to correctly install sensors to mitigate nuisance alarms, correctly terminate all connections, use the correct wire gauges, and follow "good construction" practices. Many maintenance problems develop from one of these four areas. The design of the system can also affect the maintenance. For example, many designers and most contractors will place equipment in the easiest location for the installer. This reduces cost at least for the installation contractor. When an electronic control panel for a door that has badge readers is installed, it will often be placed above the door it is controlling. This keeps wiring short and provides a known location to electronically and physically check the operation of the door. There are two potential issues with this type of installation. First, a ladder is required during a repair to gain access to the panel. Second, the door must be blocked during any repair time to keep employees, contractors, customers and visitors from trying to enter and developing a safety hazard for themselves and the repair technician. This is typically undesirable because they must go to another door or try to dodge the technician and ladder, or the repair must be performed at scheduled times only. By placing the electronic controls in a field panel area within the building, there is no inconvenience to the employees, contractors, customers and visitors. This approach does require that wires be run from the door back to the field panel location, but it is a one-time cost. This same location can have multiple doors and electronic field panels located in the same area. Field panel consolidated locations are an effective way to centralize and control access to the door controls. In larger buildings, it is very likely that there will be five or more of these data-gathering locations. In high-rise buildings it is desirable to have one or more of these areas on each floor of the building. This approach will, in the long term, reduce ongoing maintenance cost.

Testing has been briefly mentioned in this chapter. Testing is often overlooked because of the associated costs. As mentioned, NFPA 25 and 72 require the testing of fire systems. Some customers, such as the government, require testing alarms for areas of the building within the company that they occupy. An example would be closed areas that have a government clearance requirement. Testing of these areas is often monthly but if the areas are covered by a UL certification, a yearly documented test is required. There should be testing of all perimeter alarms once a year to assure proper operation and descriptors in the database. Any testing of alarms should be documented and descriptors in the database should be verified. A standardized form should be developed to record this information and provide an audit trail. It is also a responsible plan to perform testing of any safety systems, such as those associated with revolving doors or turnstiles. The benefit in performing the safety test with a third party is that it limits your company's liability associated with the operation of the equipment.

A test form should be developed that is checked off, dated and signed by the third-party representative.

The goal of any security system is to operate without failures, nuisance alarms, and false alarms. Proper design can mitigate nuisance alarms as well as system failures. The incorporation of lightning protection on power, phone lines, and wiring that goes outside of the physical building can greatly minimize weather related failures. Proper maintenance can also assure minimal false alarms and system failures. To develop the ideal maintenance program, all three facets of maintenance must be incorporated—preventive, predictive, and requested. Because it is impossible to have a system operational 100 percent of the time, it is critical to incorporate preventive and predictive maintenance to minimize requested maintenance. These preventive and predictive maintenance procedures should be increased at most companies and will minimize surprises, which in turn decrease the requested maintenance side. The maintenance plan should define the source of technical support whether in-house or provided by an outside contractor. Part of your maintenance plan must include training, spares inventory, support technicians and response planning. Downtime must be kept to a reasonable level so the Security department will not be evaluated based upon this potential weak link. Properly implementing the three legs of the maintenance triangle will reduce overall costs, improve performance, and enhance confidence in your security program at your company.

18

Security Design Process

For most security managers, a tremendous effort goes into the approval process for a new installation project. Months and maybe years go by, having areas with poor security or a Security Control Center (SCC) that is inadequate and inefficient. The frustration of dealing with these types of problems is only part of the ordeal. Major effort is expended to obtain the "buy in" of upper management to fund security projects. Security is always competing against other groups within the company for limited funding. As companies focus on their core business, it is even more difficult to designate funds for security, when it could be used by the part of the company that makes money. The Security department is considered a "necessary evil" and an overhead burden on the company. Although the Security department does not normally make a profit, it does enable other departments to do so.

When the funding does become available for that much needed project, the last thing a security manager needs is a final product that does not work as expected, overruns cost projections, or is poorly installed. There are many pitfalls that can occur during this phase. The fact most security professionals do not understand is that the level of effort spent to develop the project and receive funding is only a small part of their total effort to successfully implement a security project. In this chapter, we will look at the tasks that are necessary to obtain a successful security project installation. Typically, the assumption exists that the Purchasing department, the architect, the Facilities department, the legal group and other consultants will assure the desired results. Although their expertise is important, it is foolish to transfer responsibility for the project to these departments. Upper management will place overall responsibility on you for the outcome of the project.

To assure that the project will be successful requires that the steps up to the point of acceptance of the project were properly handled. It is important to go back to the beginning of any project and follow through each step. These steps are usually followed more closely when a new site is first being designed or the security effort is part of a large construction project; however, they apply to any project.

1. Security survey/vulnerability assessment
2. Functional requirements
3. Design
4. Procurement
5. Installation
6. Testing
7. Initial operation
8. Ongoing support

SECURITY SURVEY

This is a step in the process that should be viewed as a fresh look at the site and what is vulnerable. It is often performed on new sites or new applications or is a redo of an existing site but can be performed on any reasonable size project. The results of the survey should address potential security and safety issues such as, sensitive data protection, executive protection, safety of employees entering and leaving, crime in the area, facilities shared with other tenants, exterior lighting issues, security-in-depth for government contactors, and so on. Appendix B covers a site security audit for existing sites, but the information can apply to new projects. These concerns should be compiled into a list that should be addressed in the upcoming project. The goal is to gather all the security risks and vulnerabilities into a documented form; then a list of functional requirements can be generated. There are also software packages available to help guide you through a thorough risk assessment process. The level of detail and formality will typically be based on the size of the future corrective actions or the sensitivity of the facility.

FUNCTIONAL REQUIREMENTS

This step is often overlooked or thought to be part of the security survey, which it can be. For the purposes of this book it will be addressed in more detail. Usually a survey is performed, or, at a minimum, the security professional thinks through basic vulnerabilities and risks before designing a solution. For example, there is vehicle parking so we need cameras here, there and over there. The concept is that a risk has been defined and using a certain functional security component placed in a given location can mitigate that risk. If there is pressure to reduce cost later, the cost is reduced by removing equipment, based on thinking, "we can add cameras in the parking lot at a later date." There is no way to prioritize the functional requirements because none were developed. Components were suggested, but the actual requirement was not documented. This is the tact taken by most security professionals and many consultants. The very best solutions to address security issues are driven by proper development of functional requirements.

What are functional requirements? These are the risks and vulnerabilities expressed in word form that relate to the actual issue. Instead of saying we need cameras in the parking lot to view the lot for safety and theft, you would say something like "One requirement is to assure employee safety because of to the high crime area around the building." A list of such requirements should be generated and then listed in priority. This way as each requirement is reviewed, solutions can be developed that solve the problem and may address other requirements at the same time. If the budget is reduced, then there is a logical way to remove cost based upon removal of the lower priority functional requirements. For example, back to our functional requirement that employee safety is a vulnerability. There are several ways to address that issue: a fence can be installed, cameras can be placed in the parking lot, lighting can be added, a security officer can be visible in and around the facility, badge readers can be placed on the doors, emergency call boxes can be installed throughout the parking lot and grounds, and so on. This is not simply a word-smithing exercise; it is a way of defining and prioritizing vulnerabilities in a logical manner. This allows you to deal with budgets and management on a logical level versus arguing about cameras in the parking lot.

DESIGN

A great deal of interest exists in this step in the process, but is often poorly performed. All too often, you will have many "experts" who are all too willing to "help." The steps in the process must be built on each other. If, for example, there were no security survey or functional requirements developed, then the design step is doomed to failure. The design stage is a desirable time to have a team formed that will be stakeholders during the entire project process. This means that legal, purchasing, upper management, facilities, and so on, should be involved. The design step is itself broken into several steps. Normally the design will be broken into percent completion stages: often 10 percent, 30 percent, 90 percent, and 100 percent. Obviously the earlier problems are found or changes made, the cheaper the impact. For example, if security equipment placement changes are needed at the 10 or 30 percent point, the changes are just lines on a piece of paper. At the 90 or 100 percent point, the changes can impact the schedule and add major design/drafting rework time. For example, on a major project an architect will have a door schedule which includes having all the doors in the new building in a matrix, notes as to installation, the way the door swings, its composition, hardware on the door, and so on. If a change is made to a door at this stage, all references to the door or doors involved must be changed. This can be a major rework of the drawings and has a potential of introducing errors into the drawings. These errors can cause confusion to the contractors or costly change orders later during installation.

The security portion of most large projects is part of the drawing package that will be supplied to bidders. The security-related items can be located in Section 16 of the drawings, which is the electrical section; for example, section 16720 was fire alarms, 16760 was Closed Circuit Television (CCTV), and so on. The Construction Specification Institute (CSI) defines the various sections. They have recently modified the sections to address facilities services subgroups, which include communications and security. Most of the time the electrical contractor will bid the fire and security work as part of the electrical package. The electrical contractor does not normally perform the work, but hires licensed security/fire contractors to install the systems. (Not all states require security installers to be licensed.) One of the challenges of a solid design package is to define the tasks that will be performed by the different contractors. The building industry has standard responsibilities as far as which tasks are performed by which trade groups. (This is especially true in areas that have unions.) It is important to understand which craft does what type of work. Either you must understand or have someone involved who does understand them and provide you with any potential issues. One example is something as simple as an electrified crash bar for an emergency door exit. The normal nonunion process is that the electrical contractor would provide the wire for the electrified crash bar, the door hardware contractor would install the door, and the security contractor or the door hardware contractor would install the crash bar. There are hookup issues, responsibility issues and budget issues. Assuming all the details are provided to assure installation and wiring to be installed, as you wanted it, but the last question is where does the crash bar cost reside in the project? Is this a security cost or a building cost and have all the trades involved understood your desired result? This can, to some extent, be covered in a walkthrough that will be discussed later in this chapter.

PROCUREMENT

The bid document can take one of two basic approaches. The document can be a performance specification or a detailed design specification. A performance specification sets established requirements to which the end product must comply. The specification will not address all the details of an actual product, but what the product needs to accomplish. For example, the performance specification might require that a camera be able to view a one-foot-square target at night with only moonlight at a distance of 250 feet from the building and be able to identify whether it is a person, an object or an animal. These requirements can be tested after the camera system is installed. The other approach is a detailed design specification. In this document, it is important to provide all details needed to complete the project. In the earlier example of the camera, a detailed design document would specify the lens, its focal length, F-stop, color or black-and-white and neutral density filter (if required) as well as the model of the camera, lines of resolution, and lumen level. A detailed design specification covers all details that must be met while performance specification details the desired results. Both of these approaches have limitations, so many times the final document includes both types of specification. It is important for the bidder to know what the desired result is. It is also important to detail some of the project to make sure certain criteria are complied with.

The challenge at this stage is to find a bidder or bidders (if competitive bids are required) that are qualified, fairly priced, and have expertise in the exact environment you have for the project at hand. General contractors very often have their "pet" subcontractors they like to use who may or may not meet your desired security expertise and experience. Interview security contractors carefully, ask for references and don't be afraid to shop around. When checking references it is important to talk with people who really know how good a specific contractor is. The higher the level of manager in the company or even within the Security department the odds are they will not know or do not want to admit that a contractor did not do a good job. Prospective bidders should be able to prove that they have done similar projects with similar environments, similar scopes of work, and similar timetables. Often, national firms will show similar projects, but the portion of their company that provided the work may not be the local provider. Thus the company has the experience, but the local workers may not. If at all possible, there should be at least three bidders that are prequalified. The procurement and legal departments should verify financial viability, any existing/pending lawsuits, Dun and Bradstreet status, and whether they pay their suppliers and subcontractors in a reasonable time period (usually 30 days). Never invite a company to a bid conference that you would not want to do the job.

The goal, after the bidders have been approved, is to find the best security contractor. The best contractor will provide your company with a price and service that assures the "lowest cost of ownership" solution. If price alone is the deciding factor, the probability that you will be disappointed increases. The Procurement department should work with you to develop a list of items that are critical to the project's success. These items should be weighted and a matrix developed that makes the final decision obvious. The items used in the weighting process should be listed in the bid document, not the actual weight or percent given to each item, but the items that are important as well as the order of their importance should be listed. For example, the bid document might indicate that the following items would be used to evaluate the bid and their level of importance is in descending order: staffing, schedule, numbers of exceptions, maintenance support, price, and warranties. Another approach is to send a request for proposal. This approach allows the contractor to tell you how they would accomplish what you want done and the cost. The level of importance might be as follows: technical proposal, staffing, schedule, numbers of exceptions, maintenance support, price, and warranties. This list does not show the weight, but it does indicate that the price will not be the driving factor.

Other important aspects of the bid document are general payment schedules or plan, special company requirements, breach of contract, safety codes, any training, guidelines that must be followed, submission requirements, bonds, insurance requirements, performance clauses (if used) and so on. The Legal and Procurement departments should have a "boiler plate" that covers most of these issues in the Terms and Conditions (Ts&Cs) of the issued purchase order. If the work must be performed on the weekend or after hours, these requirements should be under the special company items. For a contractor to bid a job correctly, they must know any special requirements and how they are to be paid. All these items affect their cost and therefore affect the overall bid price.

Before the actual bids are received it is critical that pre-bid meetings be held. Mandatory pre-bid meetings will resolve many potential issues. During these meetings questions will arise that may clarify or uncover problems with the bid proposal. Either way, the potential pitfalls are identified before awarding the contract. The questions and answers during the pre-bid meetings should always be published and sent to all concerned parties. The walk-through will also assure that all potential bidders understand the project and the environment in which they will be working. Often additional questions arise during the walkthrough that must be answered and distributed in writing. Answers to all questions asked by any bidder after the bid conference should be mailed or Emailed to all bidders, so that all bidders will know the answers to all questions. When the final document is sent out for bids, it is important to set a time frame for a written response. The exact items that the bidder is to supply in their response to the "request for bid" should also be listed. The time frame should be reasonable based on the size of the project. Two weeks to a month would provide adequate time for most projects. All bidders must know the bid delivery location and contact person. Any bid supplied late should be rejected unless an extension has been granted to all bidders. Remember the clearer the project, the environment, and the expectations, the better the pricing will be to allow an "apples to apples" comparison. A bidder will increase the bid for unknowns where they would be likely to lose money.

The time to review the bids as well as the winning bid announcement time and the proposed start date/schedule should be known to the bidders. The goal is to share as much as possible with all the bidders to promote a better understanding on their part as to what is expected. This will also help them provide a more complete bid. This includes any expectations or requirements that you may have about weekend work or access requirements for the contractor to work in certain areas. Another thing to remember is that contractors make easy money on "change orders." The more detailed the specifications and pre-bid meetings are, the fewer the change orders. It is, however, almost impossible to do a project of any size without some change orders. It is also difficult to make every aspect of the project totally clear. A common problem is delegation of responsibility which must be defined, and if it is different from accepted construction processes it must be clear. As in our crash bar example: the door hardware is usually the responsibility of the contractor installing the door. These crash bars can be very expensive and become a major issue if the responsible purchasing, installing and wire termination parties are not defined in the bid document.

In the final selection of a contractor, the weighted contractor evaluation matrix should provide an obvious answer. The matrix will also eliminate feelings or other unnecessary data in the evaluation process, assuring that the contractor selection is logical and fair. A detailed check should be performed by carefully studying these bids. Any obvious oversights of a bidder, disclaimers, or product substitutions should be reviewed by Purchasing with the bidders. A sanity check is to evaluate the price spread. Qualified bidders with similar experience should fall within 10 to 20 percent of each other. A wider spread usually indicates a misconception or incomplete bid. There are times, however, when a bidder needs work to keep the crew employed or they want to "buy" their way into a company. These reasons are fine as long as the bid document locks the bidder into fixed hourly rates and markup on parts, if the relationship continues.

Once a bidder and/or a manufacturer of equipment has been selected there is a marriage bond. Like it or not, there are legal and long-term obligations that come to pass after a bid is accepted. Therefore, it is critical that care is taken in selecting the bidder. The bid document and specifications must make it clear what is to be done and how the work is to be performed and measured. Neither side sees the other's imperfections until the marriage is complete. Either both parties will enjoy a meaningful relationship or there will be a troubled marriage and/or legal issues. The way the project is bid out to a large extent will measure the success of this relationship. The level of control that you have on the security component of a large project will vary depending upon your relationship within the company and the importance of security in the entire project. Obviously, if the project is primarily a security project, you should be engaged and virtually everything discussed under this topic should apply.

INSTALLATION

The implementation segment of the multistep process includes installation, testing and initial operation. These are the areas most often thought of as "the project." In reality, these steps will be discussed separately. Each of these critical steps requires careful oversight and system understanding. The installation step is a crucial time for the security professional to be involved. It is not mandatory that you are a technical or construction expert, but what is important is that you become involved. Typically there will be weekly construction meetings held with the company's representatives, the architect, the general contractor and sometimes subcontractors. There will be other meetings between the general contractor and subcontractors that your company may not be a part of. In a large construction project, security is normally a small piece of the project, which means that it can be covered at the beginning or the end of the meeting so that your presence will not be required for the entire meeting. It is important to ask questions and be sure that the security system being installed is what you are expecting. No one in the meeting expects you to be a construction expert. By asking questions, you force the experts to think through items they may have glossed over. You should also understand the basic schedule and what is happening. For example, if you are aware that they plan to pour concrete next Monday, it is in your best interest to check that the conduits for your system that should be in the concrete are physically in place before next week. If the conduit that goes to the receptionist's desk in the lobby is not in place when the concrete is poured then you will have a very expensive modification to deal with later. The longer the project goes before the missing conduit is discovered the more cost is involved. If the lobby marble floor is laid and the desk is in place when the missing conduit becomes known the cost is major. You could argue that the conduit is the electrician's problem and that he or she should have installed it. The problem with that argument is that they will probably not go back and modify the lobby because of the delays in occupying the building, so the general contractor will give your company some type of concession that will be used to pay for something else that was forgotten (probably not part of the security project). You end up with no panic button or door release button or intercom for the receptionist unless it is wireless. Another common problem with the installation of a large job is that the first contractor to get to the site can place their equipment first. Many times the location of ductwork and cable trays may not be exactly laid out in the plans. The heating, ventilation, and air conditioning (HVAC) contractor might run ductwork in front of where a camera is to be placed. If you are keeping up with the installation, the camera location can be moved prior to being installed at the original location to avoid a partially blocked view. If the contractor installs the equipment as per the drawings and the view is blocked, there is a good chance that moving the camera will be a change order that affects your security installation budget. Keeping up with the installation step is a self-serving interest on your part. It will also allow you to see the quality of the installation. After connections are made and sensors mounted, sloppy work can get covered up. The quality of the installation will in turn affect the maintenance that the system will require in the future, as discussed in Chapter 17.

TESTING

Any testing requirements of the system should be in the bid documents. They should specify any requirements such as processing speed of the server/computer, sensor area coverage, CCTV views and quality, and so on. These should be in addition to the testing required to assure that the various security functions are properly operating and reporting. The tests should be witnessed and signed off by someone in the Security department. This is the point when many of the areas missed in the design or bid documents become obvious. For example, the bid documents should specify the desired data to be loaded into the security alarm database. What often happens is that there is no requirement, so the contractor can load whatever they want into the database and comply with the contract. The descriptor for the alarm is a good example. The contractor will often load in the architect's matrix door number instead of the descriptor you want. When the alarm from the lobby door appears at the server it might display "alarm door A765." This situation is not the contractor's problem because the contractor was not given any requirements as to the descriptors to use and the name of that area might be one the contractor is totally unaware of. All he or she can do is input something from the drawings or have you supply them with the descriptor you want. An architectural door number is not very helpful for the Security Control Center (SCC) operator, but may well comply with the bid documents. If you are not involved with the testing the contractor might finish the project and leave the site before these types of problems are discovered.

Being part of the testing step of the project will address two other issues that often arise. One is that the alarms may not report at all. The Fire Marshall will test fire alarms, but no one except someone from the Security department will care enough to assure that all security alarms work. This applies to alarms, badge reader doors, CCTV switchers, and so on. The more integrated and sophisticated the design the more testing that is needed. Some contracts require the security consultant to perform the testing. If this is desired, it must be clear in the bid documents. The other issue is speed or throughput concerns with a large system. The system may appear to be working perfectly until the building is occupied and it is tested in the real world. Many larger systems that have a substantial number of badge readers will suffer from badge processing delay time. A badge should be processed electronically in less than a second to keep the users from complaining. If there is a tremendous number of badges being read at the same time (shift changes), the server may not be able to process alarms fast enough. These types of problems should have been addressed in the performance section of the bid documents. If they were not, this oversight can be very expensive to correct.

INITIAL OPERATION

This is an important step in the project, because installation projects should include training. This is another area that should have been covered in the bid documents. Training is often not given the importance that it should be given. Training needs to be a formal documented process with hands-on practice. It is a good idea to videotape any training, because some details may be forgotten and this way they can easily be viewed again. Personnel will change, which also forces additional professional training time if there is not an easy way to view previous training. This step is where any remaining oversights in the design will usually show up. If a new SCC was part of the project, then equipment placement issues will become obvious and equipment may need to be adjusted within the console. Any problems that are discovered at this step should be addressed. They may require extra funding and/or they may be oversights from the previous stages. There is normally a 10 percent retainer on projects. The retainer keeps the contractors interested in completing the job to your satisfaction. This is the best time to resolve some loose issues. After the retainer is paid and the project is over, any changes will probably be at an additional cost.

ONGOING SUPPORT

This is the step in the process where the system should be functioning properly, the training should be complete and you should have as-built drawings in your possession. Normally, at about the same time you reach this step, there are new security requirements for some reason. The system needs additional alarms or badge readers or cameras or an intercom must be added. The support to add these functions will depend on your support plan. (Chapter 17 addressed maintenance issues and Chapter 11 addressed database issues.) Part of the plan must include what level of support will be in-house and what level an outside contractor will provide. The division of support between in-house and outside support will drive the need and level of need for outside support. It is always a good plan to have included some commonly used devices in a spare parts list as part of the initial project. Items such as badge readers, special alarm sensors and cameras should be part of that spares list. Often, a spares list includes about 10 percent of the items used in the project to be used as spares. This will depend upon budget and availability of the items that are to be ordered. This way, the delays to make a modification are minimized. Door sensors would not normally be part of a spares list because they can be available within a day. If in-house support can be utilized, the spares list might expand. For example, power supplies can fail, but not necessarily the unit that they are a part of. An intercom system might have a power supply that can be difficult to get on short notice, so it might be on the spares list even though it may need to be replaced by an outside contractor. Another option is to have the outside contractor under contract to provide any needed parts within a given amount of time. As discussed in Chapter 17, it is normally not a good idea to pay for a contract that covers any failure and provides all parts and labor on an annualized basis as a percentage of the installation project. These contracts are usually very expensive. Just a note, the warranty on a project should not start until final acceptance or commissioning of the project. This detail must also be in the bid document. A one year warranty is typical on security projects.

If you follow all the steps listed for projects and properly address each step, your project will be successful. You will have a security system that will serve your company well and reflect favorably on the Security department. It is in your best interest to be part of the process, asking questions, and understanding exactly what you are getting. When it is all said and done, the project will be considered your project, because you were the one trying to obtain funding from upper management. The quality of the operation of the system, ease of use by the employees/contractors/visitors/customers, and proficiency of the SCC operators will add or detract from the security program. Remember you do not want this project to be called "old-what's-his-name's project."

19

Special Compliance

There are always special compliance issues each of us must deal with in the applications of security functions. There are several aspects that affect the types of compliance that your company will fall under. They are dependent upon the industry in which you work, the local jurisdictions, customers, insurance carriers and the types of security functions that are in place. All industries will be affected by requirements for fire systems, privacy issues and their insurance carriers. Fire systems are code driven and overseen by the Authority Having Jurisdiction (AHJ). Everyone must protect Social Security numbers, personnel data on employees and their company's sensitive information, such as products under development or trade secrets. The health care industry is an example of an industry that has very strict requirements for securing patient's data. In fact, this industry is driven by the Health Information Protection Act (HIPA) requirements. All industries must protect data, even though they may not be in as strict an environment as the health care industry. All industries have insurance carriers that set requirements. Most large companies are self-insured to some level and have a carrier like Factory Mutual (FM) that develops proposed modifications to company facilities to mitigate losses. These carriers often visit the company locations and make suggestions/requests to address certain issues—especially fire-related issues. In this chapter, we will review basic codes and standards that affect many companies to one extent or another. We will look at the differences in codes/standards and guidelines.

It has been said that the security industry lacks standards, and developing standards is important for the industry. The security industry does lack standards, but the lack of standards applies to interchangeability of equipment more than anything else. We discussed in Chapters 1 and 4 the lack of a standard protocol between the electronic field panel and the server/computer. For example, it is not possible to change a field panel from one manufacturer to another and leave the server/computer in place. If that were possible, you could indicate at the server/computer that a field panel was being added, select the manufacturer, input the model number of the panel and the field panel would start communicating with the server/computer, similar to the way you connect a printer to your personal computer (PC). This obviously is not possible, so there is a lack of standards in place. Even the end-of-line resistor discussed in Chapter 4 is not a standard value from one security alarm manufacturer to another. Proprietary application-specific software runs on virtually all security functional equipment, which means that the software is not interchangeable—again a lack of standards.

Standards are void in many different aspects of physical drawings and bid packages. The symbols that are used by architects, integrators, alarm companies, and so on are not always standardized. Progress has been made on standardizing symbols for security, but they are not universally adopted. Even the locations of the security drawings within the construction drawing package is not always standardized. Recently, progress has been made in this area. As mentioned in several places in the book, the federal government through Homeland Security is forcing standards and to some extent, driving the security market. So progress is being made in many aspects of security standards, but this is not the type of standards that we will be discussing in this chapter. We will be discussing some of the standards/codes that are in place that affect the design and maintenance of electronic security systems. It is my opinion that understanding standards and guidelines will provide some direction and assure a minimal level of compliance. One thing to remember is that a standard/code is the minimum that is acceptable to achieve the desired end result. Many applications may require you to exceed the code requirements. For example, in most locations, a driveway is composed of steel reinforcement and 4 inches of 3,000 pounds-per-square-inch (psi) concrete. You may have an application where you want 5 inches of 3,500 psi concrete. The choice is yours because the code only requires the minimum to sustain typical vehicle loading requirements. Most large enterprise-wide security system designs will be more than a ridge placement of sensors which standards may dictate. The placement of sensors based on a standard does provide value but does not completly assure the desired level of security.

We will start our focus on two new standards that have been out for review and recently completed, which have a direct impact on security. The level of impact will depend on the ability of the National Fire Protection Association (NFPA) to force the standards across regulatory groups. The NFPA has developed standards for years associated with life safety issues, such as NFPA 70 (the National Electric Code), NFPA 101 (the Life Safety Code) and NFPA 72 (the National Fire Alarm Code). All of theses codes are used by government entities and local jurisdictions to enforce the electrical, safety and fire alarm project installation codes. The city inspects electrical wiring and requires permits to assure that the National Electric code is met. The same is true with NFPA 72. The Fire Marshall or Authority Having Jurisdiction (AHJ) in the city or county requires drawings supplied for review and permitting. Then after the fire alarm system and electrical work are completed, the AHJ inspects the project to assure compliance. There is logic in developing codes for security, much like the NFPA has developed codes for fire prevention, since few codes existed associated with the installation of security systems. Security alarm systems have been classified as low voltage systems, which avoid NEC regulations. Security, access control, as well as other functional systems operate on 12 volts to 24 volts. The two new security standards are NFPA 730 and NFPA 731. A potential problem is that both of these new documents address the AHJ. In the security field, there is not an AHJ as such. It can be argued that the building owner, the federal government or some other entity could be the AHJ. The problem is that under the standards approach that the NFPA has used in the past, the AHJ knows the codes. In fact, the AHJs decide which code will be used and which of the years the code was written will be required. Security systems do not fit very well into this type of scheme, but since few codes were written, the NFPA stepped up to the plate.

In fact, the NFPA started to write security codes in 1994, but stopped in 1995. The insurance industry re-initiated their request for codes for security, which caused the NFPA to start again in late 1995. In 1996, the effort was stopped again. In 1999 the insurance industry again requested the NFPA to proceed on the codes. In 2000, the Standards Council of the NFPA decided to proceed once again. NFPA 730 is the "what" ("Guide for Premises Security") and 731 is the "how" ("Standard for the Installation of Electronic Premises Security"). One important item to notice is that NFPA 730 is a guide and NFPA 731 is a standard. A guide provides some insight and direction, but there is no mandate on exactly how it is used, if at all. The reason NFPA 730 became a guide is that it was difficult to reach consensus across the technical groups reviewing the document. A standard on the other hand is a mandate of minimal requirements and must be followed. Wording such as "shall" contained in a standards document means there is no deviation allowed.

NFPA 730 addresses interior and exterior security from residential to industrial. It also covers a security vulnerability study. The guide looks at security based upon building and occupancy variations. The following topics are covered: (1) general requirements and facility classifications, (2) security vulnerability, (3) exterior security devices and systems, (4) physical security devices, (5) interior security systems and (6) measures to control security vulnerabilities in education, healthcare and other facilities. There will be strong supporters of this guide, as well as detractors. To some extent, the success of this document, as well as NFPA 731 will depend upon who supports them and how they are applied to various companies and installation jobs. It appears that there is support from the insurance carriers, but time will tell as to how widespread the documents will be used.

NFPA 731 is a standard, and as such, is mandatory if it is part of the requirements by the AHJ. This standard provides specifics about how to install electronic security in different types of facilities. The standard lists groups of personnel who are qualified to install security systems. The three qualified groups provided in the list (but the list is not exclusive of other groups) is as follows: (1) equipment manufacturer trained and certified personnel, (2) personnel licensed and certified by state and local authority and (3) personnel certified by an accreditation program acceptable to the AHJ. As you can see from the language, this standard is similar to other NFPA standards such as NFPA 72. The standard addresses most security functionality, but it does not address fire systems because other NFPA standards already exist for fire systems. NFPA 731 also tries to tie the installers to similar certifications and approval by the AHJ, as does NFPA 72. The problem is that some of the design/installers from the list above vary in background, capabilities, and knowledge, which is substantial enough, but when installing large enterprise-wide security systems the result might be poor. The other NFPA codes are enforced via the AHJ, meaning the Fire Marshall or equivalent in NFPA 72; but in NFPA 731 the AHJ is vague. Over time, the impact of 730 and 731 will be apparent. It is very possible that other groups will get on the bandwagon to provide "accreditation programs" for qualified personnel, and so on that will reinforce the standard.

The American Society of Industrial Security (ASIS) International has also been involved with trying to develop "standards" for security for years. They have developed certification programs for various disciplines within security: the Certified Protection Professional (CPP), the Professional Certified Investigator (PCI) and the Physical Security Professional (PSP). The PSP was an effort to address the more technical side of physical security; however, the development of standards was not accomplished. To date, their efforts have been focused more on guidelines and recommendations versus standards and codes. The reason for the approach is partly the same as what NFPA found out when addressing the issues in NFPA 730. ASIS International is presently finalizing guidelines for electronic security in several different areas and revising the technical security certification program. Since these guidelines and standards have all arrived on the scene over a recent multiyear period, it will be interesting to see where each will go and how they may blend together.

The federal government is also in the act. Homeland Security is pushing for standards. For example, HSPD-12 came from a Homeland Security Presidential Directive and forces a way to identify federal government employees and contractors. The directive requires both physical and logical security to be controlled. It also sets desired conceptual requirements. The Department of Commerce and the National Institute of Standards and Technology (NIST) developed the Federal Information Processing Standard Publication (FIPS) from HSPD-12. The new standard is FIPS 201 which assures administrative security measures, such as the identification of the person receiving the badge, assurance of a properly protected identification badge stock, and so on. The identification badge is referred to as a Personal Identity Verification (PIV) and requires the use of smart card technology. The PIV contains both contact-less and contact type smart card technology. The internal smart card devices can be separated or connected together. The fact that the federal government is developing standards within its own entities will have an effect on the security market as a whole, because of the size and impact the federal government has on industry. Many companies may incorporate the standard and it will affect the access control market to some extent. If nothing else, it will drive down the cost of smart card technology and expand smart card applications.

Underwriters Laboratories, Inc. (UL) is another organization that has been and is driving standards in security. Everyone is familiar with UL and its labeling of products in respect to life safety. Everything from toasters to computers display a UL label. UL is an independent testing nonprofit agency that certifies products. The different products fall under different UL requirements. In the security realm, it is important to utilize products with a UL label for safety reasons, but there are also some UL standards that apply specifically to security. There are requirements for installations such as UL 681 that deal with Installation and Classification of Burglar and Holdup Alarms and requirements for the Security Control Center (SCC). These UL listings are either for commercial central stations (UL 1610), proprietary central stations (UL 1076) or for an SCC that is operated by a government contractor (UL 2050). Each of the three types of central stations falls under different requirements. For the purpose of this chapter, we will look at only one of the three, but it should set the tone for the others.

UL 2050 is the standard for a government contractor's SCC. A government contractor is a company that provides services and/or products to the government. This standard is based upon and mentions other government security standards such as the National Industrial Security Program Operating Manual (NISPOM), Joint Air Force Army Navy (JAFAN 6/9) and the Director of Central Intelligence Directive (DCID 1/21). The applications for UL 2050 apply to contractors that must comply with these government security requirements. As with the other standards, the document has language of its own. For example, the SCC is referred to as a Service Center. The group that installs/maintains the electronic security systems or oversees those installations is the Alarm Service Company. The actual government contractors can be the Service Center and the Alarm Service Company or either one or neither. Government entities that have work performed, under certain conditions, at one of these government contractors' facilities can and do require that the areas where work is performed be a certified UL 2050 area. The Alarm Service Company installs the alarms and writes the closed area UL certificates and the Service Center monitors the alarms in the closed areas within the government contractor's facilities.

As with most standards the four mentioned above (NISPOM, UL 2050, DCID 1/21 and JAFAN 6/9) refer to each other and the integration of the standards can become very complex. In fact, the NEC 70 is also referred to in UL 2050. Special issues and circumstances can become somewhat subjective and an interpretation from the various standards must be made. UL makes a visit to the Alarm Service Company to review their installations on a yearly basis. Each certificate can be written for a term of one, three or five years and has a yearly fee, just as does the inspection itself. The length of time required by the inspection depends upon the number of certificates written. A certain percent of the Alarm Service Company's UL certified areas will be checked each year, as well as the SCC, which is checked for compliance each year. Any needed corrections will be listed in a letter from UL received after the inspections have been completed. The corrections must be addressed in a letter back to UL as to the resolve.

To better understand exactly what is covered in UL 2050, I will provide a quick overview. The standard addresses topics such as the number of personnel required in the SCC, the responsibility of the person responding to the security alarm, the time required for that response and the necessary documentation associated with the alarm. The standard addresses backup electrical power requirements in the field and the SCC as well as documentation requirements for a variety of tasks from training to the length of time an alarm history log must be kept. It addresses the type of alarms and coverage needed under different levels of protection. The level of protection required will vary based upon the government entity, classified material and the type of work that is being performed. Time stamps are required for alarms as well as "openings" and "closings" of the areas. There are many variations and details that we do not have room to discuss. When certification is required, the loss of that certification from noncompliance can result in the ultimate loss of a government contract.

NFPA 72 has already been mentioned as a fire standard. We need to take a look at the standard to have a basic understanding of its importance and application because fire systems are normally part of the functions in the SCC. This standard has been around for a long time and is accepted by Fire Marshalls across the country. The standard addresses the placement of sensors, their spacing, and their performance. The standard addresses initiating devices, which include smoke/heat detectors, fire pulls, etc. The NFPA 25 code defines the frequency of testing the devices and testing required when the fire system is modified. NFPA 72 also defines notification appliances, such as strobes, horns and speakers. The Americans with Disability Act (ADA) dictates the requirements of and spacing of strobes where speakers and/or horns are located to notify hearing impaired people in the event of an emergency life safety event, such as a fire. The spacing, sound requirements, light level requirements and electrical power consumption including wire gauge sizing is addressed. Sometimes there are conflicts and overlapping requirements between NFPA 72 and ADA. This topic is covered in Chapter 5 in greater detail. The standard/code is very detailed and in-depth for different types of occupancy requirements. It is modified and upgraded every three years. When there is a major fire that impacts the code, but is not actually addressed by the code, the findings of the fire investigation teams are incorporated into the future code to mitigate similar problems. The NFPA also requires testing of the electronic portion of the fire system per NFPA 72 and

NFPA 25. There are other NFPA codes that affect the design and testing of sprinkler systems. There is also International Fire Code (IFC) that many cities have incorporated versus the Uniform Fire Code (UFC). The reason for the transition is that the IFC is easier to read and understand.

There is a certification process for properly trained fire technicians and engineers. One of those certifications is from the National Institute for Certification in Engineering Technologies (NICET). There are four levels of NICET technician certifications under Electrical and Mechanical Systems Engineering Technology. There are two types of certification: one is a technician and the other is a technologist. The technician certification requires testing and work experience. The certification does not fall under the law and is not licensed by the state, but is a national certification similar to those by ASIS International for security and can be lost if certain violations occur. A license, on the other hand, is a credential granted by the state or local jurisdiction required under law to perform certain types of work. Most states have requirements for technician fire system licenses. The license holder must perform certain tasks, such as a mandatory report that goes to the state when certain situations arise with fire alarm panels, such as a red tag. (The red tag indicates that the fire system is out of compliance.) Fire codes, fire licenses and fire certifications are well established and defined.

Licenses for security are controlled in most areas at the state level. Each state can have different requirements and testing. Often the testing, when required, applies more to the laws in a specific state than installation techniques or specific electronic knowledge. The state licenses for security do provide recourse for unethical or incompetent actions. To maintain a license often requires continuing education credits to help raise and sustain the level of performance. The state also will require background checks to prevent certain types of individuals from obtaining a license in the first place. All these requirements, although beneficial, do not assure you that the person installing your security system is capable of handling the task. As system complexity continues to increase, finding competent security contractors/integrators will be a challenge.

Product manufacturers must comply with certain certifications. UL (already mentioned) produces standards for all types of products. An example in security is UL 294, which addresses access

control products; any access control product that you would purchase is UL 294 compliant. There are requirements for the manufacture of smoke detectors, and so on. Some states have special
requirements, especially in fire systems. For example, many products will indicate that they are NFPA 72 and California Fire
Marshall approved. A sample of UL listings for various products is
as follows:

1. UL 305 Standard for Panic Hardware
2. UL 365 Police Station Connected Burglary Alarm Units
   and Systems
3. UL 437 Standard for Key Locks
4. UL 608 Burglary Resistant Vault Doors and Modular Panels
5. UL 609 Local Burglary Alarm Units and Systems
6. UL 687 Burglary Resistant Safes
7. UL 752 Standard for Bullet-Resistant Equipment
8. UL 768 Standard for Combination Locks
9. UL 972 Standard for Burglary-Resistant Glazing Material
10. UL 1023 Household Burglar-Alarm Systems Units
11. UL 1034 Standard for Burglary-Resistant Electric Locking
    Mechanisms
12. UL 1484 Residential Gas Detectors
13. UL 2034 Single and Multiple Station Carbon Monoxide
    Detectors
14. UL 2058 High Security Electric Locks
15. UL 3044 Standard for Surveillance Closed Circuit Tele-
    vision Equipment

Special compliance is a very complicated and a detailed area of
study. In this chapter, we have provided a quick insight into some
of these requirements. The code documents are in themselves
lengthy and very detailed. (NFPA 730 released in 2006 is about 88
pages long.) Each topic discussed could easily be a chapter unto
itself. There is a unique vocabulary for each of the code-based entities that in many cases have been in existence for many years. In
some cases, the carryover language does not fit well with applications today. For example, UL 2050, under "Acceptable application
of transmitters," contains a listing for direct wire communications.
Direct wire can be an RS485 loop from an electronic field panel to

the server/computer as discussed in Chapters 1 and 4 or it can be an old Burglar Alarm (BA) type line that the phone company provided at one time. The BA line allowed a physical wire to connect buildings that were separated by some distance. The distance could be blocks or miles. In either case, it was a physical pair of wires that could be rented monthly from the phone company and charges were based upon distance. BA lines are still used in some locations, but they are no longer available in many cities. Another example of modern technology in the same code is referred to as a data network. This can be a LAN/WAN, Internet, Intranet, VPN, etc. There is no distinction between different "networks" as to the level of security the data network can provide. As you know there is a tremendous amount of difference in the security that can be exerted on a VPN versus the Internet.

Standards are in place to improve security functional subsystems installations and operation. Most codes were developed to address safety issues and to prevent fires. The security standards, for the most part, are relatively new and their impact will not be known for some period of time. There are guidelines that will help guide the design and installation of security systems. There are certifications by various groups to provide a required level of competence at a national level. Finally there are licensing requirements by various states. All these documents and laws were developed for the "better good." The problem with many of these attempts to make the world a better and safer place is that to design a quality enterprise-wide security solution is not guaranteed with these protections in place.

20

Trends

Discussing trends is fairly easy to do. Knowing exactly what's going to happen in the future can be another matter. Looking into a crystal ball and extrapolating where the trend will lead is much more difficult. In this chapter, I will attempt to do just that. There are some obvious directions that electronic security is headed. The part that makes the future so interesting is that it can make a major turn in direction and products will be available that today are not even known. I am constantly amazed at the new products that become commercially viable that no one even envisioned a few years ago. For an example, let's go back to the time before there were copying machines—for some of you that might seem like the Middle Ages. As a short refresher, Charles F. Carlson invented the first copy machine in 1938. (Xerography is a Greek word meaning "dry writing." Xerography became commercially available in 1950 by Xerox Corp.) An interesting note about the struggle to obtain funding to develop such a machine was the constant question from investors: Why do you need copies when there are carbons already available? What would you do with more copies? Today we could not live without the ability to make copies. This ties to the trends topic, in several ways. First, a new technology will develop other technology. Second, if someone were writing future trends, before the copying machine was invented, they would not even consider a copying machine necessary. (The need appeared to be solved with carbon copies. By the way, when you write "cc:" on a message, it literally means carbon copy.) Third, new ideas and products take time to be accepted. The time seems to be shrinking, but there is an acceptance delay.

As far as trends for the future of security electronics, one fact that cannot be denied is that every component and system will become more intelligent. The capability of motion detectors continues to get better and better. Nuisance alarms are reduced, the detection improves and the price drops. This is accomplished through newer technology, which incorporates more processing capability. Cameras are providing better quality images, with less sensitivity to unwanted lighting that can adversely affect the picture. There are Internet Protocol (IP) cameras that can be connected directly to a network. These cameras have a computer to digitally process the field of view as well as the data, and they can compress the digitized video prior to sending it to a network, thus minimizing bandwidth requirements for the intranet or Internet. IP cameras are basically a computer with a lens. They will continue to become more intelligent and be able to do more processing. Even digital IP megapixel cameras are available that can provide more detail than analog cameras. Intelligent video can process camera information and make decisions as to possible security problems, notify the SCC operator of the alarm, display the video information and record the situation. These systems will only become more capable and intelligent. This is a trend that will always be under way at all levels of systems as well as in components in security products.

IP technology is an area that has an expanding impact on Security. The IP network is a transmission medium for alarms, access control, video systems, and so on. There has been a great deal of conversation and articles on this subject. One of the changes coming to the IP area that will impact the entire world is the move from IPv4 to IPv6. This change, among other things, affects the addressing scheme used by IP. IPv4 uses 1 to 3 numbers separated by periods (000.000.000.000). This addressing pattern allows for more than 4 billion addresses. It may sound unbelievable, but there is a shortage of addresses. To solve the problem short tem, a special server called a Network Address Translation (NAT) is used to basically buffer the internal addresses that connect to it. The Department of Defense (DoD) has been pushing a new protocol standard called IPv6. IPv6 uses 8 sets of four numbers separated by colons. There are 32 numbers versus the 12 used by IPv4. This makes the number of addresses almost infinite, but remember IPv4 was considered more than enough at one time. The expanded address pool will allow the DoD to monitor soldiers and weapons in the battlefield. The impact on security and the way the IP world is viewed will change significantly when IPv6 is implemented in the private sector. Remember, the entire concept and early development of the Internet was by the government. (You may be thinking, what happened to IPv5? IPv5 is an experimental protocol and was designed to deal with streaming video.)

Most of the IP activity by security product manufacturers to date has been in the video arena. Standards have been developed, which will expand the capabilities of IP networks. One of those standards is for providing electrical power over the Ethernet (POET). This is being used by the CCTV industry to power cameras. The amount of power is limited so at present it will not power an IP Pan Tilt Zoom (PTZ) camera, but that will probably also change in the future. There have been some inroads in the access control area also. The government has driven most of the access control focus, not only on the electronic side, but also on the organizational side. The Department of Homeland Security (DHS) is already driving standards for smart cards. The government wants a single identification badge for all applications. They have forced requirements for other identification such as drivers licenses and made technology additions to passports. They are pushing for "smart" cameras. These efforts by the government since 9/11 will continue and impact the security market, products, applications and possibly standards.

IP networks are already making an impact on security in many areas. The major market, to this point, has been sending video from cameras over the network; but IP network access control systems and security systems applications will continue to increase. The push toward convergence of the Security department and the Information Technology (IT) department to work together is being promoted as the perfect solution in articles and publications. This trend of convergence is real and will expand. I do not think the transition will be as fast as it appears today for several reasons. First, there are turf issues between the Security and IT departments. Second, there is a lack of trust between the departments. Third, the IT department has not been known, up to this point, for its interest in Security. IT's view of "security" is entirely different from that of the security professional's view. IT considers security to be cyber security. Their focus has been on keeping the network operational at all costs and providing a Return on Investment (ROI). To accomplish ROI, they tend to use the latest and greatest products and technology. Security, on the other hand, tends to prefer the tried and true approach in products and technology. Fourth, the basic security philosophies and focus are different. Finally, the IT department tends to be technical and the Security department tends to be knowledgeable about physical security issues which presents a language problem. These reasons for lack of cooperation are not true at every company, but tend to be true across many companies. In many companies, the IT group has developed much more bandwidth than they need today and are looking for groups within the company to share the cost of these large networks. The extra capacity is often to allow for future needs; but with the business pressure to cut costs, IT is looking for ways to spread services and reduce costs. Because of the convenience and accessibility to the IT IP networks, there is no doubt that more products will be developed to work over IP, but the transition to a real or total convergence of security and IT will probably take a decade or more. The dream of many for a convergence between physical and logical security will take time and the convergence will happen asymptomatically, meaning it will not be 100 percent.

IP networks will allow more interactivity across an enterprise. For example, the Human Resources (HR) department will be able to add and remove employee badges from the access control security database. Timely additions and deletions in the access control database has always been a problem for the Security department. Since the HR department is usually the first and last group that an employee visits during their employment, it is logical to use the opportunity for HR supporting the access control database updates, but today they are often not part of the data entry process. Training HR personnel to enter and possibly make badges would require a new paradigm. Often, the access control system has JPEG picture files of employees which are requested for various projects, such as an organization chart or a retirement party, and so on. With an IP-based access control system, this information would be available to approved groups and individuals. Obviously some controls must be in place to address privacy and legal issues. Another application is associated with access to various areas that are restricted by badge readers. The area custodian that presently allows access to his or her area can do so by using IP and never leave their office. The process presently requires a message to the Security department from the custodian to add or delete someone's access to the area. With an IP system the custodian could sign on the access control system and be allowed to make additions and deletions to his or her area with simple password protection in place.

Voice over IP (VoIP) is another area that will impact security. New products are coming out almost monthly to satisfy the demand. This started out as a way to avoid long distance phone charges, but today many corporations are incorporating it to make all telephone installations. All audio communications used by Security today could move to VoIP. This includes intercoms, radios and telephone. There will be tradeoffs that will drive the market, but there is no doubt that VoIP will expand and will affect the Security Control Center (SCC) and the entire security operation.

Web application security software applications will continue to expand. The convenience of a Web-based application is very important to security. For example, a visitor registration program is an excellent Web-based application. Anyone within the company could have a visitor. Instead of having the visitor arrive at the lobby with no warning, the person being visited could call up the Web-based program and fill in a form. The form would include the time, date, person's name and who was being visited. The program would notify the lobby where the visitor is to arrive and print a badge for the visitor on the correct day of the visit. This provides the Security department with a log of visitors and allows a badge to be ready for the visitor in the lobby. The lobby security personnel can notify the person being visited by Email that the visitor has arrived. There can be additional automated verification that the visit application includes, such as nondisclosure agreements or classi-fied visits. Because of the convenience and easy access by everyone in the company, the applications for Web-based software will be used to address many security issues in the future.

Viruses and worms will continue to be a problem. Ten years ago few people had experienced an attack. Now virtually everyone is seriously concerned and has incorporated various types of software protection even on their computers at home. The potential impact of viruses and worms will also expand because more and more sophisticated products require computer processing capabilities. Those persons who create the computer attacks are getting more sophisticated as well. The capabilities that make security products more stable and intelligent also allow attacks from viruses and worms. Traditionally, these attacks have been associated with opening Email attachments, but other attacks exist that are based upon the software residing on network routers, hubs, switchers and even in the equipment itself. These same types of attacks will also apply to security products. There is a debate going on at this time about the possiblity of an attack against RFID tags. Any electronically based processor is susceptible to attack. A virus or worm can be loaded into the processor, causing various types of problems. These types of attacks can spread quickly and cripple an access control system, airport luggage handling equipment, and so on.

The level of complexity and sophistication causes new security installation projects to require an integrator or some other highly technical support. Often a local alarm company has been capable of performing the task, but today the task is being handled more and more by integrators. On more complicated installations, a factory-trained alarm company may be required to perform part of the installation, but in the future, more and more technical expertise will be required to install security systems. The use of IP-based products is driving that to some extent, but so is the complexity of the electronics in general. As security products get more sophisticated and intelligent, the level of expertise needed to integrate the various security functions will require a strong electronic and software background. These levels of expertise are typically lacking in most alarm companies. Many times, this level of prowess is not present in any one integrator. The integration companies will need to become more familiar with the IT side. The typical IT group is not totally prepared for this transition either. They generally do not understand the other electronic security equipment; however, it may be easier for IT to understand security electronics than for the Security alarm company or integrator to understand IT technology. The IP impact on security will also affect the manufacturers of today's products. Large network product manufacturers like Cisco, who are already heavily in the IT market, have started to sell products that are now being manufactured only in the Security market. If there is a large market and a company like Cisco is already in, they will enhance their product line to encompass new products, if there is a market big enough to justify their new direction. The security market has become large enough and enough transition to the IP infrastructure that some level of transition is inevitable for the manufacturers already in this market. Software to manage these IP security systems will also become more sophisticated and intuitive. On the CCTV side these software packages are called Video Management Systems (VMS). There are companies developing very sophisticated software for this market. The software is a must if a seamless control of accessing and controlling cameras is to be obtained. The next step is the need to record and "recall" the recorded video. The obvious transition is to a Network Video Recorder (NVR). An NVR can be in any location throughout the network.

Even fire systems, which will probably not adopt an IP network to interconnect smoke and heat detectors to the panel are moving toward IP capabilities. Detectors and fire pulls on the initiating side of a fire panel must activate an alarm within ninety seconds. There cannot be delays caused by other traffic that might be on a network. The same is true for the notification appliance side (the strobe/horn/speaker side) of a fire system. Delays on the sensing or notifying side must be controlled to assure the ninety-second code requirement. This interesting application of IP for fire systems deals with the use of IP to interrogate and monitor a network of fire panels. You can sit in your office and check for alarms and the status of fire systems in your company across the enterprise. They are adding computer port capability in fire panels that allow the port to be connected to a network and communicate using IP. This is one example of an application that was not obvious because of the thinking process associated with codes and the fact that fire systems would not use IP was obviously short sighted. This is a modern example of the thinking about carbon copies discussed earlier. The applications for IP are almost limitless.

There are other trends such as privacy concerns that will impact security products. The issues associated with safeguarding Social Security numbers bring this issue into perspective. There are several basic types of identity theft: (1) true name theft, (2) account takeover and (3) mass data compromise. If the Social Security must be safeguarded, how will other information such as that required for various biometric devices be protected? The loss of personal data does affect a company's liability. Corporation's databases such as those of the HR department have always been protected, not typically the security system and their associated databases. For example, Social Security numbers have been used in access control systems as a unique identifier for years. The Social Security number is just as sensitive in the Security department's access control database as it is in the HR database. On the other side of the privacy issue, there are a few companies that have actually implanted glass-encapsulated RFID tags in their employees. This practice has been used on farm animals and pets for years, but this practice on people is a new direction that is sure to cause a large debate. The argument at present is that the tags are voluntary only for access to extremely sensitive areas and are not in place to track employees; however, the topic will become an issue and affect security products and their applications.

Another area of privacy concern applies to Closed Circuit Television (CCTV). Cities are installing them at traffic lights to ticket red light runners as well as in public areas within the city to view possible criminal activities. Normally these are high crime areas and the argument is that the cameras will deter crime; but if crime does happen, then the incident will be monitored and recorded. This approach has been used in Europe for years. The privacy laws are different between the United States and Europe, but the CCTV implementations appear to be about the same. This trend will continue and stir up an emotional debate, the outcome of which will affect CCTV applications across society, including the way corporations install cameras at their sites.

In more recent times, another technology that has and will have tremendous impact on electronic security is wireless. Wireless security applications can apply to any security functionality that exists. Wireless is a way of sending data just like wires do, except without wires and with more convenience. There are applications where installing wiring is virtually impossible or cost prohibitive. Wireless installation will need to incorporate techniques that make eavesdropping difficult. Access control, CCTV and alarm products are all available with wireless capability. Convenience and security do not always go hand in hand, but proper steps can be taken to assure a reasonable level of security. Wireless applications are literally everywhere, not just in security. The manufacturers of automatic faucets that turn on when you place your hands in front of them are going wireless. When the faucet senses the presence of your hand, a wireless signal is sent to the control valve under the counter which activates the flow of water. At the other extreme, entire cities are providing network connectivity via wireless. The commercial marketplace will affect the security market. Two interesting developments that may be coming to the commercial market are commercial television over the Internet and power companies providing conductivity through their power network. The power companies providing conductivity through the power grid that already exist almost everywhere in the United States will spawn many new products that could be incorporated into the security market. This trend will continue. There are countless applications for wireless IP to provide security functionality from the field as well as to notify the responding officer of directions, alarms, and video. The security and functionality will also expand as new products are developed. The ideas are endless, they just require fresh thinking. Trends will provide some guidance toward new products and applications, but the actual products may well turn out to be something that no realizes they needed—just like a copy machine.

____ Appendix A
Pros and Cons of a Consolidated Database

To keep the pros and cons of each decision less complicated, three assumptions must be stated. These basic assumptions will be followed to allow the example to be more straightforward. First, the only system being converted/changed is the access control system. Security alarms may or may not be part of the changeover at a site. Second, the cutover from one system to another, required training, and day-to-day disruptions would not be addressed. (These problems will exist whenever a change is made from one manufacturer to another. The problem is not unique to selecting a single manufacturer for all company locations.) Third, the decisions made as the architecture is finalized will impact other decisions. To minimize the complexity, each philosophy will stand alone and the pros and cons of that decision will require consideration as part of a total design, the discussion of which is too lengthy to include at this time.

The access control design philosophy questions that should be considered when selecting a single technology, protocol, and manufacturer for a one-company-wide badge solution are as follows:

313

1. Should one of the larger company's existing access control platforms be used as the standard?
2. Should there be one centralized server?
3. Should there be one central data entry point?
4. Should the company security control centers (proprietary central station) be consolidated?
5. Should system architecture incorporate distributed processing?
6. Should downloads/uploads from IT systems be incorporated (HR, timekeeping etc.)?
7. Should the IT infrastructure be used?
8. Should sites have total control of their local electronic badge access authorizations?
9. Should the badge technology be magnetic stripe?
10. Should the badge technology be Weigand?
11. Should the badge technology be proximity?
12. Should the badge technology be smart card?
13. Should badge stock be controlled at a single company location?
14. Should all sites be able to manufacture their own access control badges?
15. Should keypads be used with readers on building perimeters?

Should one of the larger existing company's access control platforms be used as the standard?

Pro: Using one of the existing platform manufacturers that has a large presence already in the company will save cost and conversion time. The sites that already have the chosen platform manufacturer would more than likely support the choice and help the transition to be successful. *Con:* The best platform for a total unified electronic access control system may have a small presence or not already exist at the company. Sites may be a mixture of systems. There may be a "front-end" platform in place with varied field equipment or there may be multiple platforms in place at a given company site.

There is a potential for not achieving "buy in" by each site for a particular manufacturer. Using a market survey and choosing a platform based upon technical capabilities, expandability, reliability, price, support, financial stability, and so on can minimize the lack of support. There might be site resistance to accepting a different manufacturer that is already in place at some company sites.

Should there be one centralized server?

Pro: Helps enforce consistent data entry and reduced cost. All additions and deletions of access control for employees and contractors would most likely be controlled at one location. This may prevent multiple data entry activities at multiple sites and multiple errors, depending upon the decisions on the statements below. One source for the database allows reports to be run, encompassing the entire company, from one location. Otherwise, each site would need to run similar reports and the reports would be combined to obtain a consistent companywide view. Downtime and system outages could be minimized at a very reasonable cost, versus many different servers for backup. For example, the cost to add a RAID configuration, mirroring, etc. to one central server, which would be minimal, compared to upgrading many servers. *Con:* Sites may no longer have "total" control of their access control database. (Software partitions might be added, to assure access by a site to only change data that applied to their site.) The requirement for backup procedures, disaster management plan, backup hardware, and so on would be substantially more critical.

Note: A large, companywide, reliable Security communication network would be mandatory. There might be individual sites resistant to a central server—each site vying to be the "central" location. This could be minimized with site data entry workstations communicating with a central server, wherever it may be located. The platform server will be more complicated than if there were many stand-alone servers. There will tend to be more delay between the time badge data is entered and badge definition/activation at the different sites' field equipment than with a server at each site.

Should there be one central data entry point?

Pro: All data in the database would tend to be consistent in format, abbreviations, response instructions, access lists, etc. Full time data entry personnel at one location versus part time data entry personnel at many locations would minimize errors and be more efficient. Overall "manpower" would be reduced. *Con:* Without appropriate staffing, inputting data may take longer to accomplish based upon workload/manpower and there could be logistic problems in providing the data to a central point. These problems could be short-term, if effective processes and manpower are put in place. Standards and verification processes must be developed to ensure data is loaded consistently and correctly. Additional data entry personnel, at the central server site, would be needed if remote workstations did not connect to the server. There might be site resistance to a central data entry point. There would tend to be more delays between badge data entry and badge definition/activation at the different sites' field equipment. (Same issues as a centralized server.)

Should security control centers (proprietary central station) be consolidated?

Pro: Having fewer control centers that require compliance to UL and to other requirements/codes, as well as system upgrades, could reduce ongoing costs. The cost reduction applies to person- nel, equipment, facility space, and inspections. Company locations could establish control centers, geographically or by some other means. Security standards are more uniform across the area cov- ered by a consolidated control center, versus many stand-alone con- trol centers. *Con:* The operator in the consolidated control center cannot be as familiar with the remote site as a local operator. There will be resistance at the site level to "giving up" local control and settling for a "percieved" lower level of secruity.

Should system architecture incorporate distributed processing?

Pro: This approach provides inherent backup, redundancy, and flex- ibility. The extent of these pros depends on the manufacturer chosen. Distributed processing can increase processing speed for data access, thus decreasing time used in badge verification. (This assumes that the badge has already been downloaded to an intelligent field panel.) *Con:* Delays can exist between badge data entry and the badge data being loaded into the field equipment depending on architecture and network limitations. Badges not already in the field equipment may take longer to verify upon first badge read. As system size increases, the architecture and distribution configuration becomes more critical.

Should downloads/uploads from IT systems be incorporated (HR, timekeeping, etc.)?

Pro: Downloads could allow other databases to interface directly with the access control database. This would provide a more comprehensive and detailed database via automatic downloads from the IT network to the Security database. This reduces the amount of data entry and errors caused by loading data into multiple databases. *Con:* Could allow the access control database (badge credential numbers) to be compromised if not managed properly. The exact data files and individual databases involved must receive approvals by their owners and legal department to obtain access. This approval increases overall system (Security and IT) complexity. The network and the IT infrastructure could be used to transmit the data.

Should the IT infrastructure be used?

Pro: Using IT infrastructure will be cost effective and allow connectivity between different sites. **Note:** For companies with bandwidth capabilities that exceed the company intranet requirements and with a technically competent security department there are other options. If the IT infrastructure utilized were at the cabling level (part of the communication "pipe") and not on the company intranet level, the Security department would control access to the "Security" network and oversee the conductivity. This would provide administrative control of all hardware by the Security department. The Security department would need to assign a security network administrator responsibility to a technical security person to assure its integrity. Ideally, there would be one key person overseeing the entire

Security/IT network for problem solving and hardware consistency. The IT department often supports this configuration because it keeps the security data off the "company" network avoiding bandwidth issues. *Con:* Using the company intranet could cause bandwidth problems for IT or vice versa. IT will have control of the network as well as administrative privileges on all security servers and hardware on the company intranet. This causes issues of downtime, communication losses, integrity of the security servers and could compromise security at the server level, depending upon to whom IT gives administrative rights. Normally IT considers electronic security systems on their intranet a noncritical process. When equipment and software are added to the company intranet the IT department must test and approve them. For example, this situation creates the need for IT to test and approve all operating software, to assure compliance to IT standards and can pose possible issues associated with the software produced outside the United States. Then there are the issues associated with viruses/worms. If the security server resides on the company intranet with all the employee's office PCs, then the chances of a virus/worm attack is substantially increased.

Should sites have total control of their local electronic badge access authorizations?

Pro: Site Security is responsible to their local management for the employee/contractor authorizations they allow within the facility. Specific areas within the site, with limited access, will best be known at the site level. The local Security departments are already a focal point for access control issues at each site. If a centralized server were used, the sites would need a way to enter access data. This could be via a form sent to a central data entry point or via a local workstation from a nonserver site connected to the server. In either case, there would be data entry issues to control and standards to define. *Con:* If sites had total control of the access control system, there would be greater potential for data entry errors and nonconsistency issues companywide. When employees who frequently travel are added to the database by multiple sites there is a greater opportunity for input and deletion errors which would require access control standards to be written that do not normally exist. There might be site resistance to the lack of local electronic access control.

Should the badge technology be magnetic stripe?

Pro: This technology is inexpensive, fairly reliable, and easily programmed. Although this technology provides limited security, it is easy to reprogram badges. *Con:* Can suffer from environmental problems and abrasion due to swiping. Card life is reduced with this technology, because of abrasion to the technology itself as well as the employee/contractor picture. Exterior reader heads especially tend to get dirty and require frequent cleaning. The magnetic data on the badge can be inadvertently erased. It is also easily counterfeited.

Should the badge technology be Weigand?

Pro: This technology is moderately priced, reliable, and factory preprogrammed. Manufacturer strictly controls distribution, coding and badge production for any given customer. A proprietary standard may already exist at company sites and the numbering scheme may be large enough for the entire company for as long as 10 years, without repeating numbers. (A ten year period is somewhat arbitrary, but badges are distributed faster than anyone plans for and repeat numbers cause problems in the database.) This technology provides a high level of security. It is very difficult to duplicate. The manufacturer physically sets Weigand wires in a unique pattern for each badge before the badge is shipped to the customer. Weigand readers are hermetically sealed and are not subject to most environmental issues (rain, frost, magnetic fields caused by plant electrical systems, lightning, etc.). *Con:* The numbering scheme is set at the manufacturer and cannot be altered by the end user. The technology requires swiping the badge through a reader. There is some abrasion to the employee/contractor picture if protective film is not employed.

Should the badge technology be proximity?

Pro: This technology is moderately priced, reliable, and partially preprogrammed by the manufacturer; provides medium security; and is fairly difficult to duplicate. The technology allows "hands free" badge reads at short distances. Readers are not subject to most environmental issues (rain, frost, abrasion). A proprietary standard may exist at company sites and the numbering scheme is large enough for the entire company for years, without repeating numbers. (A ten-year period is somewhat arbitrary, but badges are distributed faster than anyone plans for and repeat numbers cause problems in the database.) *Con:* Distance between badge and reader for reliable badge reads is normally 3 inches or less. This technology is susceptible to high levels of electromagnetic fields that can destroy the badges. Reader placement (on metal or wood) can adversely affect the "read" distance between the badge and the reader because metal will absorb some of the reader's Radio Frequency (RF) energy.

Should the badge technology be smart card?

Pro: Smart card is an "up and coming" technology. Many IT departments are considering smart cards for controlling access to the IT network. Smart cards could be partitioned to accept both Security and IT data, allowing the same card to do both. With card/badge storage capability of 128 Kbits+ (128,000 bits+) many partitions are possible. (The manufacturer has limits on the maximum number of partitions.) Going to one new standard for both IT and Security could save money. *Con:* Security could lose control of the data being entered on the smart card, if not properly partitioned and/or if IT wants overall control. If Security was the only data entry controlling the card, personnel would need to be added to make the constant changes necessary from an IT standpoint. IT could control their own data entry, on their partitions, by downloading that data each time the badge was used to activate a computer. Loss of the card would add to the vulnerabilities with Security and IT, resulting in possible compromises. "Hackers" can read smart cards but with cryptographic techniques built into the badge, the problems are minimal. IT will probably want a contact-type card and Security would want an RF, contact-less type card. Contract-type smart cards suffer the same abrasion and cleaning issues as magnetic stripe and Weigand technologies and will need to be replaced more often.

Should badge stock be controlled at a single company location?

Pro: Better control of badge stock material minimizes badge stock compromise from falsifying undocumented stock. Better pricing and support from the badge manufacturer is possible because they have only one specific customer to deal with. Usually a manufacturer will require a company to order through a distributor to minimize the extra support required when dealing with an unknowledgeable end user. Corporate agreements that assure a set price, but allow anyone in a Security department to order using the agreement may or may not be as effective from a cost or manpower standpoint. An inventory of badges at a central location provides a reliable supply to company sites that make emergency request for more badges. A single company location minimizes many potential problems arising at many different company sites at the same time when requesting badges. These problems would include badge initialization (a procedure that must be performed by the badge manufacturing company prior to shipment), lost shipments, manufacturer delays, and quality problems. *Con:* Places burden on the single company site to keep up with badge stock and to carry and distribute cost of companywide inventory. Requires one company site to assure quality of badge stock and act as an interface with the manufacturer and other sites.

Should all sites be able to manufacture their own access control badges?

Pro: Allows for a practice that may already be in place. Most sites will normally be manufacturing their own badges today. Some larger sites make badges for small sites to minimize cost of badge-making equipment or they outsource the task to an outside company. When badges are manufactured at each site, the problems associated with shipping (electronically or physically) data and photos to a central point are eliminated. This would allow badges to be manufactured at the closest point of use, allowing faster processing and distribution. *Note:* By having the protocol protected by the manufacturer and/or by the stand-alone badge programmers (except for magnetic stripe), each site could manufacture their own badges. Safeguards are already in place to protect the protocol for Weigand and proximity. Each site could be assigned a unique site code for any of the above technologies. *Con:* More cost efficient to have one site or maybe three geographical locations (East, West, and Central) set up to manufacture badges. JPEG files of employee/contractor pictures must be shipped to a different site or sites to manufacture the badge. Credential numbers must be correctly matched to pictures to assure that the finalized badge matches the picture with the correct employee. This is accomplished by using a unique identifier such as a Social Security number, and so on. Finished badges must then be shipped back to the requesting site. This process contains all the potential issues of shipping cost, delays, and loss as well as potential security compromise. There might be site resistance to the lack of local badge manufacturing.

There is also cost associated with purchasing printers to manufacture the badges: cost of ribbons and laminate for the printer (plus associated maintenance), labor cost to make the badge, cost for photo equipment and the labor to take a visual image of the employee/contractor, and cost for the space for the badge room. Since the cost is recurring and usually more than planned, care must be taken when deciding the badges' appearance, technology and manufacturing process.

Should keypads be used with readers on building perimeters?

Pro: Can incorporate an activation and a deactivation feature during changes in National Security Level changes. When the Security Level is heightened the keypads can be activated, requiring a badge and pin number be used to a slow access. Provides additional documentation for security. Improves perception of a "harder" target and can improve employees' confidence in security. Minimal additional hardware cost (additional wiring). Provides higher level of security through a secondary validation (prevents lost badges from being used by others). *Con:* Slows movement of people through entry/exit points. There can be resistance by employees due to the requirement of remembering an additional number. Added cost for hardware and administrative support to keep database updated. There are inconsistencies between different system manufacturers as to number of bits and requirements to use the # or * symbol at the beginning or end of the bit pattern or not at all.

Appendix B
Security Audit

When most people hear the word "audit" they immediately think of being audited by the IRS. This is not an experience anyone looks forward to. In fact, each year there are legitimate deductions not taken because of the fear of being audited on the part of some taxpayers. The actual meaning of the word accurately describes the tax review process. The idea is to evaluate and scrutinize one's performance. Webster defines an audit as "a methodical examination and review." Audits are viable instruments for evaluating all kinds of processes; therefore, it is logical to perform security audits.

The performance of a security program can be weighed and measured by standards through the use of an audit. Most large organizations perform some type of security audit to assure a minimum level of compliance. The audit is effective from the standpoint of evaluating security, but can cause difficulties in two critical areas. The first area of difficulty is in minimizing stress of the actual audit process and in developing an atmosphere of teamwork between the auditors and those being audited. Typically the audit, based on rules and adherence, is an "us versus them" environment, even under ideal conditions. The second critical area of difficulty is in the ability to gather information that would allow the standards or rules to be modified. A standard audit does not allow for flexibility. There are rules and findings that must comply with the audit criteria. A subsequent report must be written that summarizes the level of compliance. Deficiencies are listed and a plan must be developed to correct them. Audits have typically been a stressful negative process.

Another option would be to gather information about security processes used in other facilities within the company and formulate the data. This approach can result in a list of "best practices" that can set standards for Security operations. Finding the "best practices" used at many different facilities within an organization allows for an internal benchmark for security. In turn, these best practices can be distributed to all sites and enhance the security of the entire organization. This approach does not imply that the evaluation of a facilities security program must no longer meet some minimal standard. Many audit best practices must be part of the total security evaluation.

The goal is to develop a teaming approach with the company site being audited. The audit process should be driven by corporate support. The team members can be composed of a corporate audit member and member or members from other company locations, as well as physical security at the audited facility. The audit members should include a physical security expert and a technical security expert and/or business process expert. The membership of the team should change over time, which will modify the view the team brings to the evaluation. Different combinations of personnel will slightly change the focus and assure all aspects are covered and facilitate in finding a "best practice." If each site feels they are part of the evaluation team and that they are an important part in setting security direction, the evaluation process will be a success. It is impractical to believe that a given set of standards will cover all possible situations and facilities. It is also important when you have security personnel at multiple remote locations to incorporate their ideas and concerns to develop "buy in." The evaluation process is just a tool composed of two components, an audit and best practices.

The correct balance of an audit and best practices is difficult to obtain. The balance will be unique for different industries. The prevailing culture of an industry should drive the implementation of these two concepts into an effective security tool. If left to the discretion of an individual facility, the level of security might not be adequate. So the audit component of the balanced evaluation is essential to assure a minimal level of security across the enterprise. To be effective, best practices, local buy in and the audit function must be part of the internal evaluation.

To perform an internal security evaluation, it is important to follow several basic steps. First, an audit notification should be sent to the site to be audited. This assures that all personnel that will participate in the audit are aware of the day and time. Second, a list of audit questions should be sent to the facility that will be evaluated. Third, the team should meet with security representatives at the facility prior to starting the evaluation. (The audit questions should have been answered prior to the visit.) At this time, the evaluation team includes the local team member or members. This approach assures that a holistic view is obtained.

The audit needs to address a long list of questions. The general list for a manufacturing facility might be as follows:

1. Activities of the facility
2. Organization—key personnel
3. Number of physical security personnel—shifts
4. Officers' general background and experience
5. Pre-employment checks
6. Officers: contract or employees
7. Number of guard posts
8. Special training—first aid, emergency etc.
9. Security posture: Proprietary, DoD, Industrial
10. Local control center
    a. Number of cameras, monitors, etc.
    b. Intrusion/fire alarms
    c. Access control
11. Entry/exit checks
12. Facility population
13. Product and stock inventories
14. Scrap disposal
15. Emergency response/disaster recovery plan

Then each of these topics should be broken down into additional detail. For example, access control should cover the following:

1. Types of badges: standard?
2. Badge recovery or cancellation process for terminated employees or lost/stolen badges
3. Visitors: authorization, log, escort, average number
4. Service personnel—log, average number, sponsors' approval process
5. Special access for equipment—cameras, equipment moving
6. Access control electronics—manufacturers, number of badge readers, assistance buttons, data base entry, revolving doors or turnstiles, etc.
7. Key control—storage, responsible party, number of master keys and assignment of keys
8. Combination locks—locations, periodic changes
9. Gates—controls, locations

Fourth, the team should review the answers to the above questions and participate in a facility walkthrough. After the walkthrough is complete, processes should be discussed. For a given process, there should be written documentation that proves that a process is being followed. Fifth, the team should then ask questions regarding specific concerns observed, understanding the use of equivalent solutions, and ask questions to find best practices.

After a baseline of security has been established from the audit, best practices can be obtained. This concept primarily deals with the process security uses to perform tasks. The audit covers the procedures security has in place. Best practices deals with the operational approach of solving security problems. To obtain the best practices information, questions about handling certain security issues must be asked. Many different processes should be evaluated to find a best practice. One sure way to verify a process and possibly find a best practice is to address specific issues. For example, if there has been a security incident at another facility, one of the best practice questions would deal with the approach this facility would use if a similar incident occurred. The goal is to obtain the different approaches used at several facilities to solve the same security incident. Another way to obtain a best practice is asking questions about overcoming limitations of equipment or practices, which are already known to exist at another company location. Operational communications is an area that has always had problems. It is possible that a facility has developed a better way of dealing with the communications to the officers as well as other first responders. An example of this is the use of an RF transmitter that sends floor plans to the responding officer's vehicle. The floor plans include shortest path to alarm area, best building entry point, and exact location of the alarm. Another example is the use of "man down" notification equipment to assure communication to the Security Control Center (SCC). This equipment provides quick response to a person who has fallen or been hurt and needs assistance. The need for this procedure develops out of the desire for protection of employees who are working alone (usually on a late shift or in an area that has few employees present).

The previous examples are implementations or enhancements to solve specific security communication issues. On the audit side of an evaluation, the facility may or may not have the physical hardware or policies in place to meet the edicts of the audit, but there is often another approach that meets the intent of the audit standard. By using best practices data gathering, the security evaluation will take on a much softer appearance. It will also allow a facility to have a best practice even though they may have deficiencies pointed out by the audit. The evaluation team will be positively received by the facility and allowed to gain knowledge from the facility if the audit/best practices approach is used.

Ideally, the physical security representative will also have members of the local facility to help clarify and answer questions. Any issues or concerns still remaining should be brought to the physical security representative's attention. If serious enough, the security violation should then be presented to the management of the facility to assure knowledge of the issue at a high management level. Finally, it is important to assure there are no surprises when the final report is distributed. The final report will include best practices, equivalencies, and any deficiencies. If security deficiencies are part of the report, then a time frame for each action item must be included. Site management should receive a copy of the final report along with the security manager.

A quality internal evaluation will be performed in a nonintimidating manner when the audit/best practices process tool is used. The tool allows other site representatives to view the site security program from an unbiased perspective. The goal is to understand a facilities approach to meet the intent of company standards and gather best practices information. Each facility has the capacity of a best practice. As the information is gathered from different facilities, lists of improvements develop. The best practices list should then be distributed to all facilities including the corporate office or site. This makes the evaluation a living process providing continual improvement for the entire organization. Even the effort expended to prepare for the evaluation and answering the audit questions is of value. This early effort allows for improvement and understanding of security processes prior to the evaluation. The combined process of the audit/best practices assures a positive internal security evaluation is achieved with buy in from all participants. Providing feedback to upper management allows the local security personnel support for needed improvements. This report can include a grading scheme; however, a grading scheme requires a published weighted scale to prevent the score from being overly objective.

_____ Appendix C
Integration Tips

The operator's viewpoint is critical for integrating and fine-tuning electronic security functions. There are several tips you should consider when starting an integration project.

1. Establish a project team.
2. Assure a single point of responsibility.
3. Perform frequent inspections.
4. Design for future expansion.
5. Install the system for ease of maintenance.
6. Purchase the system as if it is a marriage.
7. Assure compliance with all codes and "Authorities Having Jurisdiction."
8. Make training mandatory.
9. Specify the documentation of application software.
10. Supply as-built drawings.
11. Consider ergonomics as a critical part of the project.
12. Make performance specifications and special requirements part of the contract.
13. Ask lots of questions.

Establish a project team

A strong project team should cover all disciplines to assure every aspect and angle of the project has been evaluated. This team should start at the security survey stage and continue through system test and activation. The members and some of the disciplines may change as the project progresses through the different phases of the project. Some team members may be from within the company, some may be from outside, but all areas of expertise must be present at one time or another. The minimum areas of expertise that need coverage are Technical Security, Facilities, Security Operations, IT, HR, Legal, Accounting, Management, Profit Centers, and Project Management.

Technical Security, Security Operations, and Facilities should be part of the initial team. When the security survey starts, these organizations or groups are critical to include in the team. One of the typical problems with a security survey is that it misses key inputs from Facilities, Management, and Profit Center. Generally, Security is succinctly aware of what needs to be corrected. Security management is needed on the team for a holistic long-term view. A Facility representative is needed to represent heating, air conditioning, power, parking, and building accessibility issues. Often Purchasing, Management, Profit Centers, HR, IT, and Legal get involved early on in the team effort. They may want to actually meet regularly as team members or receive a periodic update.

Assure a single point of responsibility

This is true on both sides of the project fence. On the company side the security managers should be the responsible party. Not only are they the system owner, but they will also inherit the blame if the system does not work whether they are recognized as the responsible party or not. For larger projects that might include the construction of a major building, the security component may be a small part of the project. There is normally someone within your company who is the contact point. That person is the responsible party for you. This is often the Facility's project manager. On the other side of the fence, there must be one person who makes the final decisions and commitments. In larger projects, this person is usually the architect. If there is not a legally responsible party on the construction side of the fence, then the finger pointing will never end and the company will receive a substandard system, a non-functioning system, a system that is way over budget, or all the above.

Perform frequent inspections

There is an old adage that goes like this: "You get what is inspected, not what is expected." This is where a good architect, general contractor, or a project manager earns their money. They should constantly inspect all aspects of the project. The company should also be inspecting to ensure that what they receive is what they are paying for. If the company does not have the expertise to inspect the project, then they should hire someone to directly represent their interests. (This is the role of the architect or security consultant in many projects.)

Design for future expansion

No matter how well the system is planned, there is no way to be able to estimate its size five years into the future. Security systems always expand. Features such as electronic access control often expand to ten times their original size after five years. As employees become aware of the convenience of badge readers they don't want to use keys or remember keypad numbers. They want to use their access control badge that they must already carry for identification. Employees will also request that electronic access control be added to areas that Security never anticipated, thus adding to the system's size. Expansion room must be left in every electronic field panel as well as the system's total capacity. The Security Control Center (SCC) will also expand in functionality over time as new requirements are added. This expansion usually requires additional equipment. Even though manufacturers are always reducing the size of their hardware while expanding its capability, additional space will be needed in the SCC. If you, as the security manager, must request capital funding to upgrade your system a few years after installation, management may look for a new security manager.

Install the system for ease of maintenance

Ongoing maintenance will be a large part of the system's cost after the warranty lapses. To minimize the labor associated with maintenance, the system must be properly designed and installed, as discussed earlier. It must also be installed with maintenance issues in mind. For example, many contractors will install power supplies for access control strikes, magnetic locks, and so on above the doors. So maintenance personnel must use a ladder to check for electrical power on both sides of the power supply before they can proceed with troubleshooting. If the power supplies were in a designated security equipment room/closet, then the power could be checked without a ladder thus reducing time spent gaining access to resolve a problem. (In addition, ladders in front of doors tend to block employees as they enter or leave the building.) To further troubleshoot, the SCC operator can activate a door release from the SCC while the technician observes the field panel that is in the same room as the power supply. This will eliminate running back and forth between the door and the equipment room to test the system. The reason many of the maintenance reducing efforts are not installed is because they initially require more installation effort and at times are slightly more expensive. Contractors will usually install the project in a way that is easiest for themselves at the time of installation, with little thought given to future maintenance.

Purchase the system as if it were a marriage

Once the security/access control/fire systems are purchased, the owner is now married to the manufacturer or manufacturers. Since there are no standard information protocols, the owner is committed to the manufacturer or its representative for support and products. Any support, improvements, enhancements, upgrades or maintenance must be supplied through the recently purchased manufacturer. If service or system operation or lack of expandability becomes a tremendous problem most companies will limp along, because of the financial impact of replacing the system. (After purchasing a system, it is painfully expensive to replace it.) In most cases, only the sensors can be left and everything else must be removed and new equipment and software installed. To avoid this frustration and expense, the manufacturer must be carefully selected. The selection process must include the consideration of local alarm companies or the local group that is part of a national company in order to have the support that will be needed on a local level. The selection of a local installation/maintenance/support company may be more important than the selection of the manufacturer. Many systems will meet most requirements, but an alarm company that is the representative of the chosen manufacturer and supposedly factory trained may provide very poor support. If they do, then another local alarm company could be used for labor support as long as the second company or the original alarm company can purchase the equipment from the manufacturer and provide it to you. It is also prudent to investigate the references supplied by the manufacturer and installation/alarm company to minimize this potential problem in the first place.

Assure compliance with all codes and "authorities having jurisdiction"

The system designer (architect, security consultant, etc.) should handle these requirements for your project. It is critical to provide language to this effect in your contract documents. These items are covered with topics such as "workman-like quality," special insurance requirements, and so on. This way, if something is overlooked it will be the designer's or installer's responsibility to correct the problem. Also codes are continually changing and each city uses a uniform or international building and fire code. These codes are tied to different releases of codes. NFPA 72 is a good example in the fire industry. This code is updated on a periodic basis. The city where your company is located could easily be 1 to 6 years behind the latest release. The difference in accepted versions may impact the system design.

Make training mandatory

Training is critical to the success of any project. When new equipment and software are installed, the SCC operators, data entry personnel, and internal maintenance personnel need to understand the system. Training also promotes "buy in" for the new system by these personnel. As discussed earlier, the goal of the new system is to allow the

SCC operator to be effective in his or her job. Security personnel cannot be very effective when quality training is not provided. The Information Technology (IT) department in many companies realizes that the lack of training is a problem when a new software package is purchased and provided on the company network for employees. The employees do not know how to use their new program, which causes people to be very frustrated and the IT call center or "help desk" to become overrun with requests. Usually the deadlines, which incorporate the new software or equipment, continue whether the personnel knows how to use the system or not. For this reason the IT department has come to realize training is necessary. Not everyone that is intuitive knows how to use new software packages. The SCC operators are no different. Training means real "classroom" type training. It should include videotaping the training to be used as a refresher course at a later date. The lack of training is an area for major dissatisfaction with a new system, thus dooming the project.

Specify the documentation of application software

The security, access control, and fire systems run on application-specific software that is proprietary. If the system manufacturer goes out of business, you are stuck with a system that cannot be upgraded or modified without software documentation. It is important to require in the contract that system documentation be available if such a situation develops. The application software should be thoroughly tested and provisions added to the contract allowing for modifications. In the past, the application software source code from the manufacturer was placed in an escrow account in case the manufacturer dissolved their corporation. This was some protection, but source code is of little value if it is not extremely well documented. Most companies in the security industry today are fairly small, based upon the standards used by large companies. In many cases, the security department purchasing the equipment is larger than the manufacturer. This is changing as large nationally known corporations acquiring small security companies.

Supply as-built drawings

The intent is always to correct the documentation when the project is complete. To protect oneself, the contract should withhold final payment until the documentation is complete. (This amount is usually 10 percent.) The bid documents must also specify what documentation must be supplied and the type of format that is required. It is always important to have correct drawings. It is also a good plan to request a software file, such as CAD version X. This software should be in a format used by the Facilities department, which will allow future changes to be easily added. The configuration changes to the drawings can be accomplished in-house or via another contractor.

Consider ergonomics as a critical part of the project

One of the first concerns that arise with ergonomics is in the SCC. With the goal of integration being the effectiveness of the SCC operator/operators to use the system, it is important to develop an environment that is conducive for the operator to work in. This includes noise level within the SCC, the appearance of the SCC, the chair the SCC operator uses, workstation height, lighting, air conditioning, background noise level and equipment layout. All these areas should be addressed in the design of the project. The console layout should be mocked up and the operators should make recommendations before the SCC console is built. After the system is installed and operational, it is a good idea to videotape the operators as they work to refine the system layout and modify the equipment or software to add to the operator's efficiency. The time when efficiency is critical is during emergencies. A poorly designed control center will cause tempers to flair and high turnover within the department.

Make performance specifications and special requirements part of the contract

Everyone is aware of the importance of a well-written contract. The contract should address everything from payment schedules to safety requirements. A well-written contract covers what is to be done as well as how it is to be done. The fewer items left to interpretation the fewer change orders during installation. Two areas often overlooked are performance specifications and special requirements. A performance specification assures that the hardware and software will provide the desired functionality for the company requesting the installation. The performance specification should represent the companies' anticipated needs as well as assure future loading. It should be as demanding as possible to assure the desired results, but fall within the stated manufacturer's specification.

Any special requirements the company wants the contractor to adhere to must be stated. For example, the company may want some areas where the system is to be installed be performed on the weekend. Or if clean rooms are part of the facility the contractor may be required to "smock up." All special requirements should also be part of the bid documents to assure that all contractors know what is required. There should not be any surprises; they cost money, time and/or contract problems, which all have negative impacts on the project. For this reason the performance specifications should also be part of the bid documents.

Ask lots of questions

As a security professional, you may not know all the technical or construction detail that is part of most projects. It is important that you ask questions and receive answers to assure yourself that the contractor, architect, security consultant, project manager, and alarm contractor know what they are doing and what you want done. There are questions that should be asked before going out to bid and applies to all areas of the project: "How long is the warranty? When does the warranty period start?" The answers, or what you want these answers to be, should then be added to the contract. There are questions to ask during construction. The team is a great source of answers to questions that should be addressed to assure no area is overlooked, such as, "How do the wires get to the lobby receptionist desk?"

An electronic security integration project can be a major challenge for any company, but with proper planning, a solid team effort, open exchange of information with prospective contractors, and a well-written contract the odds of success are substantially improved. The goal of the project is to implement a system that allows the SCC operator or operators to perform their task efficiently in an ergonomic environment. These tips should provide some ideas on ways to increase the likelihood the project will provide the results that you desire.

Appendix D
Technical Security Job Grades

Company X
PROFESSIONAL/INDIVIDUAL CONTRIBUTORS
& MANAGERS
TECHNICAL SECURITY
FUNCTIONS/RESPONSIBILITIES

Security—Technical Security

Develops, designs and administers technical security systems and procedures for Company X or Company customer security systems/network(s). These security systems/network(s) can be unclassified, proprietary, and/or government classified. Must be able to study and implement security systems/network regulations that apply to company operations. Coordinates with government agencies to obtain rulings, interpretations, and acceptable deviations for compliance with regulations. Prepares manuals outlining regulations and establishes security systems/network(s) policy. Conducts security systems/network(s) education classes. Will assist in investigations of security system and network violations and preparation of reports. Provides engineering design and supervision for installations of security systems for Company X buildings, government project closed areas, Security Control Centers, etc. Manage the ongoing designs, installations and maintenance of Company X security, fire, access control, CCTV, intercom, and other related electronic security systems/communications/networks. Prepares manuals outlining regulations and establishes technical security policies. Conducts technical security classes.

Security—Technical Security

Table D-1

Classification Title	Job Code
Technical Security Specialist I	A01
Technical Security Specialist II	A02
Senior Technical Security Specialist	A03
Principal Technical Security Specialist	A04
Consulting Technical Security Specialist	A05
Consulting Technical Security Specialist	A06
Team Leader I Technical Security	A02
Team Leader II Technical Security	A03
Manager I Technical Security	A04
Manager II Technical Security	A05
Manager III Technical Security	A06
Sr. Manager Technical Security	A07

Table D-2: Technical Security Responsibilities and Requirements

Job Title	Responsibilities	Qualifications
Technical Security Specialist I (A01)	Operations Level Entry level exempt position requiring close supervision from technical security manager. • Assistant in technical security design, installation, and maintenance • Troubleshoot technical system problems • Help in project management • Assist with technical security audits • Oversee maintenance of security systems databases • Develop technical evaluations • Prepare reports as required by the technical security manager • Perform technical security functions as assigned	• Accredited (4 year) Bachelor's degree • 0 years related experience • General electronics background • Basic technical knowledge
Technical Security Specialist II (A02)	Operations Level Perform duties under general supervision. Responsible for all duties of a Technical Security Specialist I, plus:	• Accredited (4 year) Bachelor of Science degree

Continued

Table D-2: Technical Security Responsibilities and Requirements (Cont'd)

Job Title	Responsibilities	Qualifications
	Oversee technical security on a *small* (less than 1,000 person) site or sites • Provide cost management for projects • Manage installation and maintenance projects • Conduct technical security audits • Conduct security system project design reviews • Perform technical security functions as assigned	• 2 years related experience • Proven electronics background • Project management experience • Skills emphasizing technical security
Senior Technical Security Specialist (A03)	Operations Level Perform duties under general direction. • Technical Security *Assistant* for a *Company Segment* • Technical Security *Manager* for a *small Company operation* • Oversee technical security on a medium site or sites (less than 3,000 people) • Manage, design, and provide cost management for multiple coexisting projects	• Accredited (4 year) Bachelor of Science degree • 4 years related experience • Strong electronics background • Proven technical security related experience • Some formal technical security training • Proven project management experience

Continued

Consulting Technical Security Specialist (A05 & A06)	• Review technical security requirements for compliance, efficiency, and standardization • Coordinate technical security issues with plant engineering, security operations, and management • Perform technical security functions as assigned	• Accredited (4 year) Bachelor of Science degree • *12 years related experience* • *Strong electronic background* • *Extensive technical security and project management related experience* • *Strong formal professional technical security training* • Registered Professional Engineer or Master's degree • *Viewed as a technical security subject matter expert by Company*
	Corporate or large Segment Level Perform duties under consultative direction. • Technical Security *Manager* at the *large Company segment or corporate level* • Act as consultant for all technical security issues affecting the entire segment • Develop technical security procedures • Provide technical advice and assistance throughout the segment • Interface with all levels of plant management, security and information technology • Primary technical security expert for cross-company projects	

Table D-2: Technical Security Responsibilities and Requirements (Cont'd)

Job Title	Responsibilities	Qualifications
Team Leader I Technical Security (A02)	Operations Level Accomplish tasks through direct supervision of predominantly skilled nonexempt employees. • Oversee technical security on a small (less than 1,000 person) site or sites • Provide cost management for projects • Manage installation and maintenance projects • Conduct technical security audits • Conduct security system project design reviews • Perform technical security functions as assigned	• Accredited (4 year) Bachelor of Science degree • 2 years related experience • Proven electronics • Proven project management experience • Skills emphasizing technical security
Team Leader II Technical Security (A03)	Operations Level Accomplishes tasks mainly through the direct supervision of predominantly highly skilled nonexempt and entry level exempt employees. • Technical Security *Assistant* for a Company Segment • Technical Security *Manager* for a *small* Company *operation* • Oversee technical security on a medium site or sites (less than 3,000 people)	

Continued

Manager I Technical Security (A04)	• Manage, design, and provide cost management for multiple coexisting projects • Review technical security requirements for compliance, efficiency, and standardization • Coordinate technical security issues with plant engineering, security operations, and management • Perform special assignments in relation to total protection of facilities and personnel • Train and develop subordinates • Perform security functions as assigned	• Accredited (4 year) Bachelor of Science degree • 8 years related experience • Strong electronics background • *High technical security related* experience • *Moderate* formal technical security training • High project management related experience • Strong communication skills
	Operations Level Accomplish results through lower level subordinate supervisors or through related experienced exempt employees. • Technical Security Manager for a *large Company operation or medium segment level* • Review Segment and Company technical security requirements for compliance, efficiency, and standardization	

Table D-2: Technical Security Responsibilities and Requirements (Cont'd)

Job Title	Responsibilities	Qualifications
Manager II Technical Security (A05)	• Primary interface between security, plant engineering, information technology and management for technical security issues • Act as principal contact for all technical security issues • Implement technical security procedures throughout the segment • Provide technical security technical training at the operations level • Coordinate technical security issues between segments • Perform security functions as assigned Operations Level Accomplish results through subordinate supervisors, or exempt specialist employees • Technical Security *Manager* at the *large Company segment level* • Act as consultant for all technical security issues affecting the entire segment	• Accredited (4 year) Bachelor of Science degree • 12 years related experience • Registered Professional Engineer or Master's degree • Strong electronics background • *Extensive* technical security

Job Grade	Description	Qualifications
Manager III Technical Security (A06)	Operations Level Generally accomplish results through lower management levels. • Technical Security *Manager* at the *large Company segment or corporate level* • Negotiate security waivers and exceptions with government security representatives • Act as consultant for all technical security issues	• Accredited (4 year) Bachelor of Science degree • 14 years related experience • Registered Professional Engineer or Master's degree • Strong technical background • *Extensive* technical security and project management
Sr. Manager Technical Security (A07)	Segment or Corporate Level Responsible for results and effectiveness of a function. • Negotiate contracts for technical support • Technical Security *Manager* at the *large Company segment or corporate level* • Acts as consultant for all technical security issues affecting the entire segment and/or corporation • Develop technical security procedures	• Accredited (4 year) Bachelor of Science degree • 18 years related experience • Strong technical background • *Extensive* technical security and project management related experience • *Extensive* formal professional technical security training

_____ Appendix E
Interviewing

It is time to hire a new employee so you begin the process by filling out the justification forms in order to receive approval. With completed forms the process starts to justify the need. This can be a painful and slow process while work stacks up and the existing employees attempt to make an effort to cover the extra work. Obviously, the need for an additional employee has existed for some time or it would be impossible to justify the need for extra support. After a seemingly slow and stressful process, management approval is finally obtained and the requisition is passed to the Human Resources (HR) department. You are now at the point of where the real work starts. The effort used up to this point will prove to be the easiest part.

There are several preliminary efforts that can be in place to provide some level of screening which will help to assure that the right person is hired to fill the requirements. The goal of any hiring process is to sift through the applicants and arrive at the end with several qualified candidates. These preliminary screening efforts are often written about and there are a number of companies today that provide such services. The quality of the screening will depend on the companies providing the service and the type of employee who is being evaluated. The approach used for selecting an electrical engineer or security technician will be different from the process used to find a security officer. The level of intrusiveness to the applicant that the screening process provides will also depend on the industry's practices. Drug testing, personality profiles, background checks, verification of technical training or college degrees, and aptitude testing can all be part of the services provided by the HR department or by an outside company.

One way to proceed in the search for a qualified employee is by using a temporary agency. By using a temporary agency, you will have first-hand knowledge of the potential employee as they perform the work you have assigned. This can be a slower process, but it enables you to view their degree of success at the particular job you wish to fill. One thing that must be in place in this situation is a legal agreement with the agency allowing you to hire the employee while they work for you. This also changes the approach to justification of need.

A second approach in the search for a qualified employee is the use of networking. This requires the person doing the hiring to be aware of possible candidates in other related jobs. When an opening arises, candidates can be notified and if interested will be open to applying for the position. Professional organizations are a great source for finding qualified people to fill new positions. Often the use of contract labor leads to finding the right person for the job, and once again you are able to see the person perform before fitting them into your organization. If these approaches are not options, then you are left with starting at the beginning with the HR department.

The following is a list of potential screening categories, which allows the HR department to refine the number of resumes:

1. Years of experience
2. Education
3. Background
4. Interests
5. Special skill sets

The HR department typically will obtain resumes of people who are interested in working in a given field. The approach used to obtain the resumes will vary depending upon what the company deems an effective approach. These can vary with combinations of the following:

1. Classified ads
2. Radio/TV
3. Billboards
3. Referral bonuses
4. College recruiting
5. Internet
6. Recruiting firms
7. Mail in resumes

Often, a company receives a substantial number of resumes either "mail in" or via the Internet. The company will then scan the mailed in resumes into a database and the HR personnel will evaluate the resumes based on key words that allow them to electronically sort through the database. The sorted resumes are then sent to the manager. Each resume should be reviewed and analyzed to assure that HR understood your requirements. There will be some resumes that are not a good match for obvious reasons. After reviewing each resume, any thoughts should be documented in the form of written notes. If the applicant is interviewed, the notes will help you perform a more effective interview. If the applicant is not interviewed, the notes will remind you of your reasoning if any issues arise at a later time.

Before interviewing the applicants, each resume and the associated notes should be reviewed in order to develop questions that may be of value in understanding the applicant's strengths, weaknesses, personality, and skills. Before the actual interview, any specific guidelines your HR department publishes should be reviewed. During the interview it is important for the applicant to visit with team members and the supervisor. The supervisor should be the first contact when the applicant arrives and should develop an environment that makes the applicant feel comfortable. This would include small talk such as their trip or difficulty in finding the site, and so on.

Sometimes the HR department performs some level of interviewing and screening before the supervisor is involved. These steps apply no matter what level of screening exists prior to the meeting of the applicant and supervisor. Whether the applicant interviews with the supervisor and peers at the same time or individually can be debated. The approach suggested in this appendix is that the supervisor interviews the applicant first, then the applicant meets with the other team members (peers) and interviews without the supervisor. It is, of course, the supervisor's responsibility to introduce the applicant to each team member and develop a comfortable atmosphere with the team members before leaving. After the team members interview, it is a good idea to continue a dialog in a nonbusiness atmosphere. A good solution is to go to lunch or dinner. This will allow the applicant to be more himself or herself and allow you to see the applicant in a different environment.

During the first interview between the supervisor and the applicant important information can be exchanged. The applicant can understand the job, the way the job fits into the organization, the team members they will work with, and general expectations. The supervisor can see the applicant and their responses before they have had a chance to receive feedback from other employees in the company. This is an important stage for the supervisor. Questions should be carefully formulated based upon his or her resume. The following is a list of questions to choose from that will provide some insight into their last or present job:

1. How can your skills and abilities meet the needs of this position?
2. What skills do you think you bring to this job?
3. What are your strong points as an employee?
4. What was the most enjoyable part of your previous position?
5. Why did you leave your last position?
6. What do you find most rewarding in your job?
7. What do you find most frustrating in your job?
8. What are your career goals?
9. What do you see as your weaknesses?
10. How would you describe your manager's style?
11. How do you handle your work-related stress?
12. What and who have motivated you in the past?
13. What are some of the things you look for in a job?
14. If you could have an ideal job, what would it be?

15. How were you able to demonstrate teamwork in your previous position?
16. How many hours are you accustomed to working in a week?
17. Tell me about your last performance appraisal.

The questions above will provide some insight into the applicant's personality and work ethics. When questioning the applicant, observe facial expressions, body language, voice inflection, and so on to help in understanding the answers. Interpreting body language requires specialized training so you must not put too much emphasis on their interpretation. If an applicant folds his or her arms, it can be a sign of defensiveness or simply that the applicant is comfortable. It is important to weigh the answers in the context of the interview. The goal is to understand the environment where the applicant has worked or is working, and then to understand the applicant. When there is a real understanding of both the environment and the person, it is time to shift the focus to the opening that exists. The goal is to evaluate the applicant as if they were working in the company culture. This will help to determine the likelihood of whether the applicant will work successfully or not. Some deeper questioning is necessary at this point. Some questions to pick from would include the following:

1. Why are you interested in this company?
2. What is your understanding of this position?
3. How much do you know about the company?
4. What do you believe are your qualifications for this job?
5. Why do you believe you are qualified?
6. How might your skills be improved?
7. What areas would you like to improve?
8. In the context of this job, what does service mean to you?
9. What does quality mean to you?
10. When were you previously responsible for doing this kind of work?

There are legal issues that must be considered when interviewing. Certain questions cannot be asked because the answers could allow an applicant to be discriminated against. There are also no reasons why the interviewer should need to know the answers to these types of questions.

The list of lawful questions is as follows:

1. Applicant's place of residence.
2. How long a resident of this state or city?
3. Are you legally authorized to work in the United States on a full-time basis?
4. Inquiry into the academic, vocational, or professional education and the public or private schools he or she has attended.
5. Have you ever been convicted of a felony? If so, application must show when, where and disposition of the offense.
6. Inquiry into work experience.
7. Names of applicant's relatives already employed by this company.
8. Can applicant perform the essential functions of the job with or without reasonable accommodation?
9. Stating the work schedule and asking whether he or she is willing to work that schedule.
10. Asking applicant if there is a problem with their ability to do manual labor, lifting and other essential physical requirements of the job, if any.

The following is a list of unlawful questions:

1. Birthplaces of applicant's spouse, parents, or close relative.
2. Birthplace of applicant.
3. Maiden name of married woman applicant.
4. Requirement that an applicant state his age and submit proof in the form of a certificate of age or work permit issued by the school authorities.
5. Inquiry into an applicant's denomination, religious affiliations, church, parish, or religious holidays observed.
6. If not a citizen of the United States, does applicant intend to become a citizen of the United States?
7. Inquiry into languages applicant speaks or writes fluently.

8. Do you live with your parents? If not, with whom do you live? What family do you have?
9. Inquiry into medical or work comp history or disability status.
10. Credit history, including bankruptcy.

After completing the interview, the supervisor would then escort the applicant to the team interview. Depending upon the amount of time the supervisor used during the interview process, a break could be necessary at this point before proceeding. This could be accomplished with some sort of refreshments or by giving the applicant a quick tour of the area where they would be working.

The team members should have already reviewed the resume. They should have developed some questions on their own and the supervisor should have discussed with the team members these questions, or at least the general areas that he or she planned to discuss with the applicant. The team members should pick questions and use a similar approach as the supervisor. The importance of this interview is again to exchange information. For the applicant, it is a way to understand and get to know at some level the people that they will be working with. It also allows the applicant to double-check the information obtained from the supervisor. A wise supervisor will tell the team members and applicant to be open and honest in their answers. There is no benefit in hiring someone who leaves in a month because the job, the environment, or peers were misrepresented. It is important to remember that the applicant, as well as the interviewers, has expectations and knowledge to share.

After the applicant leaves, all interviewers should meet and discuss the applicant. Notes should be taken to jog memories for the time when a final selection is made. The notes should include the applicant's actual answers as well as feelings or intuitions. It would be ideal, if it is possible, to have this review before the nonbusiness meeting with the applicant takes place. This way the interview can continue in a very relaxed environment and concerns or questions can be investigated further.

It is beneficial to interview as many applicants as possible one after another. This allows each interviewer to clearly remember and compare applicants. Many times this is not possible so note taking becomes even more critical. It is also possible that the first round of interviews will narrow the potential employees to two or three. If this develops the process starts again, but the environment must be changed to evaluate the applicants in a new light. This might include having the applicants attend a staff meeting or a team meeting. This would allow the applicants a better idea of the actual working process they will be a part of. It allows the interviewer to watch the applicants and see how they operate. Depending upon the type of job being filled and the expectations of the job the applicants could be asked what they would recommend on a certain issue during or after the meeting.

In order to be successful in hiring an applicant who plays a critical part in your team and the company it is imperative to be an effective interviewer. Often it is not possible to hire from a pool of contract labor, temporary personnel, or from other networking contacts. This means that your interviewing skills must be effective in order to assure that you get the type of employee that best suits the position you have available. Even with HR screening the final decision is yours. You and your team members will be the ones who benefit most from using the interviewing process to its fullest advantage in hiring the perfect employee to work in your environment.

Index

A

Access control, electronic. *See* Electronic access control

Access control philosophy, 4–5

Audit, security. *See* Security audit

Automation process. *See* Process, automation

B

Badge making, 19–36
  all sites pros and cons, at, 321–322
  anticounterfeiting measures, 23
  appearance, 22–24
  appearance considerations list, 22–23
  binary breakdown of protocol diagrams, 26, 27
  colors, 23, 24, 32
  cost, 19, 32
  lamination, 32–33
  manufacturing process, 31–36
  numbering, 24–25

printer costs, 322
printers, 31–32
protocol, 25–26, 27
reasons for, 19–21
replacing system questions, 35
stock, 23, 31, 32, 320–321
summary, 36
technologies, primary, 28
technology, 24–31

Badge rooms
  cost of badges and, 19
  delays in, 16
  multiple, 16
  space cost, 322
  system support and, 10, 11, 12
  typical components, 33–34
  typical room photograph, 34

Badges. *See also* Badge making
  culture and, 4
  data storage, 2
  distribution, 34–35
  frequency problems, 12
  life cycle, 185

355

About the Author

Bob Pearson has over 35 years experience in electrical engineering and electronic security systems design, installation, testing and maintenance. He has a BSEE from Texas Tech University with graduate studies at University of Southern California, and is a Registered Professional Engineer. He has been a continuing education instructor for George Washington University, Washington, DC and published numerous articles in *Security Management, Access Control and Security Systems*, and *Security Technology and Design* magazines. He is a member of National Standing Architecture/Engineering Council of ASIS International and has presented numerous seminars at the national and international conferences and workshops. He has worked for various companies in the private and defense sectors as a digital design engineer and he has been a Senior Member of the Technical Staff for the Digital Systems Design Group of a major defense contractor. He has also worked at the corporate level as manager of a large technical department with worldwide responsibility. He has performed international security surveys and provided electronic security systems for key personnel. He was selected as the business manager of a proposed Commercial Security Business Unit for one of those corporations. He designed and installed a computer driven security system for the protection of nuclear weapons assembly plants and was a security consultant for the National Strategic Oil Reserve. He is a Licensed Security Consultant.